Earning Money
From Your
French Home

A Survival Handbook

by
Jo Taylor

Survival Books • London • England

First published 2006

Survival Books Limited,
26 York Street, London W1U 6PZ, United Kingdom
☎ +44 (0)20-7788 7644, 🖨 +44 (0)870-762 3212
✉ info@survivalbooks.net
🖥 www.survivalbooks.net
To order books, please refer to page 317.

British Library Cataloguing in Publication Data.
A CIP record for this book is available
from the British Library.
ISBN 1 901130 93 2

Printed and bound in Italy by Legoprint spa.

ACKNOWLEDGEMENTS

I would like to thank all those who contributed to the successful publication of this book, in particular the staff at the head offices of Gîtes de France and Clévacances, my Comité Départemental du Tourisme and UK holiday agencies too numerous to mention individually. Special thanks go to Alan Taylor for his patience, my own *gîte* guests for putting up with not having their lawn mown quite as often as it should have been this summer, Stephen Buss for his advice and information on holiday letting agencies, and everyone else who provided information or contributed in any way. I would also like to thank Joe Laredo (editing), Catherine Wakelin (proofreading), Kerry Laredo (dtp) and, last but not least, Jim Watson for his great cartoons and maps.

TITLES BY SURVIVAL BOOKS

Alien's Guides
Britain; France

The Best Places To Buy A Home
France; Spain

Buying A Home
Abroad; Australia & New
Zealand; Cyprus; Florida;
France; Greece; Ireland; Italy;
Portugal; South Africa; Spain
Buying, Selling & Letting
Property (UK)

Earning Money From Your Home
France; Spain

**Foreigners Abroad: Triumphs
& Disasters**
France; Spain

Lifeline Regional Guides
Brittany; Costa Blanca;
Costa del Sol; Dordogne/Lot;
Normandy; Poitou-Charentes;
Provence-Côte d'Azur

Living And Working
Abroad; America;
Australia; Britain; Canada;
The European Union;
The Far East;
France; Germany;
The Gulf States & Saudi Arabia;
Holland, Belgium & Luxembourg;
Ireland; Italy; London;
New Zealand; Spain;
Switzerland

Making A Living
France; Spain

Other Titles
Renovating & Maintaining
Your French Home;
Retiring Abroad;
Shooting Caterpillars in Spain;
Surprised by France

Order forms are on page 317.

WHAT READERS & REVIEWERS

When you buy a model plane for your child, a video recorder, or some new computer gizmo, you get with it a leaflet or booklet pleading 'Read Me First', or bearing large friendly letters or bold type saying 'IMPORTANT – follow the instructions carefully'. This book should be similarly supplied to all those entering France with anything more durable than a 5-day return ticket. It is worth reading even if you are just visiting briefly, or if you have lived here for years and feel totally knowledgeable and secure. But if you need to find out how France works then it is indispensable. Native French people probably have a less thorough understanding of how their country functions. – Where it is most essential, the book is most up to the minute.

LIVING FRANCE

Rarely has a 'survival guide' contained such useful advice. This book dispels doubts for first-time travellers, yet is also useful for seasoned globetrotters – In a word, if you're planning to move to the USA or go there for a long-term stay, then buy this book both for general reading and as a ready-reference.

AMERICAN CITIZENS ABROAD

It is everything you always wanted to ask but didn't for fear of the contemptuous put down – The best English-language guide – Its pages are stuffed with practical information on everyday subjects and are designed to complement the traditional guidebook.

SWISS NEWS

A complete revelation to me – I found it both enlightening and interesting, not to mention amusing.

CAROLE CLARK

Let's say it at once. David Hampshire's *Living and Working in France* is the best handbook ever produced for visitors and foreign residents in this country; indeed, my discussion with locals showed that it has much to teach even those born and bred in l'Hexagone. – It is Hampshire's meticulous detail which lifts his work way beyond the range of other books with similar titles. Often you think of a supplementary question and search for the answer in vain. With Hampshire this is rarely the case. – He writes with great clarity (and gives French equivalents of all key terms), a touch of humour and a ready eye for the odd (and often illuminating) fact. – This book is absolutely indispensable.

THE RIVIERA REPORTER

A mine of information – I may have avoided some embarrassments and frights if I had read it prior to my first Swiss encounters – Deserves an honoured place on any newcomer's bookshelf.

ENGLISH TEACHERS ASSOCIATION, SWITZERLAND

HAVE SAID ABOUT SURVIVAL BOOKS

What a great work, wealth of useful information, well-balanced wording and accuracy in details. My compliments!

THOMAS MÜLLER

This handbook has all the practical information one needs to set up home in the UK – The sheer volume of information is almost daunting – Highly recommended for anyone moving to the UK.

AMERICAN CITIZENS ABROAD

A very good book which has answered so many questions and even some I hadn't thought of – I would certainly recommend it.

BRIAN FAIRMAN

We would like to congratulate you on this work: it is really super! We hand it out to our expatriates and they read it with great interest and pleasure.

ICI (SWITZERLAND) AG

Covers just about all the things you want to know on the subject – In answer to the desert island question about the one how-to book on France, this book would be it – Almost 500 pages of solid accurate reading – This book is about enjoyment as much as survival.

THE RECORDER

It's so funny – I love it and definitely need a copy of my own – Thanks very much for having written such a humorous and helpful book.

HEIDI GUILIANI

A must for all foreigners coming to Switzerland.

ANTOINETTE O'DONOGHUE

A comprehensive guide to all things French, written in a highly readable and amusing style, for anyone planning to live, work or retire in France.

THE TIMES

A concise, thorough account of the DOs and DON'Ts for a foreigner in Switzerland – Crammed with useful information and lightened with humorous quips which make the facts more readable.

AMERICAN CITIZENS ABROAD

Covers every conceivable question that may be asked concerning everyday life – I know of no other book that could take the place of this one.

FRANCE IN PRINT

Hats off to *Living and Working in Switzerland*!

RONNIE ALMEIDA

THE AUTHOR

Jo Taylor is originally from Devon, where she attended art college, subsequently working in graphic design and advertising. She has lived in Normandy since 1993, running a B&B and *gîte* business in addition to being a freelance designer and illustrator (💻 www.blue-moondesign. co.uk). This is her first work as writer for Survival Books; she has illustrated *Brittany Lifeline* and *Provence-Côte d'Azur Lifeline*.

CONTENTS

1. EARNING MONEY FROM YOUR FRENCH HOME   15

2. GÎTES   35

3. BED & BREAKFAST   113

4. LONG-TERM LETTING 165

5. YOUR HOME AS BUSINESS PREMISES 197

IMPORTANT NOTE

France is a large country with myriad faces and many ethnic groups, religions and customs. Although ostensibly the same throughout the country, many laws, rules and regulations, especially those associated with doing business, are open to local interpretation. Laws and regulations are changing at a considerable rate as France grapples with the task of homogenising its legislation. In particular, many of the French organisations responsible for the regulation of holiday accommodation operate on an autonomous basis, and the rules set by one department can be quite different from those set by the next. The costs and prices mentioned in this book were correct at the time of writing but should be regarded as examples only, as these may vary from one region or department to another.

I therefore cannot recommend too strongly that you check with an official and reliable source (not always the same) before making any major decisions or undertaking an irreversible course of action. However, don't believe everything you're told or have read, even – dare I say it? – in this book! Always check and double check things yourself.

To help you obtain further information and verify data with official sources, useful addresses and references to other sources of information have been included in all chapters and in **Appendices A to C**. Important points have been emphasised throughout the book **in bold print**, some of which it would be expensive or foolish to disregard. **Ignore them at your peril or cost.** Unless specifically stated, the reference to any company, organisation, product or publication in this book doesn't constitute an endorsement or recommendation.

AUTHOR'S NOTES

- Times are shown using the 24-hour clock; for example, two o'clock in the afternoon is written as 14.00.

- His/he/him/man/men (etc.) also mean her/she/her/woman/women (no offence ladies!). This is done simply to make life easier for both the reader and, in particular, the author, and isn't intended to be sexist.

- British English is used throughout, but American English equivalents are given where appropriate.

- Warnings and important points are shown in **bold** type.

- French words and phrases are given in brackets in *italics* (usually in the singular).

- The following symbols are used in this book: ☎ (telephone), 🖶 (fax), 🖳 (internet) and ✉ (email).

- Lists of useful addresses, further reading and useful websites are contained in **Appendices A**, **B** and **C** respectively.

- Maps of France showing the departments and regions and transport networks are in **Appendix D**.

- Tables showing scheduled airline services between the British Isles and France, including contact details of airlines and airports, are provided in **Appendix E**.

- Official organisations and their requirements are detailed in **Appendix F**.

INTRODUCTION

France's beautiful and varied landscape and relaxed lifestyle have wide appeal, and over the last couple of decades thousands of foreigners have bought property there. Buying a home in France continues to be at the top of many wish-lists but, increasingly, property owners want to make the most of their home and benefit from it not just for their own use, but also to make money. If you're thinking of buying a home in France and earning money from it, this is the book for you.

The purpose of *Earning Money From Your French Home* is to provide you with information to help you make the most of your home as a source of income. Whether you plan to buy purely for investment, let your property short or long term, run a bed and breakfast business or use your home as business premises, this book is essential reading. It includes comprehensive guides to short- and long-term letting, including the legal and financial implications; the advantages and disadvantages, pitfalls and 'trade secrets' of running *gîtes* and bed and breakfast accommodation; a guide to setting up a business in your home; plus comprehensive tax information and much more.

Information is derived from a variety of sources, official and unofficial, not least the experiences of foreigners who have bought property in France and earned an income from it – with varying degrees of success. *Earning Money From Your French Home* is designed to make your investment in a French home more profitable and less stressful. It will save you valuable time, trouble and money, and repay its modest cost many times over! (For complementary information, this book's sister publications, *The Best Places to Buy a Home in France*, *Buying a Home in France*, *Living and Working in France*, *Making a Living in France* and *Renovating & Maintaining Your French Home* are also highly recommended reading – see page 317.)

France is one of the world's most popular holiday destinations and a wonderful place to invest in a home – few countries can compete with its stunning scenery, charming villages, delicious cuisine and fine wines, not to mention the seductive French lifestyle, with its emphasis on relaxing and enjoying yourself. I hope *Earning Money From Your French Home* will help you make the right property investment and enjoy it to the full!

Bon courage!
Jo Taylor
November 2005

1.

Earning Money From Your French Home

Buying property abroad has never been as popular as it is today. There are endless magazine articles and television (TV) programmes about buying a home in the sun, whether for permanent living or as a holiday home. What could be better, in addition to realising your dream of buying property in France, than to earn income from it? Whether you're just dreaming, planning a purchase abroad with a view to investment, already have a holiday home in France, from which you wish to earn money, or are planning a permanent move, this book will help you explore the potential of your investment.

More than a million properties in France are owned by foreigners, half of them British, and an increasing number of people are jumping on the bandwagon: the total is rising by around 30 per cent per year. Property exhibitions, magazines and websites offer an overwhelming choice of properties, from small stone ruins to substantial farmhouses and magnificent *châteaux*. Buying an overseas property used to be a popular choice for older people, who often buy a holiday home with a view to later making it a permanent residence for a peaceful retirement. Nowadays it's increasingly buyers under 40 who are investing in property in France, with the aim of revitalising their lives and starting up a business or generating an income from the property itself.

WAYS OF EARNING MONEY

There are essentially three ways of earning money from a property (in France or elsewhere), detailed below.

Capital Growth

The property is purchased as an investment, as you believe that you will make more money by tying up capital in a property and re-selling it in a number of years' time than by saving or investing it elsewhere. In recent years, many people have invested in property to provide an income in their retirement. For information about buying purely for investment, see page 21. You may want to earn an income from your investment property by letting it long term. **Chapter 4** deals with long-term letting.

Holiday Home

If you want a holiday home in France, but cannot afford for it simply to be left empty when you aren't using it (i.e. for most of the year), you could let it as self-catering accommodation to earn income to pay the mortgage or, if you're fortunate enough to have been able to buy it outright, to cover the running costs and/or provide 'pocket money'. **Chapter 2** deals with letting property as self-catering holiday accommodation.

Business Premises

If you want to live permanently in France, but cannot or don't want to get a job there and therefore must make money from your principal home, you may make your home your business premises, by starting a business and operating as self-employed (see **Chapter 5**), by using spare bedrooms for bed and breakfast (B&B) accommodation (see **Chapter 3**), or by converting a building or two to self-catering accommodation (see **Chapter 2**) in order to pay the mortgage, cover running costs, etc.

RESEARCH

If you haven't yet bought a property, you're in the best position to turn your purchase into a viable business proposition. You can choose the region, the area, and the specific property with your requirements in mind. You can choose to buy an existing business, or to buy a property with one or more buildings specifically with conversion in mind.

You might have visited a region that you think will make an ideal location for a holiday accommodation business, but before rushing into buying a property, you must carry out detailed research – leaving behind the rose-tinted spectacles. It's a good idea to take one or more holidays in the area you've chosen; once you've been a customer, you're more likely to appreciate what is needed to satisfy the holidaymaker. Visit at times outside the holiday season – that delightful sunny country hideaway might not be as welcoming in the cold, wet, muddy winter.

Once you've chosen the area, consider renting for a while before buying, so that your capital isn't tied up while you're researching and finding properties for sale.

Don't believe all you see and hear in TV programmes or magazine articles – many were made some years ago, and prices and availability may be seriously out of date; articles may be biased to encourage you to buy in an area, and TV programmes may paint an artificially rosy picture. Earning money from a property in France isn't as easy as it looks, and an article or programme seldom points out the pitfalls, hardly touches upon the legal processes involved and never explains the, often fundamental, differences between French legal system and culture and those of other countries.

If you're considering buying to let long term (i.e. for over three months), note that the law is far more stringent than for short-term or holiday lets, and is strongly biased towards the interests of the tenant. In many areas, including long-term letting, French law has completely different principles from British law, for example – this cannot be overstressed – and you must find out exactly what's involved before committing yourself to long-term letting. The minimum term for an unfurnished let is three years (six years if you're trading as a company), and allowable reasons for termination are severely limited. You must take expert legal advice and be very careful when choosing tenants.

MAJOR CONSIDERATIONS

Good investment properties generally include the following:

- A property that's under-priced.
- A property with a large garden, part of which can be built on sold as a separate building plot.
- A property with the potential to add value such as a loft conversion, annexe or extension.
- A property in an up-and-coming area.
- A property with good transport links (road/rail) or planned links.
- A property close to good amenities (shops, leisure facilities, parks, etc.).
- A home near a good school (e.g. an international school).
- A property with well proportioned rooms.
- A period or character property.
- A large property that can be converted into apartments or split into two semi-detached homes or terraced homes.
- A reasonably priced apartment in the centre of a major town or city.
- A property with off-road parking or a garage (particularly in a city).
- A waterside property, particularly in a popular resort.
- A property in a university town.
- A property in a historic or tourist town.

SURVIVAL TIP

If you plan to live in a property for a long time, it's best to buy a home, not simply a 'good investment'. Nevertheless, it pays to have one eye on the investment potential of a home, as you never know when you may need to sell!

Poor or indifferent investments generally include the following:

- A property that's over-priced.
- A small studio or one-bedroom apartment.
- A property in a rundown area or an area with high unemployment.
- An unusual, poorly designed or 'individual' house with limited appeal.
- An apartment attached to commercial premises (e.g. above a shop).
- A house near to any source of noise such as a busy motorway, airport or factory.
- A home susceptible to flooding.
- A property in a town without private parking and no nearby on-road parking.
- A nondescript 'modern' home.

Main reasons letting businesses fail include the following:

- Paying too much for a property (e.g. taking on too large a mortgage).
- Purchasing a property in an unsuitable location for your market.
- Underestimating the cost of refurbishment or modernisation required to bring it up to the required standard.
- Underestimating other expenses, such as taxes, advertising, running costs, insurance.
- Underestimating the time allowed for renovation, restoration and decoration required to bring the property up to the required standard.
- Overestimating the rent you can charge.
- Overestimating occupancy (i.e. the number of weeks or days the property will be let) or the amount of time it will take to achieve the desired occupancy level.
- Failing to allow for problems, such as tenants who cause damage or demand refunds.

 Running a *gîte* or a B&B is hard work and not suitable for those looking for an activity compatible with semi-retirement.

Market

If you're planning to let to holidaymakers, you should bear in mind (although you shouldn't need reminding) that tourism is a fragile industry, being affected by a host of factors outside the control of property owners, travel agents, tour operators, airlines and other 'service providers'.

One of the most influential factors is the economic climate of both the host country and those parts of the world from which its clientele is attracted. People's spending power (and habits) change in line with their wealth and their sense of financial security. A downturn in the economy of, say, the US or the UK, not to mention a currency devaluation or stock market crash, can cut your clientele in half virtually overnight. On the other hand, of course, you may find new markets in countries where the economy is booming, such as China.

Needless to say, people's propensity to travel – especially by air – is affected by political unrest and, particularly, global terrorism. Even a bad air or rail crash can dissuade holidaymakers from travelling abroad.

The holiday industry is also affected by the weather – one summer's reported floods, heat wave or hurricanes can have a serious adverse effect on the number of bookings received the following year.

To these one can add such factors as changes in school holiday dates, transport price rises (caused by rising fuel costs, for example), outbreaks of disease or mere anti-French feeling . . . the list of things that can make your dream turn sour is long! Nevertheless, come rain or shine, people go on holiday each year and France is the top holiday destination in Europe, with over 70 million tourists every year.

If you're intending to let long term, your market will be a very different one. Rented accommodation, both furnished and unfurnished, is in demand in cities and towns throughout France – for business people, and students who want to be near a college or university. Only 57 per cent of French people own their homes, so there's continuing demand for rental accommodation (see page 167).

Regulations

If you let a property, you should be aware that there are separate laws governing long-term unfurnished accommodation, long-term furnished accommodation and holiday lettings, i.e. furnished lets of less than six months (see **Chapters 2, 3** and **4**).

Owning and operating a *gîte* or B&B accommodation isn't usually considered a commercial activity by the French authorities (although you must pay tax on the income), provided you don't operate on a scale that necessitates setting up a trading company or registering as a business. Operating as an individual rather than trading through a company usually means lower taxes and social security payments. A property with five (in some areas six) or more rooms to let for B&B, or accommodating more than 15 people, is classed as a commercial business and is more expensive to establish and operate.

Income

When buying to let, you must ensure that the rental income will cover the mortgage (if applicable), outgoings and vacant (void) periods. If you're planning to let a property, it's important not to overestimate the income, particularly if you're relying on letting income to help pay the mortgage and running costs. Buyers who over-stretch their financial resources often find themselves on the rental treadmill, constantly struggling to find sufficient income to cover their running costs and mortgage payments – you're highly unlikely to meet your mortgage payments and running costs from rental income alone.

Yields vary considerably with the region or city and the type of property. The yield is your annual profit on your investment, usually expressed as a percentage of its cost or of its current value, and can be used to compare the effectiveness of your property as an investment with that of other investments, such as savings and shares. You must take into account all outgoings – purchase price, purchase fees and taxes, mortgage payments, local taxes, income tax, maintenance and repairs, utility bills, marketing, etc. – and balance these against your projected rental income in order to estimate your potential profit.

SURVIVAL TIP
Most experts recommend that you don't purchase a home in France if you must rely on rental income to pay for it.

Bear in mind also that you must pay French income tax on earnings from a letting business, even if you're a non-resident. If you're a French resident, you must also make social security contributions, which are higher than in many other countries and considerably higher than in the UK, for example.

 It's difficult to make a living providing holiday accommodation in most areas, as the season is too short and there's too much competition (the market is saturated in many regions).

BUYING FOR INVESTMENT

Investing in property is attractive as long as property values rise faster than inflation. Not long ago, buying property in France (and in most other countries) wasn't perceived as a good investment compared with the return on income that could be achieved by investing elsewhere. The property slump of the '90s caused many overseas buyers to lose money – and even to lose their French homes. In recent years, however, many investors have lost money on the stock market and lost confidence in pension funds and companies, while property has become a more attractive investment proposition. In the last five years or so, in particular, French property has been an excellent investment, prices having performed well in many parts of France. Some properties in parts of Paris and the Côte d'Azur have doubled in value, far out-performing the stock market and all forms of savings.

As a rule of thumb, property values in France double every seven years, although in recent years in some areas a similar increase has occurred in as little as three or four years (i.e. annual price rises of around 20 per cent), even without the owners making any improvements. Even in rural areas, where in past years prices didn't rise substantially, a price increase of 10 to 20 per cent per year isn't uncommon. This is partly due to the increase in the number of foreigners buying – in one area of the department of Manche (Normandy), 19 per cent of all sales in 2004 were to British buyers.

Nevertheless, property values are affected by a myriad of factors and can plummet almost overnight, so a property investment should be considered over the medium to long term: a minimum of five and preferably at least 10 or 15 years. Investments can be risky over the short to medium term – unless you get an absolute bargain or add value without spending more than you could hope to recoup when selling.

SURVIVAL TIP
**Whatever the state of the property market,
the best way to make money when selling property is
to not pay too much in the first place!**

When buying for investment, you must also take into account that capital gains tax will be payable when you sell the property, as it won't be your principal residence (see page 219) and, if you let it, that you must pay income tax on your earnings (see page 212).

SURVIVAL TIP
**Before buying for investment, think how easy
a property will be to sell – if it will be easy to sell,
it will also be a good investment.**

Buying Off Plan

Many people buy properties off plan and sell on completion to make a quick profit. Usually the earlier you buy off plan the better the deal, as developers are keen to bank some money before they start building. You sign a preliminary contract and pay a booking deposit – 5 per cent if the building will be completed within one year, 2 per cent if it's to be finished within two years. Your purchase is protected under the *Code de la Construction et de l'Habitation*. For further information, refer to *Buying a Home in France* (Survival Books – see page 317).

WHERE TO BUY

If you're buying with the intention to let a property, consider your target market. A popular choice for foreigners buying in France is to cater for the holiday trade, mainly letting as self-catering accommodation (see **Chapter 2**) or running a *chambres d'hôtes* business (see **Chapter 3**). Such properties should obviously be situated in areas popular for tourism.

The most recent French government statistics on the top tourist destinations in France show Corsica as the most popular, then the Mediterranean coastal regions – Languedoc-Roussillon and Provence-Alpes-Côte d'Azur. These are followed closely by Brittany, Lower Normandy, Aquitaine, Poitou-Charentes, Rhône-Alps and the Auvergne. Next come the Pays de la Loire, Midi-Pyrénées, Limousin, Bourgogne, Franche-Comté and Alsace. The lowest figures are for Centre and the northerly regions – Upper Normandy, Picardy, Nord-Pas-de-Calais, Champagne-Ardenne and Lorraine.

Paris is the most popular tourist destination in the world, but the Paris region is, surprisingly, also in the lower group. This could be because the figures are based on the number of overnight stays (visitors to Paris tend to stay for only a few nights). Nevertheless, property in Paris lets well, with a potentially longer season than many other areas. The figures include French nationals as well as those from other countries. French residents generally go south and to Corsica for their summer holidays. Those who live in the south of the country go north for a cooler climate or to visit relatives or friends, and city dwellers go to the country.

Bear in mind that these statistics include hotel accommodation as well as *gîtes* and *chambres d'hôtes*. There's a growth market in 'green tourism' (*le tourisme vert*), as urban residents seek peace and quiet in the countryside.

 In many popular holiday areas, the rental market is now saturated, and owners are unable to find enough customers to generate sufficient income.

The letting season is longest in Paris, where you can let year-round either as holiday accommodation or for longer lets and may achieve 35 weeks' rental. Southern France, particularly the Côte d'Azur, is the next most popular for letting and you may be able to let an apartment for 30 weeks or a villa for 25 during the spring, summer and early autumn. In Normandy and Brittany, if you're within 30 minutes of the coast (and within an hour of a Channel port) and your marketing is efficient, you can also achieve 30-plus weeks. In other coastal areas, the summer season may be limited to around 20 weeks. Inland properties are generally restricted to a maximum of 16 weeks and in some areas the letting season can be as short as ten weeks. **However, you're unlikely to achieve this many weeks' occupancy and you should budget for around half these figures, even when letting full time.** The Alps are a special case, as there are two letting seasons, summer and winter; however, properties in ski resorts are astronomically expensive.

Properties close to an airport have good letting potential, but airlines (especially budget operators) change routes frequently, or even go out of business, and you shouldn't rely on a particular airline service for your clientele. In any case, flying isn't for everyone: families with small children and/or a lot of luggage will find flying expensive or inconvenient, or both.

You may dream of owning a country hideaway, far from the madd(en)ing crowd. But if you're buying with a view to catering for holiday trade, make sure it isn't **too** hidden away. Your guests won't return (or recommend you) if they spend hours finding the place or must drive miles along unmade roads or halfway up a mountain to get to it – and every time they want to go anywhere.

Details of French tourism statistics and further information can be found on ⌨ www.tourisme.gouv.fr. This book's sister publication, *The Best Places to Buy a Home in France* provides details of each of France's 22 regions, including property prices (see page 317).

WHAT TO BUY

Once you've decided on the best area to buy in, you must make sure that you purchase the right type of property for your chosen purpose. If you're planning a holiday letting business, you will need an attractive property that people want to come and stay in – this may seem like stating the obvious, but many people buy cowsheds which, when converted, still look like cowsheds. They may be beautifully renovated and equipped, but the point at which you sell a holiday is when the client sees the advertisement. Saunas, luxury kitchens and video games machines don't sell holidays – photographs do. A pretty house with stunning views and a swimming pool (that does make a difference), even if fairly basically equipped, will let well. A luxuriously appointed property that looks like a barn or a concrete toilet block won't, unless you spend an unnecessary amount of time and money in marketing.

For long-term lets you must find out what type of property is in demand in your chosen area. One way of doing this is to ask local estate agents, most of whom also deal with property letting.

If you aren't intending to live in France, don't buy a huge property that requires a lot of maintenance – paying a caretaker or property manager will eat up your profits. Even if you're planning to become a French resident, don't be tempted to take on too much or you may regret it later.

SURVIVAL TIP
If you're combining a desire for a more relaxed lifestyle with a plan to run a letting business to help finance it, don't forget the lifestyle side of the equation!

Land

Most people's dream French property is a picturesque country cottage with extensive land and gardens, and it's often tempting to acquire a vast amount of land. But too much land is usually a liability, **not** an asset. Bear in mind the costs, time and hard work involved in maintaining such a property. If you don't live there all the time, who will do this work? If you want a tidy garden, the lawn will have to be mown twice a week at some times of the year (everything grows **much** faster in France than in the UK, for example) and you will spend all your holidays hacking away the undergrowth. Allowing a farmer to use the land might seem a good idea, but this often has legal implications, in some circumstances leading to his having rights of tenancy and even first refusal on the land should you decide to sell. If you plan to live in the property, dreams of self-sufficiency are all very well, but you don't need ten hectares (or even one hectare) of fields to keep a few hens and grow a few vegetables!

Buildings

Another frequent mistake made by foreign buyers, in whose home country such properties are either scarce or too expensive, is to purchase a property with several outbuildings, which are often in a poor state of repair. What will you do with them? Do you have the finance, skills, energy and motivation (and can you obtain the planning permission) to convert them into holiday accommodation units? The average person's experience of do-it-yourself will not be sufficient to undertake a major restoration project. If not, they will need constant maintenance just to keep them from falling down, which costs time and money. If you're in an older age group, consider whether you're prepared to take on the burden of never-ending property maintenance – will you still be able to cope with it in ten years' time? Many owners will tell you that they never foresaw the amount of work and money that's absorbed by a restoration or renovation project and advise others against it!

Community Properties

Many properties are community properties, i.e. an apartment or house in a development where there are shared facilities. Properties are owned outright, but ownership of communal areas (staircases, lifts, gardens, etc.) is shared with other owners. Check before buying an apartment that letting is permitted and what restrictions apply (you may be required to notify the community 'manager', for example). You must also inform your insurance company if a property is to be let.

Old or New?

The 'perfect' French property may be a traditional house or cottage at least 100 years old, made of stone, brick and wood. But new properties can be an excellent alternative as an investment, often working out cheaper than an older home, particularly when the cost of renovation is taken into account (see below). There are other advantages to buying new: new buildings must be sold with a ten-year guarantee, with a further two-year warranty on equipment, and must comply with modern building regulations.

Renovation

The secret to making money on property is buying what nobody else wants to take on (at a knockdown price) and turning it around. When looking for a property that needs refurbishing or modernisation or one where you can add value with a loft conversion, annexe or extension, it's essential not to pay too much for it. **One of the most common mistakes that people make is to pay too much for a restoration property and to underestimate the cost of the work required.** If you buy a ruin for restoration, you must be prepared to spend a lot of money and probably a lot more than you bargained for, as a major restoration almost never comes in on budget! It will also take you much longer than planned. **It isn't always easy to get a loan on a property requiring complete restoration.**

You must check that you will be allowed to make the alterations you have in mind, as planning regulations can be restrictive, especially in historic or scenic villages or towns.

If you're planning to buy a property that needs renovation or restoration, you should arrange for a builder to inspect it and provide a quotation (add **at least** 25 per cent for unforeseen problems). You must know **exactly** what you plan to do before starting work and to have architect's drawings for all structural alterations. This can add a further €2,000 to €3,000, even for a simple barn conversion. You must also know how much each job will add to the value of a property – so that you don't waste money doing non-essential work that adds little or no value – and obtain an accurate valuation of what the restored property will be worth. Spending too much money on renovation is a common mistake.

A property must be well renovated, but there's little point in spending a fortune on a designer kitchen, fancy bathrooms, double glazing, conservatories and power showers if they're out of character with the property, or if the sort of tenant or buyer you can expect to attract won't be interested in paying for such things. You must keep all the receipts to offset against capital gains tax when selling, and therefore the work must be carried out by registered tradesmen, not 'on the black' by people working illegally.

Somewhere between the estimated value after restoration and the cost of renovation is the amount you should pay for a property. For example, if the restored value is estimated at €300,000 and the cost of restoration will be €100,000 (allowing for contingencies), you should pay no more than €200,000 – much less if you want to make a reasonable profit. You must allow for budget over-runs and the fees associated with buying and selling, if you plan to sell as soon as the restoration is completed. **You must also bear in mind that the property market could fall by the time that you're ready to sell.**

For more information on renovating a home, refer to *Renovating & Maintaining Your French Home* (Survival Books – see page 317).

CASE STUDY 1

Living in Buckinghamshire, near London, we had always enjoyed holidaying in France because of the variety of beautiful regions, food and wine and the humane lifestyle. In 1995, we were inspired by a holiday in a B&B in the Beaujolais area, where we realised that this was a way we could work together to earn a living: Bob was an architect/interior designer who had worked in the fashion business and had renovated several home before, as well as being a wonderful cook, and I, Celia, enjoy meeting people and interior design and furniture and painting.

Although we loved the Beaujolais area, which had the most beautiful scenery (and not bad wine), it had a Continental climate and we knew that to run a holiday business we needed a warmer, Mediterranean climate. This, we discovered, started below the town of Valence, in the Drôme region. We holidayed there, to check it out, as it was then fairly unknown; most people careered down to the Luberon and the south coast. We found it beautiful, with affordable property and well situated in relation to motorways, airports and the towns of Lyon, Valence and

Avignon. We loved it and felt that we'd discovered a new holiday destination.

We had a very specific brief to follow in searching for a house or farm:
- It should be in a semi-rural area.
- It should have a potential habitable space (including renovated lofts and agricultural buildings) of 500m².
- It should be built of stone (and the stonework should be exposed).
- It should have a lovely view.
- It shouldn't be too far from basic amenities and services.
- It should have not more than 1ha (2.5 acres) of land.

We saw around 50 properties in the space of two years (using all our holidays to search) and were happy to find a farm that needed total rebuilding, which meant that we could plan exactly how to use the space available. It had two habitable rooms and a collection of filthy, semi-ruined agricultural buildings. We bought it in 1997.

It was a good choice, and Bob redesigned the space to suit our business needs and give us the income we needed: five *chambres d'hôtes* and two *gîtes*.

We marketed mainly through the Chez Nous homeowners' catalogue published in the UK and a Canadian website called 'En France'. Chez Nous, which cost around £700 per year, has provided 80 per cent of our clientele, and En France, costing around £100, a further 10 per cent. The remaining 10 per cent consist of friends and acquaintances. We have an 80 per cent return rate, but must always keep new people coming, so we continue to advertise with these two companies.

Several cheap or free internet sites haven't been worthwhile – we've had maybe five bookings from them in total. We may consider one of the leading (and more expensive) sites if Chez Nous, which also has a website, should ever slow down.

In general, we've had delightful customers, but we're absolutely dedicated to making sure that their holiday is really good. This involves being always available – virtually 24 hours a day between April and October – to give advice, suggest trips, organise wine tastings, walks, pony rides and visits to artists' studios, etc., as well as preparing and serving breakfasts and evening meals. We steal around one-and-a-half hours to rest in the afternoons, but otherwise we're committed to the business and have no social life at all (one of us manages to go to church on Sundays).

Our worst experience was a Swiss couple who appeared trustworthy (Range Rover, cashmere sweaters, etc.) and stayed for six weeks in one of our *gîtes* and left without paying. Screaming children can be painful for other guests, so we normally suggest that families with small children stay in one of the *gîtes*.

We were reasonably pleased to have a good number of bookings in our first year, and those people who returned plus new visitors gave us a healthy second year. The only glitch was that, having stated our prices in sterling, we lost a substantial amount in 2002/3 on account of the poor exchange rate to euros. We quote all prices in euros now.

We think the fact that we cook evening meals, everyone eating *en famille*, is one of our greatest attractions, which people return for – but which makes life exhausting! Often, couples want to have interesting company to interact with over a home-cooked evening meal (including vegetables from the garden) in the courtyard, with plenty of good Côtes du Rhône wine.

We encountered some mystifying rules relating to planning permission, which proved painful when we were trying to build extensions to ex-farm buildings – inflexible, unreasonable old rules which don't apply today but **are** applied, as that's how it has always been done!

Our biggest problem initially was trying to get advice on how to run the business within the French system. Talking to as many people as possible is important. Had we not needed to have the VAT on all the building work refunded, which necessitated setting up a formal business, we would certainly not have become an *enterprise*, but remained private individuals, paying normal income tax. The very high social charges we must pay for widows', orphans' and unemployment benefits, as well as for healthcare, eat into our profits – on an escalating scale, the more we earn. It makes us want to reinvest our money to reduce our profit, on which the charges are calculated.

However, the healthcare is very good – as long as you can pay for a complementary insurance (this costs us €1,700 per year), which tops up what the state pays.

Employing staff is very painful and expensive: it necessitates the completion of umpteen forms for various bodies, and you pay out virtually double the employees' wages to cover their social charges. The system encourages employers to pay people cash in hand, which doesn't seem right.

With hindsight, we're glad to have calculated accurately the income we expected to generate from the size of property we had (ten weeks' letting is a good initial projection). It's easy to romanticise about growing one's own vegetables, living from the land, etc. and getting by on next to nothing, but life isn't much cheaper in France than in the UK (electricity is madly expensive), and it's important to be realistic about how much you must earn.

Couples with children must really enter the French social security system, but an older couple can take out private medical insurance, have a private income without registering with the Chamber of Commerce, and be liable just for income tax. This would have been our ideal scenario but, once committed, it's difficult to withdraw unless you move or close your business.

We require the extra income from B&B and meals, as we have a mortgage. But when it's paid off, our aim is to have self-catering accommodation only, which is generally filled in high season. Offering B&B and meals can extend the season at both ends (May and September) and is worth the enormous commitment and relentless effort while you're fit enough to manage it.

We started with dinner seven evenings a week, now it's five and next year perhaps it will be four. However, many customers come especially for the camaraderie and fun at dinner time, so there's a fine balance to be made.

Also, we try not to be too upmarket, as attracting a five-star-hotel-type person, who's picky and demanding, can give you lots of headaches. Our prices are reasonable and we attract a wide variety of people, including window-cleaners, lawyers, chip shop owners and teachers, all of whom mix unexpectedly well. And they're all on holiday to enjoy themselves, which makes our job easier!

We offer the following advice to others contemplating a similar business:

- Make sure the location and climate are right to attract visitors throughout your planned season – and to suit your planned lifestyle. Bear in mind that there's never much business to be had in winter, when France can be cold, so it isn't worth opening.

- Add 20 per cent to all projected costs; there are many unexpected expenses.

- Make sure you have enough money to create the accommodation from which you intend to earn a living; we worked on renovation for 20 months with no income.

- Be prepared, if you do B&B with meals, to have no other life during the season and to be working relentlessly. You can look forward to a tranquil winter!

- Stay out of the formal business system as far as possible, but do have an accountant to fill in all the forms for you.

- Create a private space for yourselves — especially your own sitting room.

- Make sure, above all, that your own accommodation gives you what you've dreamed about when living in France. You have to live there 12 months a year; your visitors are there only for very short periods.

Bob & Celia Christmas, La Roche Colombe, route de Manas, 26450 Charols (☎ 04 75 90 48 22, 🖳 www.larochecolombe.com)

TOP TEN MONEY-EARNING TIPS

If you're considering investing in French property:

- Do your research and choose the area carefully according to your needs and expectations.

- Ascertain the letting potential in the area you've chosen by talking to agents and local people and by searching internet holiday sites.

- By the same means, get an idea of the rental you can charge.

- Don't buy a property that's unsuitable for the purpose you have in mind, however attractive it might appear. Viewing houses for sale is one of the later stages in the process – not to be done whilst on a sunny holiday!

- Do your sums carefully, then reduce your expected income and increase your anticipated costs by 25 per cent and do them again.

- Ensure that you have enough information to make a dispassionate decision.

- Ensure that you're aware of all the risks involved and that you're comfortable taking those risks.

- Ensure that you can afford to tie up your capital for as long as it takes to show a profit.

- Research your market and give yourself the best possible chance of attracting tenants, but don't overestimate occupancy levels, particularly in the first few years.

- Acquaint yourself with French inheritance laws and how they may affect your property ownership.

For further information on buying property, refer to *Buying a Home in France* (Survival Books – see page 317).

2.

GÎTES

The French word *gîte* means, literally, resting-place, shelter or lodging. It has become the generic term for what is known in the UK and elsewhere as a holiday cottage or, more generally, self-catering accommodation, mainly resulting from its use by the organisation Gîtes de France (see page 55). Furnished self-catering accommodation in France is generally referred to as a *gîte* and can be anything from one or two converted outhouses to a large luxury property with a number of self-contained apartments and cottages. In this chapter we deal mainly with the popular conception of a *gîte* – a rural self-catering cottage.

Running one or more *gîtes* is a popular choice for those relocating abroad because the legal implications of setting up an accommodation business aren't as restrictive as those for other types of business in France. In general, setting up as self-employed involves a huge amount of bureaucracy and paperwork which is difficult enough for French people to wade through – even more so if you aren't fluent in French and unfamiliar with the process. *Gîtes* aren't considered a professional activity, so it may not be necessary to register them as a business if you're operating on a small scale. It makes sense to have a number of units, thus reducing the running cost per unit and spreading the cost of installing amenities such as a swimming pool, but bear in mind that you may then have to register (see **Registration** on page 53). In any case, you do, of course, have to pay tax on the income earned (see page 212).

SURVIVAL TIP
You won't earn enough to live on unless you have
a number of luxury *gîtes* with a pool.

Gîte owners generally fall into three categories:

● Those who buy expressly with the purpose of running a business: as an investment.

● Second-homeowners (whose principal residence is in France or in another country) who let their holiday home when they aren't using the property themselves.

● Those who live in France and have spare buildings on the site of their principal residence to convert in order to supplement their income. (This is a popular choice among UK residents.)

Running a *gîte* business can be rewarding and pleasurable, as well as helping to contribute towards the running costs of a property. For the third category of owner, it's less intensive than running a bed and breakfast (B&B); with a little consideration and care in setting up, you can preserve your privacy and enjoy your own home.

CASE STUDY 2

We ran a successful marketing company in Northamptonshire with 100 employees, but when the opportunity arose to sell the business to a larger American company, we seized the chance to provide our children (then aged eight and six) with a bilingual upbringing and a taste of other cultures. Linguistically, we were well prepared: Tim had a degree in French and economics, while Chloe had A Level and business French qualifications.

Our main business is the running of a *gîte* complex on the Dordogne/Charente border, which we took over in a rundown state and developed. Currently, it consists of three *gîtes*, to which we've recently added an on-site restaurant. This has proved attractive to many British and some French customers. The business is better each year than the last, although we sense that it's getting harder as more rental properties come on to the market.

We had little trouble in making the transition in July 2001, although the timing of sales of three homes in the UK was a challenge. We put this down partly to realising that bureaucracy is really just a matter of understanding a different culture and system. We're sure that anybody arriving in the UK for the first time would struggle similarly with council tax, road fund licences, speed cameras and the Inland Revenue. It's a surprise that émigrés to France don't expect the bureaucracy to be difficult. Difficulties come from not knowing – and you never know what you don't know!

Opening the restaurant brought its own share of red tape. We had to learn about live music licences, the four different kinds of drinking licence, restaurant licences and health and safety inspections by the sapeurs-pompiers. Similarly, with the change in the European law on septic tanks and new legislation on pool safety – you just have to discover it somehow and then deal with it.

In addition to running the *gîtes*, Tim manages the letting of properties we own as investments in the UK and US, while Chloe works part-time at a French language school in the local town. Tim also lectures to courses for people considering going into the *gîte* business, from which the following advice to participants, including what to do and what not to do, has been adapted:

- Make a friend of the mayor, who's responsible for adherence to the laws in his commune. In some senses, what he says goes.

- Ask for help at the *mairie*, from other *gîte* owners, magazines, websites, helplines, etc.

- Avoid:
  - Disregarding all the advice given.
  - Buying in the 'wrong' area (e.g. with inadequate attractions to prompt return visits or recommendations).
  - Buying the 'wrong' property (too big or small, with too much land).
  - Overspending on purchase and renovation.
  - Not leaving sufficient financial 'cushion' for unexpected expenditure.
  - Not allowing sufficient funds to live on while building the business.
  - Undertaking too much renovation for the time (or money) available before the first holidaymakers arrive.
  - Underestimating the time required for renovation (always slower than you think).
  - Making false economies on furnishings, fittings and appliances.
  - Extravagant advertising.
  - Inadequate monitoring of advertising response and failure to adjust accordingly.
  - Overestimating the length of the rental season.
  - Vague rental terms and conditions, which can lead to misunderstandings and disputes.
  - Insufficiently clear directions to the property.
  - Underestimating the time and energy required for thorough cleaning on changeover days.
  - Inattention to detail in presentation, advertising, administration, etc.
  - Neglecting safety issues (e.g. notices around the pool).
  - Not having a complaints procedure (e.g. how, how soon and to whom faults should be reported).

- Skimping on insurance, particularly public liability.
- Creating unnecessary hostility (e.g. unclear or petty restrictions on where to park or sunbathe, when the pool may be used), which can make guests feel unwelcome.
- Expecting the French to do things the English (or any other) way – they won't!
- Making too little effort to learn French or improve your French.
- Struggling alone.
- Forgetting to enjoy the experience!

Tim and Chloe Williams: *Gîtes* (☎ 05 45 78 65 80, ✉ timdwilliams@wanadoo.fr); *Gîte courses* (💻 www.gitecomplexes.co.uk)

If you intend to register your *gîte* with Gîtes de France or Clévacances (see page 53), they send a representative to inspect the property and advise you on facilities required and planning application procedures and costs, as well as providing an estimate of the income you can expect to earn. It might be possible to use this service even if you don't plan to register with these organisations in order to help you with your planning, although you may consider this unethical.

THE MARKET

It's impossible to estimate the number of *gîte* and related self-catering properties in France, as many are independently run and not subject to any central registration. The following figures apply **only** to those properties registered with Gîtes de France (see page 55), the majority of whose clients are French.

- There are currently 42,000 owners of *Gîtes Ruraux* and 55,000 properties; on average, a further 2,200 are created each year.

- 30 million days' holiday are taken in *Gîtes Ruraux* each year, which means that the total (French) market for *Gîtes Ruraux* is around 3 million people.

- The average rental period is 17.33 weeks per year, with guests staying 1.5 weeks on each visit (in other words, roughly half of guests stay for one week and half for two), and the average annual occupancy rate (the number of weeks' rental as a percentage of the number of weeks the *gîte* is open) is 43.4 per cent.

- The average cost of creating a *Gîte Rural* is €58,000, including building works and interior furnishing and decoration.

- Overseas visitors represent one fifth of Gîtes de France's clientele – mainly English and Belgian, but also Dutch and German.

- The average weekly rent is €387 during the high season and €259 during the low season, the average weekend rate €154.

Gîtes are extremely popular with families, mainly couples aged between 25 and 44 with two children under 15, who live in cities and own their own homes. 50 per cent of customers are middle-management or senior executives and professional people; 18 per cent work in offices. Although customers remain loyal, only 15 per cent go back to the same *gîte* on a regular basis, whereas 72 per cent choose a different location within the Gîtes de France network every year.

Recent reports state that the *gîte* market is reaching (or in some areas has already reached) saturation point, with more accommodation available than there are clients – in some areas there are as many as five *gîtes* for every potential booking. Moreover, interest in buying French property has never been higher, and a lot of prospective buyers will be considering converting one or more buildings to accommodation use. It's therefore more important than ever to research the market – you need to know what makes a successful letting business, why some *gîtes* are let for over 30 weeks per year while other owners are struggling to achieve five or six weeks' occupation.

As demand has increased, so too have the expectations of clients. Whereas in the past a *gîte* was perceived as a fairly basic form of holiday accommodation, nowadays a higher level of comfort is expected and many holidaymakers expect a 'home from home' with all the amenities that implies – and of a much higher quality than in the past.

You stand a better chance of success if you:

- Identify your target market and keep it as wide as possible, always looking for ways to expand and extend your season.

- Do some research into how people choose their holiday destinations (weather, culture, facilities, easy travel, etc.).

- Anticipate clients' requirements.

- Exceed clients' expectations.

- Adapt with a changing market – improve facilities, add a pool, etc.

- Maintain contact with clients.

- Foster word-of-mouth promotion.

- Give your business the personal touch.

French or Foreigners?

It makes sense to target as many potential clients as possible. However, spreading your marketing too thinly can reduce its efficiency. One of the prime considerations is to decide whether to specifically target French guests, in which case registering with Gîtes de France, Clévacances and/or your regional or departmental tourist board is recommended – 80 per cent of their customers are from within France. Most French people are quite traditional in their holidaying habits, the greatest demand being for the last week of July and the first two weeks of August, and the Easter and Whitsun (*Pentecôte*) holidays. If you have French clients, you must of course be able to read, write and speak French (including answering the telephone!). If you aren't fluent in French (which is increasingly being made a requirement of registration with tourist boards, etc.), it's better to concentrate on attracting clients who speak your language, which may in any case allow you to sell a larger number of weeks.

ADVANTAGES & DISADVANTAGES

Running a *gîte*, as compared with running any other business in France, and particularly bed and breakfast accommodation (see **Chapter 3**), has a number of advantages and disadvantages. Advantages include the following:

- Tax breaks (legislation in France favours anything to do with the tourist industry and in particular *gîtes*).
- No formal qualifications or experience required.
- No special permission/licence required (unless your business is large enough to need to be registered – see **Legal Considerations** on page 50).
- No need to be on site to cater to guests (as with B&B), you can even run your business 'remotely' (e.g. from another country), although you will need a caretaker and other maintenance staff).
- Guests largely look after themselves (unlike B&B guests).

Possible disadvantages include the following (some apply only to a property you use yourself as a holiday home):

- The cost of purchase: a property suitable for use as a *gîte*, especially if it needs extensive modernisation, can cost €80,000 or more, in addition to the cost of your home (see also **Buying an Existing Business** on page 48).
- The cost of maintaining the property to a high standard, including caretaking expenses.

- Not enough income to live on unless you have a number of *gîtes* or a complex.

- Having to decorate and furnish your property to appeal to others rather than yourself.

- Having to remove your personal belongings when renting.

- The possibility of having your property damaged.

- Not being able to use the property in peak season, when most of your income is generated, or for as many weeks/at the time of year you want.

- Having to take all your holidays in the same place.

- Having to spend the majority of your time when in your holiday home doing repairs and maintenance, gardening and decorating.

QUALIFICATIONS & EXPERIENCE

Unless you have a reasonable grasp of French – including reading and writing – you will find it very difficult to navigate the rules and regulations, cope with tax forms and deal with the never-ending bureaucracy for which France is famous, and you will be severely limited in the number of French clients you can attract. Unless you have good French, it's therefore virtually essential that you learn the language or improve your skills **before** starting a *gîte* business. Even if you're using an agency and dealing mainly with English-speakers, you still have to deal with paying your property and income taxes, negotiate with builders, suppliers, architects, etc. If you're intending to let to French people, speaking their language is a must.

Other tasks you must be able to do efficiently and professionally include cleaning, building maintenance, gardening, and laundry. You can of course employ others to do these jobs but, if you choose to do so, bear in mind the costs when putting together your business plan.

You must be able to smile and be nice to strangers – even if you don't like them! This may seem obvious, but you must be realistic about the prospect of sharing your idyllic home and/or pool with other people. You may enjoy socialising, but it's an entirely different thing to have people staying with you who aren't your friends – they may have little in common with you (apart from liking France). Ask yourself how you will cope with a people-carrier driving onto your lovingly maintained lawn, disgorging a quantity of disgruntled teenagers or tired but overactive toddlers who then run amok in your flowerbeds and start wrenching branches off your beautifully pruned shrubs (having arrived three hours later than expected, when you'd planned a much-needed evening out), or with the reluctant partner who moans from the moment of arrival – he or she would much rather be in a modern apartment on the Costa del Sol than facing two weeks in a 300-year-old cottage in rainy Brittany . . . Your job will be to smile, welcome them, sympathise, and enable them to make the most of their stay so that, if they don't return (heaven forbid!), at least they put in a good word for you among their friends and relatives back home. You must be prepared to deal diplomatically with any badly behaved children, broken appliances, leaking roofs and any other problems, both real and imagined. Whether problems are within your control or not, they're ultimately your responsibility to resolve, as you're providing a service for which your guests are paying. In short, you must be able to put yourself in the place of your clients and act as you would expect your host to act. Note, however, that some people will attempt to obtain a refund by complaining about almost everything, including the size of the pool or fridge and a lack of air-conditioning equipment or tennis court. You must decide (in advance) whether you will budget for 'goodwill' refunds in such cases or whether you will refuse a refund and accept that these clients will give you a bad reference (they probably will anyway!).

WHERE TO BUY

This is probably the most important factor in determining whether your business will succeed or fail. There are still some areas of France where you can buy a lovely old farm building that has barns ripe for conversion to *gîtes* at what might seem to be a reasonable cost. If you find one, ask yourself why someone hasn't already bought it with the same intention. Do people holiday in this area? Will the costs of renovation and/or conversion be too high? Will you even obtain permission to do so?

SURVIVAL TIP
If you're buying in France with a view to setting up
a business, you must buy where other people want to go
on holiday, not necessarily where you want to live.

Although location is paramount, it's impossible to give details of the best locations in France to set up *gîtes* beyond a few more or less obvious generalisations, such as coastal areas tend to be more popular than inland departments – with the exception of Dordogne. Anyone, anywhere can probably let the last two weeks of July and the month of August; you need to find something to attract holidaymakers outside these few weeks. It's therefore essential to carry out detailed research at regional, departmental and local levels.

For example, the Brittany and Normandy regions are particularly popular among *gîte* clients – they're both well served by the Channel ferry ports, have plenty of attractions and usually book up faster than properties in areas further south, with coastal locations booking first of all. Brittany has over 25 per cent (3,000km) of the French coastline (nowhere in Brittany is more than an hour's drive from the sea). The main disadvantage of these two regions compared to the south is the variable weather.

The department of Mayenne is an example of a poor area for letting: although adjacent to Normandy, the number of holiday weeks per property let there is a fraction of the neighbouring department. Holidaymakers have heard of Normandy, there are few that know of Mayenne. Delightful though it is, it has none of the advantages mentioned above, neither does it enjoy the hot climate of places further south and the seaside is a long day trip.

Look for undiscovered potential – areas such as the Dordogne are saturated (some owners report that, although several years ago they could easily let 20 weeks, they're now struggling to fill six). For example, there's currently a shortage of holiday accommodation in Meuse and Ardennes, where properties suitable for conversion to *gîtes* are available from around €50,000 to €150,000 and properties for extensive renovation start at around €20,000. The World War One (WW1) battlefields and monuments, the attractive countryside and the easy accessibility for British holidaymakers on short breaks all create a demand here.

If your preferred area is somewhere you've been on holiday, it's likely to be a popular spot – but how many *gîtes* are there already, and what about the low season? If you aren't familiar with the area or areas you're considering, find out what attractions it has to offer and when they're available (many are closed or have limited opening times out of season).

The majority of holidaymakers go to places they've heard of, for one reason or another. Even if wanting to get away from it all, and wishing to spend a week or two in an isolated rural idyll, they will choose one area over another on account of local attractions – e.g. there may be a famous historical town, good bathing beaches, spectacular scenery or sporting facilities nearby. Of two equally pretty cottages in a brochure, it's the one near the sea or a tourist hotspot that gets more bookings.

Most *gîte* bookings are for a week or two weeks as opposed to B&B, where people often spend a night or two or three in several different locations. *Gîte* letting is therefore more dependent on there being plenty of interest in the surrounding area, with day trips to major attractions being possible.

If a property isn't within half an hour's drive of the coast, it's worth seriously considering installing a pool. Some of the better agencies won't even consider taking a property on unless it has a pool or is near the coast. Installing a pool can add €20,000 or more to your set-up costs and a great deal to your running costs, but a much higher rental can be charged and/or more weeks can be sold.

For further information on where to buy and a guide to the regions, refer to *The Best Places to Buy a Home in France* (Survival Books – see page 317). In particular, you should consider the following factors.

Climate

Properties in an area with a pleasant year-round climate such as the Mediterranean coast and Corsica have a greater rental potential, particularly outside the high season (subject, of course, to the level of competition). This is also important should you wish to use the property yourself outside the high season; for example, you could let a property during the summer months, when rental rates are at their highest, and use it yourself in May or October and still enjoy fine weather.

Proximity to an Airport or Ferry Port

For holidaymakers from overseas it's a great advantage for a property to be situated within easy travelling distance of a channel ferry port, major airport or *TGV* station. Many holidaymakers would prefer not to travel more than 45 minutes to their destination after arriving in France. Some may choose a combination of air transport, train and hire car. Make sure you choose an airport with frequent flights from the UK, if that's where you intend to advertise. Many visitors from the US and other parts of the world travel via the UK; others come via Paris. **It isn't wise to rely on an airport served only by budget airlines, as they may alter or cancel routes at short notice.**

Accessibility

The journey to your property should be easy – both the long haul (ferry trips or flights) and the drive from the port or airport. If it's in the country where signposts are all but non-existent, you must not only provide a detailed map with plenty of landmarks, but you may also need to erect signs (for which permission might be necessary – see page 86). Holidaymakers who spend hours driving around trying to find a holiday home are unlikely to return or recommend it!

For those who don't travel by car, it's an advantage if a property is served by public transport (e.g. local buses) or is situated in a town where a car is unnecessary. If a property is located in a town or development with a maze of streets, you should provide a detailed map. Maps are also helpful for taxi drivers, who may be unfamiliar with the area.

If you're in a rural area that's poorly served by public transport (buses may run only on Wednesdays), be sure to advise your potential guests that their own car (or a hire car) is necessary. If you won't be living in or near the property, it should be easily accessible to you so that you can carry out necessary repairs and maintenance.

Attractions

People who choose *gîte* holidays usually want a week or fortnight's holiday in one location. (Many have two weeks' holiday, spending the first in one place and the second in another.) This makes the type of location rather different from that needed for a hotel or B&B, where a lot of clients are passing through for one or two nights.

The property should be as close as possible to a major attraction (or more than one), e.g. a beach, theme park, area of scenic beauty or well known tourist town, but the type of attraction depends on the sort of clientele you wish to attract. If you want to let to families, a property should be within easy distance of leisure activities such as theme parks, water parks, sports activities (e.g. tennis, golf, watersports) and nightlife. If you're planning to let a property in a rural area, it should be somewhere with good hiking possibilities, preferably near one of France's many natural parks. Proximity to one or more golf courses is an advantage to many holidaymakers and is an added attraction outside the high season, particularly in northern France, where there may otherwise be little to attract visitors in the winter. Properties in coastal regions (or departments within those regions) will always let well (subject to competition).

WHAT TO BUY

If you haven't yet bought a property, you're in the best position to make your *gîte* business a viable proposition. You can choose the region, the area, and the specific property with your requirements in mind. You can choose to buy an existing business (see page 48), or to buy a property with one or more buildings to convert (see page 49). Once you've chosen the area, consider renting for a while before buying, so that your capital isn't tied up while you're researching and finding properties for sale. It's wise to take one or more *gîte* holidays before setting up your own business – once you've been a customer, you're more likely to appreciate what is needed to satisfy the holidaymaker!

Carry out some research by asking agencies that let properties in that area (see list on page 95) what their criteria are and what type of property most of their clients are looking for. They will advise on the best type of property, number of bedrooms, whether or not you need a swimming pool to generate sufficient bookings, and the level of comfort required by their clients. They will tell you what will let the best in that area.

If you want to register your property with an agency such as Gîtes de France, ensure that the property meets its criteria (see **Registration** on page 53 and **Appendix F**). Consider also the following factors:

● **Access** – Rural locations are desirable, but remember that many people's idea of the countryside is idyllic rather than realistic. A great deal of the country is covered in mud – if your property has access by a private lane or drive, it must have a hard surface or gravel. Although your guests may arrive in a four-wheel drive vehicle, this doesn't necessarily mean they expect to be driving off-road!

● **Noise** – What are the neighbours like? Neighbouring farms can be noisy and smelly places. Incessantly barking dogs, crowing cockerels and loud farm machinery don't make for the ideal peaceful holiday retreat. Will the farmer be escorting his herd of Holsteins down your quiet lane at 6am and 6pm for milking? Cows in neighbouring fields cause smells and flies. Cockerels crow early in the morning, as soon as they see light. (If they're your own, you will be used to it, but do keep them shut in until a reasonable hour so that your guests aren't disturbed.) If the property is adjoining another, whether your own home or another *gîte*, it must be sufficiently soundproof so that guests won't be disturbed by others' activities at any time of night or day.

● **Garden** – In general, the type of person booking a *gîte* holiday is looking for peace and tranquillity. A typical *gîte* is a detached cottage with two to four bedrooms and its own enclosed garden or grounds. Avoid buying a property with too much land; your guests are unlikely to spend their time playing cricket or strolling around the grounds – and they certainly won't help with the gardening! Nevertheless, people staying in *gîtes* won't want to go out every day, so they must have a private outdoor area – preferably a sunny garden – in which to relax, eat, play and generally enjoy their holiday. It's preferable that this space is enclosed, especially if you cater for families with young children.

● **Buildings** – Costs of maintenance are proportional to the property's size; big isn't always better! On the other hand, there's good demand for large properties sleeping 10 to 15 people. These are suitable for two or three families taking a holiday together or larger groups such as walking enthusiasts and other clubs and organisations. They book early for the high season, as large groups have to co-ordinate their arrangements well in advance. Although you can obviously charge a lot more for a property of this size, you may not let as many weeks, as there's less demand outside school holidays. For maximum flexibility, you could consider two smaller adjoining units, which can be let individually or as one large property.

- **Swimming Pool** – Whether or not to install a swimming pool is one of the most important decisions to make, as this can double your income. If you cannot afford, or have decided not to install a swimming pool, consider buying an above ground pool. In today's competitive market, many agencies won't consider promoting properties without pools unless they're very near the coast.

The old adage of buying the worst property in the best location might work, provided it has the potential for renovation and conversion within your budget, but it's obviously preferable to find a property that's suitable for the purpose. For further information on buying property, refer to *Buying a Home in France* (Survival Books – see page 317).

BUYING AN EXISTING BUSINESS

Instead of setting up a *gîte* business from scratch, you can buy an existing business – there are plenty on the market. The major disadvantage of buying an existing business is the cost: an established *gîte* business with a good income will cost you at least €200,000 and possibly as much as €400,000. This cost is obviously in addition to the cost of your principal residence. You also won't have the freedom to arrange and style the accommodation as you would wish. On the other hand, there are several advantages to buying an existing business, including the following:

- You won't have to spend time and money renovating or adapting buildings for use as *gîtes*.

- You will (or should, if you buy a successful business) have guaranteed income from the word go, which reduces your marketing costs and lessens the risk.

- You won't be setting up in competition to existing *gîtes* and so further diluting the market, but will in effect be buying a slice of the market.

The various French property magazines (see **Appendix B**) carry advertisements, and businesses can be found via the internet (see **Appendix C**); a website that specialises in *gîte* properties is 🖥 www.gitecomplexes. co.uk.

You should look for a business that has room for expansion – e.g. space for a pool, or a building that could be converted into a games room or an additional accommodation unit. Above all, check that the owners aren't exaggerating their profits or the potential of the site; ask for detailed accounts for the past few years. Do your own independent research, and ask the right questions, including the following:

- Are there confirmed bookings for the coming season?
- How do they market the property?
- Do they keep a database of previous customers and their comments?
- Does the price include the fixtures and fittings?
- Does the price include any of the furniture? If it does, is it worth buying or would it need replacing?

If possible, buy a business in the autumn, to give yourself time to settle in, make any necessary alterations, do some marketing and (if necessary) improve your French before welcoming your first guests the following spring.

CONVERSION

Probably the most common conversions for *gîtes* are farm buildings, which can make ideal letting properties. On the other hand, such buildings may be in a poor state of repair, not having been used for decades, and lack basic services such as water and electricity. When buying, you must ensure that planning permission is obtainable, even making it a condition of purchase, and ensure there's sufficient land for drainage, a pool and other utilities. Planning permission is a complex subject and is beyond the scope of this book; for detailed information, refer to *Renovating & Maintaining Your French Home* (Survival Books – see page 317).

If you're converting a building or buildings that are part of a property where you live yourself, consider privacy –yours and that of your guests. Your guests are on holiday, you aren't, and some will waylay you at any time of day (or night) for a long chat when you need to be doing other things. If possible, plan your conversion so that you both have private outdoor space and you have an entrance away from that of the *gîte*. This way your guests won't feel that they're being scrutinised every time they leave or return (and nor will you!).

When considering a property for conversion, don't overestimate its size by planning to cram in as many bedrooms as possible; bear in mind the space required for the rest of the building. There's no point having sleeping space for eight people if you can only fit in a dining table that will seat six, or if half of your guests have to stand to watch television.

Note that large farmhouses with plenty of outbuildings in good repair are now few and far between in many parts of France. It may be preferable to buy a small village house, which is easier to maintain and service and can be sold at any time should the need arise.

Converting a Property You Already Own

If you already own a property and want to convert one or more buildings into *gîtes*, there are a number of points to consider:

- Are you able to obtain planning permission?

- Are you in a region and location where the number of weeks you can let makes it a viable proposition?

- If you aren't near the coast, are you prepared to install (and maintain) a pool – and are you able to?

- Do you have noisy neighbours or barking dogs nearby? Or seasonal nuisances such as farmers working combine harvesters all night in the harvest season?

- Is the building itself suitable and does it meet the relevant standards (see **Appendix F**)?

- Will your existing *fosse septique* cope with the extra load?

- Will it photograph well? This is the first impression people have of a holiday property: they browse photographs, **then** read the price, **then** the details.

Above all, draw up a detailed budget for the project, and expect start-up costs to exceed your most pessimistic prognostications!

LEGAL CONSIDERATIONS

Before establishing a *gîte*, it's wise to obtain legal advice and contact your *mairie* regarding local regulations. Various rules and regulations apply to the letting of property in France and, if you're buying a property with the express intention of setting up *gîtes*, you should make sure that permission will be granted before you buy or make obtaining permission a condition of purchase.

Registering a holiday let property as a business isn't necessarily obligatory; other types of registration are optional (see **Registration** on page 53). If you're planning to buy a community property (e.g. an apartment), you must check whether there are any restrictions on letting. If you have a mortgage on the property, it's essential that you have written permission for the letting from the lender.

If you're considering letting your property long term (e.g. during the winter), you should be aware that lets of more than three months are subject to different rules and regulations (see page 178).

Holiday Rental Law

In general, short-term furnished rentals are exempt from the *Loi Mermaz* (1989), which is designed to protect the rights of long-term tenants in unfurnished accommodation (see **Chapter 4**), but a number of other laws apply and you should check your legal situation with a lawyer. The main points of holiday rental law are explained below. Further information can be obtained from:

● Your local (departmental or regional) Office du Tourisme or Syndicat d'Initiative – listed in yellow pages under *Offices de Tourisme* – and the national tourist board website (🖳 www.tourisme.gouv.fr).

● Your local Centre de Documentation et d'Information de l'Assurance (listed on 🖳 www.ffsa.fr).

● The Fédération Nationale des Agents Immobiliers (🖳 www.fnaim.fr).

● The Syndicat National des Professionnels de l'Immobilier (SNPI, 🖳 www.snpi.com).

Contracts

The booking is made by signing a contract or by a simple exchange of letters. Two copies of the contract or letter must be signed when the deposit is paid (see below). One copy must be given to the client, who must agree to the clauses contained in it. A description of the accommodation must be included if it doesn't have an official grading. The contract or letter must also detail the following:

● The duration of the rental.

● The price (which must not vary with the number of occupants).

● The responsibilities of the owner and tenant, which can be anything you choose, e.g. what the owner should provide and that tenants should leave the accommodation as they found it, not invite friends and family who aren't listed as guests, and supervise children while swimming.

● The deposits and guarantee, if applicable (see **Deposits** below).

● The cancellation conditions.

● Details of the *taxe de séjour*, if applicable (see page 218).

Property Description

You (or your representative), on being asked, must give every client a signed description, containing:

- The address of the property.
- The grading category (if applicable).
- The nature and standard of the property.
- The arrangement of the interior and the furnishings.
- The terms and price of the rental and any supplements.

Deposits

Booking Deposit: As far as the French are concerned, there are two types of booking deposit (*dépôt de réservation*): *arrhes* and *acompte*. If the client pays an *arrhes*, he loses it if he cancels – at any time; if the owner cancels, he must pay the client twice the amount of the deposit. If the client pays an *acompte* and he cancels, he must pay the whole amount due; if the owner cancels, he can simply return the deposit, but the client may claim damages. If the type of deposit isn't specified, it's assumed to be an *arrhes*, so it may be to your advantage to specify that it's an *acompte*. If your contract is in English and simply uses the word 'deposit', you should stipulate the conditions under which it may be returned in full or in part.

If you, the owner, take the booking deposit, there are no restrictions: you may charge as much or as little and take it as far in advance as you wish. If an intermediary (e.g. an agent) is handling the transaction, the deposit cannot be more than 25 per cent of the total price or be taken more than six months in advance.

Security Deposit: You should also take a security or guarantee deposit (*dépôt de garantie*), in case anything is damaged or broken. In the case of a booking made without an intermediary (e.g. an agent), you should ask for the deposit to be paid on entering the property (and provide a receipt). You have the right to bank the deposit. In the case of a booking made with an intermediary, the deposit is collected by the intermediary; the law restricts the amount to 25 per cent of the rental and stipulates that the deposit cannot be taken more than six months in advance. The intermediary may charge you commission on the deposit. The security deposit is usually returned at the end of the stay, less an amount for breakages and other unusual costs incurred as a result of the tenancy. The contract must specify the time for the deposit to be returned.

Cancellation

A booking may be cancelled, even if an advance payment has been made, but the consequences depend on whether the deposit was an *arrhes* or an *acompte* (see **Deposits** above).

REGISTRATION

Registering as a Business

Registering a *gîte* as a business isn't necessarily obligatory (unless the income is your only or main source or over €23,000 – see **Chapter 5**), but there are many grey areas here. In the past, the tax authorities have regarded up to three or four *gîtes* as non-commercial (more than that and you must register with the Chambre de Commerce), but requirements (as in so many matters in France) vary from one department to another.

Recent reports suggest that the French government and tax authorities are investigating foreign owners and internet property rental sites in order to clamp down on unregistered businesses and tax evasion. As the present situation is so confusing and involves so many variables, the best action to take is to visit your *mairie*, where you will be directed to the relevant authorities for **your** situation in **your** department.

Tourist Board

The simplest form of registration is to request an inspection and grading from your local Comité Départemental du Tourisme. Many tourist offices won't publicise your accommodation unless it's graded under their own system or registered with Gîtes de France or Clévacances. It may, in fact, be a Gîtes de France or Clévacances representative who performs the inspection, as they work closely together. This requirement is becoming increasingly frequent – ask your Comité Départemental du Tourisme for advice on whether it applies in your area. Some tourist boards charge for inspections, others don't, and the registration fee varies. Similarly, some charge for advertising (e.g. around €15), while others don't.

Gîte Organisations

There's no obligation to register with any of the recognised *gîte* organisations, but depending on your target clientele it may be to your advantage to do so. The best known accommodation 'label' in France is the Federation Nationale des Gîtes de France et du Tourisme Vert (normally referred to as simply Gîtes de France), a national organisation formed in the early 1950s (see page 55). Another government-approved organisation, Clévacances, was introduced in 1997, and it regulates *gîte* and B&B accommodation (see page 58). Unlike those of Gîtes de France, Clévacances properties aren't exclusively rural. There are a few smaller organisations, including the following:

- **Accueil Paysan** – Mainly for farmers with a subsidiary letting business (see **Appendix A**).

- **Bienvenue à la Ferme** – Also mainly for farmers with a subsidiary letting business (see **Appendix A**).

- **Fleurs de Soleil** – Deals with upmarket self-catering accommodation, but has only around 400 properties and is little known (see page 128 and **Appendix A**).

Advantages & Disadvantages

There are advantages and disadvantages to registering with an officially recognised organisation. The advantages include the following:

- You're 'buying into' a recognised brand name, which appears on your publicity material and signs. (According to a poll carried out by the Institut Français d'Opinion Publique on the reputation of tourism businesses, the brand name Gîtes de France appeared third, below only Club Méditerranée and Nouvelles Frontières.)

- You benefit from the organisation's promotional and publicity material (catalogues, internet site, etc.).

- Your accommodation will be known to meet certain recognised standards, which reassures clients.

- You will attract a greater number of French visitors (who constitute 80 per cent of the market).

- You may not be able to advertise your *gîte* with the local tourist board unless it's registered.

- You might not have to pay *taxe d'habitation* on the *gîte* (see page 216).

- You might be eligible for a grant (see **Grants & Services** on page 57).

- You can use the organisation's booking system.

- You're supplied with documentation (e.g. contract forms).

- You can obtain free advice (e.g. on setting up your business).

- You have access to financial and legal assistance.

Disadvantages of registering with an officially recognised organisation may include the following:

- The cost of registration (see below).

- The cost of adapting your premises to meet their standards.

- If you take advantage of a set-up grant from Gîtes de France (see page 57), you're tied to the organisation's booking system for a considerable time – up to ten years – and these systems are often less than 'user-friendly'; for example, to book accommodation via Gîtes de France's site, you must input the name of the department (not just the region) you're interested in, how many people will be holidaying and what dates you're interested in, and go through half a dozen screens before you can even **see** any properties!

- Clientele are on average 80 per cent French, and the French are 'conservative' in their choice of holiday periods, which may limit the number of weeks you can sell.

- Marketing is mainly aimed at the French, although the major organisations have increased their overseas marketing in recent years.

- Pricing is structured around French holidays, so that high season is limited to around six weeks in the summer.

- Rents are often lower than can be obtained by direct marketing focussed on British and other overseas clients.

- Adherence to their grading standards, some of which may seem odd to non-French people, e.g. you need provide only a two-ring hob (and no oven or kettle) for fewer than six people, but you must have a pressure cooker, an electric food mixer and a salad spinner (see **Appendix A**).

 You may be asked to house people who have been evicted from social housing for several months in the low season. If they have no fixed abode, it may be difficult or impossible to get rid of them, so you should take legal advice before accepting tenants on this basis.

As the majority of the clientele of Gîtes de France and Clévacances is French, you would be able to fill the last week of July and the first two weeks of August ten times over, but bookings might be sparse for the rest of the year. Gîtes de France has reciprocal advertising with some British agencies (see page 99), but not all *gîtes* appear in the overseas advertising, making this somewhat of a lottery.

You can, however, choose to take your bookings privately, while benefiting from Gîtes de France accreditation; Gîtes de France grades your property and supplies contract forms and the familiar green signposts, but you take bookings directly and arrange your own publicity, including advertising at your local tourist office (many tourist offices won't advertise a *gîte* unless it's registered with one of the recognised organisations).

Gîtes de France

The original aim of Gîtes de France (GdF, La Maison des Gîtes de France et du Tourisme Vert, 59 rue Saint-Lazare, Paris 75439 Cedex 09, ☎ 01 49 70 75

75, ⌨ www.gites-de-france.fr) was to help struggling farmers earn a supplementary income and to encourage economic growth by revitalising dying rural areas; its properties are therefore rural. (With the advent of industrialised farming, many smaller agricultural businesses were failing to keep up, and farmers' children were moving out of the business; the nature of their properties meant that they had spare rooms and buildings, and GdF offered advantageous set-up grants, government subsidies and allowances for their conversion to tourist accommodation.) As GdF is allied with the Ministry of Tourism, properties are graded in conformity with the national classification defined by a law of 1st April 1997 according to a rating system of *épis* (wheat ears), similar to the more familiar star ratings for hotels.

GdF sends a representative to inspect the property and advises you on planning procedures and costs, and provides an estimate of the expected rental income.

Gîtes de France has an office in each department capital and, as these are autonomously run, many of the regulations and standards are specific to a department (see **Appendix A** for addresses).

Categories: *Gîtes Ruraux* (the plural of *rural*) is the main category of *gîtes* with GdF; there's also *Gîtes d'Étape* and *Gîtes de Séjour*, which are for large groups, and *Gîtes d'Enfants*, for children. Within the *Gîtes Ruraux* category are the following sub-categories. If your *gîte* qualifies as a *Gîte Bienvenue Bébé*, for example, it's 'flagged' as such in the GdF brochure, to attract those looking for baby-friendly accommodation.

● *Gîtes Accessibles aux Personnes Handicapées* – Must have wheelchair access approved by the Association des Paralysés de France.

● *Gîtes Bienvenue Bébé* – Offering all equipment necessary for the care and comfort of babies up to two years old, i.e. cot, highchair, potty, changing facilities, enclosed garden, protected electric sockets and stair gate.

● *Gîtes de Caractère* – *Gîtes* in buildings particular to their region, carefully restored and preserved, ranging from old farms to *manoirs* and *châteaux*.

● *Gîtes de Charme* – Selected for their 'charm'.

● *Gîtes à la Ferme* – As the name suggests, these are situated on a working farm belonging to the *'Bienvenue à la Ferme'* network.

● *Gîtes de Jardin* – Those where the proprietors share their knowledge of gardening.

● *Gîtes de Mer* – Must be within 2km (1.2mi) of the coast and within 10km (6mi) of a seaside resort, with equipment suitable for seaside holidays, including deckchairs, beach games and parasols.

● *Gîtes de Neige* – 'Snow *gîtes*', which must be no more than 15km (11mi) from a ski station.

● *Gîtes Panda* – *Gîtes* situated in regional or national parks, offering nature trails and wildlife watching, under the jurisdiction of the World Wildlife Foundation.

● *Gîtes de Pêche* – *Gîtes* with fishing facilities, information and equipment hire available nearby.

Additional labels are available, including *Séjours Équestres* for *gîtes* offering riding holidays and *Séjours en Vignoble* for those on wine-growing estates, offering information about viticulture, tours of the winery and wine tasting. GdF also gives its label to campsites and to *chambres d'hôtes* (see **Chapter 3**).

Costs & Conditions: There's an annual contract and fee, which varies by department; for example, in some departments the fee is €15 for each rental, in others it's 50 per cent of the cost of one week's rental in high season per year.

Properties must usually be available for a minimum of three months of the year – again the requirement varies by department.

If you've accepted a grant (see below), it's obligatory to be signed up with GdF's booking service, normally for eight to ten years (the duration varies by department). There's a clause in the agreement whereby you agree not to sign up with any other booking services, which can be very restrictive.

Costs and conditions vary from one department to another and you should seek advice from the relevant regional office (see **Appendix A** for addresses).

Grants & Services: If you choose to register with GdF, you can apply for a grant to convert your property (see **Financial Considerations** on page 59), which must be applied for before you start work. There are also tax concessions available, including possible exemption from *taxe d'habitation* on the *gîte* if it's part of your main residence (e.g. an outbuilding you've converted, on the same site as your main house).

GdF publishes the following guides (a total of 2 million copies are printed annually), in which your accommodation is listed as appropriate:

● **Departmental Guides** – One for each department.

● **Regional Guides** – One for each of the following regions: Auvergne, Corsica, Normandy (Upper and Lower combined) and Midi-Pyrénées.

● **National Guides** – One for each of the accommodation types listed above.

Once you're registered with GdF, you may use its booking service (*service de réservation*), whereby GdF in effect acts as your agent, handling all bookings and contracts between you and your clients, although you aren't obliged to. It's possible register with GdF if you live outside France, but you **must** in this case have an agent or caretaker nearby to deal with maintenance and to handle changeovers.

Grants, concessions and services vary from one department to another and you should seek advice from your departmental office (see **Appendix A** for addresses).

Clévacances

The other official French organisation regulated by the Ministry of Tourism is Clévacances, which has two main categories of accommodation: *La Location Clévacances* for self-catering accommodation, and *La Chambre Clévacances* for B&B (see **Chapter 3**). There are around 24,000 *gîtes* registered in 80 departments. Unlike Gîtes de France, Clévacances handles urban as well as rural properties, including houses, flats and maisonettes.

Properties are graded with one to five *clés* (keys), a similar system to GdF's *épis* or tourist board stars. The standards for the various grades are detailed in **Appendix A**. You will notice that French priorities can be different from those of the British or Americans, for example – even for the lowest grade, your property must have a pressure cooker, but it's permissible to have a two-ring burner rather than a proper cooker; and a salad spinner is considered more important than a kettle! Three main criteria are taken into account, as follows:

● The environment, i.e. the quality of the building, the site and its surroundings and absence of nuisances such as noise and smells.

● The quality of the interior, i.e. comfort, furnishings, decoration, facilities, and the arrangement and function of rooms.

● The welcome and assistance offered by the owner or caretaker.

For an inspection by a Clévacances representative (which costs from €100) you must apply to the relevant Comité Départemental de Tourisme or the local tourist office. The inspection must be made in the presence of the owner or caretaker (and possibly an inspector from the Comité Départemental du Tourisme), and the inspector prepares a report, which is submitted to the departmental *préfecture* for assessment and grading (according to the ministerial decree for standards in tourist accommodation).

Subject to a satisfactory inspection, you receive accreditation from Clévacances and a grading of one to five *clés*. If your property isn't accepted, you must pay a forfeit fee of around €40. The annual registration fee, payable in October, is around €70. (Charges vary from one department to another; ask at your Comité Départemental du Tourisme). Further information is available from the Clévacances website (⌨ www. clevacances.com).

FINANCIAL CONSIDERATIONS

Mortgages

If you require a mortgage to buy your French property, where and how you obtain it depends first on whether you're resident in France or in another country.

If you're resident and your main income is earned in France, you should normally take out a French mortgage. 'Buy-to-let' mortgages aren't a familiar concept in France, with the exception of leaseback schemes (see page 190).

French mortgages are normally granted only for residential properties, which can include second homes. They may be granted for properties used for holiday letting, but the (estimated) letting income won't usually be taken into account and you must provide proof of other income, e.g. a pension, to obtain a loan; if you're self-employed, you must supply a minimum of two years' accounts. Letting income is usually only taken into consideration if the property is rented on long-term contracts (see page 183).

If you're a foreign resident, you have three options:

- Borrowing against assets in your home country.

- Taking a second mortgage on (or re-mortgaging) your principal residence in your home country.

- Raising a mortgage in France.

For the first two options, you would obviously need to take the advice of your existing lender. It's also wise to do this if you opt to raise a mortgage in France, as many foreign lenders have reciprocal arrangements with French institutions. Many even have French sister companies such as the UK's Abbey National (see ⊒ www.abbey-national-france.com) and HSBC, whose French equivalent is Crédit Commercial de France (CCF).

When you let the property, you can deduct the mortgage interest from your French tax declaration. Your assets and liabilities will be in the same currency, so fluctuating exchange rates won't result in negative equity. A French mortgage is usually calculated on one third of your net income, less any payments such as those for existing loans, mortgages and credit cards. If you're a non-resident, you will generally be able to borrow around 70 per cent of the price of the property, although some lenders might consider a higher percentage. The minimum amount is usually around €40,000, and the normal repayment term is 15 years, although longer terms are increasingly common. Loans are usually repayment mortgages; 'interest-only' mortgages are rare in France.

For example, HSBC/CCF offer a capital repayment mortgage over 5 to 15 years, with variable, fixed or capped rates. The minimum you can borrow is €50,000, and this can be up to 80 per cent of the purchase price or the estimated value of the property (excluding legal fees), whichever is lower. The arrangement fee is generally 1 per cent of the amount borrowed.

Further information about French mortgages can be found via the internet (e.g. 💻 www.europelaw.com, 💻 www.frenchentree.com and 💻 www.french-mortgage.com) and in *Buying a Home in France* (Survival Books – see page 317).

Viability

If you're a second-homeowner, you might just want to earn a little extra money from your property, which would otherwise be standing empty, and you may be tempted to let for a nominal rent to be sure of attracting clients. Bear in mind, however, that there's little point in letting if you barely cover your costs (marketing, cleaning, etc.) and that you might as easily obtain the going rate. If you do under-charge, you won't make yourself popular with those in the area who are trying to make a living from *gîte* rental!

If you're running your *gîte* as a business, bear in mind that you might be up against competition from second-homeowners who let at low rates, even in high season, which will obviously make it more difficult for you to charge a commercially viable rent. In any case, one *gîte* won't generate enough income to live on and, however many you intend to run, you must budget carefully. To ascertain the viability of your *gîte* business, you must first establish the following:

- Your initial capital outgoing, including the purchase price of the property you intend to buy and the cost of restoration or renovation, equipment and fittings.

- Estimates of the fixed and variable expenses you expect to incur each year relating to the property and business. Fixed costs include your mortgage payments, most maintenance expenses, taxes and insurance which would decrease per unit when spread across the number of weeks sold. Variable costs are those that change according to the number of weeks (and/or units) sold, e.g. agent's fees, cleaning and laundry costs, wages, consumables, maintenance and (re)decorating, repairs, marketing. Void periods (when the property is unoccupied, between lets) also count as expenses.

Then you must estimate your gross annual revenue, i.e. your earnings before expenses and taxes, which depends on the number of weeks you let and the rates you charge (see **Letting Rates** on page 62). Before you can set your rates (unless, of course, you use an agency that sets them for you), you should take into account the following factors.

Supply & Demand

There's a fundamental relationship between price and quantity: consumers buy greater numbers of a product at a lower unit price than at a high price. For example, if the price of a week's rental is €200, you might sell 15 weeks; if it's €400, you might sell ten weeks; if it's €600, you might only sell five. Based on these assumptions, you would take most money by charging €400 (15 x €200 = €3,000, 10 x €400 = €4,000 and 5 x €600 = €3,000).

The actual number of weeks you can sell at each rate depends largely on demand, which in turn is dependent on the competition. There might be other *gîtes* in the same area, other similar properties in the same brochure or on the same website, properties that offer added value in terms of facilities (e.g. a pool) or have an established clientele. Identify what the competition is charging and take this into account when pricing your property.

Gross & Net Revenue

Using the above example, if your costs were €50 per unit per week, your net revenue would also be highest at a letting rate of €400. (Gross revenue – cost = net revenue.) Whereas your gross revenue is the same with the highest and lowest rates, your net revenue isn't. At €200 per week your net revenue would be €3,000 – (15 x €50) = €2,250. At €600, your net revenue would be €3,000 – (5 x €50) = €2,750. At €400, it would be €4,000 – (10 x €50) = €3,500.

Break-even Point

The next step, based on a reasonable projection of fixed and variable costs, is to establish your break-even point, which is when takings are equal to costs. This is the minimum you will need to charge **before** you start to make a profit. Experiment with differing prices and numbers of weeks using the equation $P \times N = F + (V \times N)$ where P is the price, N the number of weeks, F the fixed costs, and V the variable costs.

Yield

The yield on a property is the profit on your investment (after the deduction of expenses, but before tax), which can be compared with the gain on other types of investment, such as shares. Generally, the cheaper the property, the higher the yield. For example, if you buy a property for €100,000 and the gross receipts for your letting in one year total €12,000, your gross yield is

12 per cent (12,000 divided by 100,000 = 0.12, multiplied by 100). If you buy a property for €200,000, you're unlikely to be able to let it for €24,000 to achieve the same yield; you might only take €16,000 in which case your gross yield will be 8 per cent.

Expenses (see above) must be deducted from your gross income in order to calculate your net income and net yield. For example, if you buy a €200,000 property, earn €16,000 a year in rent and have annual expenses of €6,000, you have a net income of €10,000. Your net yield is therefore €10,000 divided by €200,000 = 0.05, multiplied by 100 = 5 per cent – but bear in mind that you still have to pay tax on your net income. Note that you should always use the current market value of a property to calculate the yield.

If your property is divided between your own accommodation and one or more *gîtes*, base your calculations proportionally – for instance if you paid €480,000 for the whole, and your own house is worth one third of that figure, your yield should be calculated on the remaining €320,000.

Letting Rates

After taking into account the above factors, research what other owners are charging – find similar properties sleeping the same number and with the same facilities as your accommodation and make a note of the prices, bearing in mind, of course, that they might not actually have any bookings! Some sites have availability calendars, which you can use to check which ones are letting well. Also, check with agencies – they know which type of property lets for what amount in which locations and can advise on what to charge. Take an average figure and see how this works in your calculations (see above).

Letting rates vary considerably according to the time of year, the area, and the size and quality of a property. A house sleeping six in an average area can be let for around €750 to €1,000 per week in high season. A luxury property in a popular area with a pool and accommodation for 8 to 12 can be let for between €4,000 and €6,000 per week in high season. If you're letting to the non-French market, high season generally includes the months of July and August and possibly the first two weeks of September. The mid-season usually comprises June, September and October (and possibly Easter, Christmas and New Year), when rents are usually around 25 per cent lower than in high season; the rest of the year is low season. Rates are much lower for winter lets, when you shouldn't expect to earn more than around €500 per week or €2,000 per month in most regions for a *gîte* sleeping six.

Extras

It's acceptable to charge extra for certain services, including the following:

- **Heating** – You can charge a fixed figure at certain times of the year according to the climate in your area or, if electric, read the meter on arrival and departure. Many owners include an allowance (e.g. 8kwh per person per day) in the rental price that covers lighting and hot water, any surplus being charged for heating. This is fair – some guests leave all the radiators on all the time with the windows open while others are more conscious of the cost and of energy conservation.

  If the heating system is wood or coal-fired, combustibles may be included in the rental price or charged at cost, or you can supply an initial quantity and charge thereafter.

- **Cleaning** – *Gîte* clients are normally expected to leave the property clean, and most contracts include a clause to the effect that a charge will be deducted from the security deposit if excessive cleaning is required. Some agencies advertise that cleaning is included, but this doesn't mean the property should be left filthy. Other agencies might sub-contract through travel companies in other countries and not send clients full booking conditions of each stay (e.g. Americans on a tour of Europe). If this is the case, make sure the guests are aware of any requirement to clean before they leave.

SURVIVAL TIP
Make sure any extra charges are clearly
stipulated in the contract.

Grants

Grants are available to set up *gîtes* (and other types of holiday accommodation) in certain areas. Grants may be funded by the Conseil Général or sometimes the Conseil Régional, and the availability of grants, conditions of eligibility and amounts offered vary greatly from one department to another: some have no provision for grants whatsoever, while others can award 30 per cent of the cost of setting up a *gîte* business. As a general rule, to be eligible for a grant a property must be in a commune of fewer than 1,500 inhabitants.

In all cases, applications must be made through Gîtes de France. The first step is to contact your departmental GdF office, a list of which can be found in **Appendix A**. GdF sends an inspector, who evaluates the property's suitability and advises you on all aspects of running a letting business, including the demand for rental accommodation in your area. He prepares a dossier with your proposals and presents it to the main office. You must await the decision of the organisation **before** starting work. Note also the following conditions:

- There's a time limit of two years for the completion of work associated with a grant from GdF.

- Grants are conditional on the accommodation provided meeting certain standards (see **Appendix A**), and properties are assessed annually.

- A typical basic grant is equal to around 30 per cent of the cost of work (up to a maximum of €5,000) excluding taxes.

- Grants are usually paid only on completion, although 50 per cent is sometimes paid halfway through a project.

- Grants from GdF are conditional on the property being available to rent by them for a set period – usually ten years, but longer or shorter in some departments. If you sell within this period or the property is unavailable for letting, you must repay the grant.

For further details, contact Gîtes de France, La Maison des Gîtes de France et du Tourisme Vert, 59 rue Saint-Lazare, Paris 75439 Cedex 09 (☎ 01 49 70 75 75, 🖳 www.gites-de-france.fr).

Taxation

An important consideration for anyone running a *gîte* in France is taxation, which includes property tax, income tax and in some cases other local and special taxes (see **Chapter 6**). **You must declare tax in France on all income from property letting, irrespective of where you live.**

Before buying a property for letting, you should obtain expert advice regarding French taxes. This will (hopefully) ensure that you take maximum advantage of your current tax status and that you don't make any mistakes that you will regret later.

OTHER CONSIDERATIONS

Insurance

You must notify your insurance company that you're letting the accommodation and obtain appropriate cover for your *gîte*. It's a legal requirement to have adequate public liability (*responsabilité civile*) and fire insurance once you've bought your property. When you start letting, this should cover your clients, but check whether it includes a guarantee for *recours de locataires contre le propriétaire*, which applies when a client causes water or fire damage. You should also have comprehensive household insurance (*assurance multi-risques habitation*).

Notwithstanding the above, it's wise to advise your clients to have an adequate comprehensive insurance policy, including public liability, personal injury, loss/theft of property, holiday cancellation and vehicle breakdown. (French residents might have a clause called *villégiature* in their own household insurance policies, which covers them while on holiday.)

Extra insurance is required for swimming pools – consult your insurance company. General information regarding insurance can be obtained from the Centre de Documentation et d'Information de l'Assurance (CDIA), 26 boulevard Haussmann, 75311 Paris Cedex 09 (🖳 www.ffsa.fr).

Fire Safety

You should have fire extinguishers and fire blankets (check between lets that they haven't been used and that the 'use-by' date has not passed) and smoke alarms (check the batteries and test them between lets). Check with your insurance company and letting agency (if used) for any further fire safety requirements.

Waste Disposal

Provide clear instructions for rubbish disposal (e.g. that it's to be left in tied bags at the end of stay, or the location of nearest community bin if you're in an area that has that system) and the location of the nearest bottle bank, etc. If you're in a rural area, warn guests that bags may be torn apart by wild animals if left in an exposed position.

Keys

You will need several sets of spare keys, as some will inevitably get lost. If you employ a caretaker, his address should be on the key fob and not that of the house. If you let a home yourself, you can use a 'keyfinder' service, whereby lost keys can be returned to an agency by anyone finding them. You should ensure that 'lost' keys are returned, or you may need to change the locks (in any case it's wise to change external locks periodically if you let a home). If you arrange your own lets, you can post keys to clients in your home country, or they can be collected from a caretaker in France. To avoid problems with keys, it's possible to install a keypad entry system, but you must obviously arrange for the code to be changed after each let and for clients to be advised of the code.

Documentation

Supply a folder containing the following:

● A list of places to visit in the vicinity (in good weather and bad).

- A list of local markets.

- A list of restaurants in the area with a description of each, days on which they're closed, their telephone numbers and approximate menu prices.

- Local emergency numbers – fire, police, ambulance, taxi, etc. – and details of health services such as a doctor, dentist and hospital or clinic.

- Numbers for general assistance such as a repairman, plumber, electrician and pool maintenance person (you may prefer to leave the telephone number of a local caretaker, who can handle any problems if you aren't on site).

- The location of the nearest shops and petrol stations, with opening times.

- House rules, such as where children are/aren't allowed to go, stressing the safety aspect and possible dangers (e.g. falling into the pool).

- How things work, e.g. kitchen appliances, television/video/CD/DVD player, heating and air-conditioning, pool safety equipment.

- If appropriate, a little history of the area and the buildings.

You should also make the following available:

- Leaflets and brochures of tourist attractions in the area – obtainable from your local tourist office.

- Maps – national, departmental and local.

- Guide books – e.g. *Le Petit Futé* and a Green Guide.

- A visitors' book (*livre d'or*) for guests' comments.

It's surprising how many visitors have inadequate maps and guide books (or none at all!), and providing these helps to forestall a barrage of questions (how to find places, when attractions are open, etc.). It's a simple matter to check that they're still on the premises at the end of each let.

Extras

It pays to provide a 'welcome pack' for each set of guests. This can be anything from a bunch of flowers and a bottle of wine to a hamper of food basics – coffee, tea, milk, sugar, cereals, bread, etc. Don't include the provision of a welcome pack in your contract, but make it a nice surprise ('added value'). If you put it in the contract, people will ask you exactly what it contains, e.g. the quality and brand names of the products!

Any other little extras you can think of to increase your guests' enjoyment (and exceed their expectations) will encourage them to return and to recommend your accommodation to others. If you know that one of their children has a birthday during their stay, for example, buy a card and a small present. At Easter, give Easter eggs to children (or follow the French tradition of hiding them in the garden for children to find). Let guests know that you're available to help (if you are!) if there's anything they need or have forgotten to bring, e.g. a plug adapter (don't leave these in the *gîte*, as they will 'disappear').

Smoking

Many holiday lets are now non-smoking, but this limits your letting potential to some extent – smokers won't book a non-smoking property (hopefully!), but non-smokers will probably book even if you don't stipulate that it's non-smoking. You cannot police it, so it might be preferable to have a few restrictions such as no smoking in the bedrooms, or leave ashtrays out on the terrace or in the garden.

Animals

Allowing animals should be seriously considered. Since the introduction of 'pet passports', it has become easy for travellers from the UK to take their dogs and cats on holiday with them. You could have a higher number of lets if you allow pets. Nevertheless, it's best to accept them only if your *gîte* is fenced; town dogs might regard your chickens as dinner or find the nearby field of sheep an irresistible temptation and be shot by the farmer. They might also run into the road. There are several disadvantages, not least that they might mess indoors, or leave hairs, causing allergy reactions in future guests. Check with your insurance company if you decide to allow pets.

Children

The largest group of clients who book *gîte* holidays is families, and not allowing children drastically reduces your letting potential, although children can cause more damage than adults or pets! If you decide to admit children, you should do your best to make your property child-friendly and can even apply for GdF's *Bienvenue Bébé* accolade (see page 56). However, your property might simply be unsuitable. You might have beautifully landscaped gardens unsuitable for children's play, or the property may not be fenced, or you might have reasons for not wanting shrieking babies and toddlers at unsociable hours! If you have a *bijou* little cottage that sleeps two, for example, you can target your advertising at couples wanting a peaceful getaway. Some people don't let to families with children under five because of the risk of bed-wetting. Let enquirers know in advance whether or not the property is enclosed and if there are steep stairs.

Groups

Problems can arise if you let to large groups, particularly same-sex and younger people (e.g. a football team). If you don't wish to let to such groups, you can stipulate that they aren't permitted (or that the property isn't suitable) or simply say that you're fully booked.

Disabled Access

If your property has disabled access, including wide doors, and no steps to at least one bedroom and bathroom, this can be a good selling point. Most agencies will have provision for emphasising this in their advertisements (GdF has a special category for properties suitable for the disabled – see page 56), and there are some that specialise in this area, e.g. Access Travel (UK ☎ 01942-888844, 💻 www.access-travel.co.uk).

FACILITIES

Clients expect certain facilities – particularly a swimming pool, telephone and television. There are many considerations to be made in respect of these, detailed below.

Swimming Pool

Having a swimming pool can significantly increase your letting potential and your income; it also significantly increases your costs, and you must weigh up the advantages and disadvantages before deciding whether to install a pool and what type of pool to install.

To maximise your letting, a pool is essential – and some letting agencies won't handle properties without a pool – unless the property is near a beach, lake or river where swimming is possible. It's usually necessary to have a private pool with a single-family home, but a shared pool is sufficient for an apartment or townhouse. You can also ask higher rent for a property with a pool – you can charge up to double for a property with a private pool.

Cost

According to a report by the International Swimming Pool Exhibition, the cost of installing or building a private pool varies from €6,000 to €18,000, with an average of €12,500. The price depends mainly on whether the pool is prefabricated or custom built. The report also indicates that annual pool maintenance costs €587 and chemical products (de-scaling, pH control, algaecides, chlorine and bactericides) €247. This means a total cost of around €20,000 over ten years, or €2,000 per year (without allowing for inflation) that must be recouped in **extra** net letting income just to break even. These figures exclude the cost of heating a pool, which can add thousands of euros per year.

The most economical option is a kit, which costs from €4,000 to €14,000 depending on size. They come with prefabricated sections for the vertical structure, a liner and filtering and purification equipment. The seller will be able to recommend installation companies. For a medium budget, you can buy a fibreglass shell, made in one piece, which must be installed by specialists. This costs between around €9,000 to €18,500. A more luxurious option is a cast concrete pool, costing from €15,000 upwards, which also requires professional installation.

Your budget must include the excavation, the purchase and installation of the pool itself, accessories, maintenance products and pool cleaning equipment, safety systems (see below), heating equipment if applicable, steps and terraces, landscaping, electricity and water supply and, if applicable, fuel for heating the water.

Further information is available via the internet, and the following websites are particularly useful:

- 🖥 www.eauplaisir.com – This site has a lot of practical information, a readers' forum and a newsletter, as well as product descriptions.

- 🖥 www.irrijardin.com – Irrijardin offers a wide range of products and the site provides comprehensive information.

Regulations

Note that new safety regulations regarding pools used by the public, including pools at private homes that are let for holidays, came into force in 2004 (see below). Make sure you understand the regulations before installing a pool or letting a property.

Location: You aren't normally allowed to build a pool nearer than 3m to a boundary or within view of a road – the sight of half-naked bathers is believed to be the cause of many road accidents! Check with your town hall what local regulations apply.

Planning Permission: Planning permission is required for any construction over 20m^2 (there's little point in installing a pool smaller than this).

Safety: A recent law requires that certain types of pool must be equipped with an approved safety system (*un dispositif de sécurité normalisé*). Pools inside a building and inflatable or demountable above-ground pools are exempt from the requirement. All other pools must have at least one of the following systems:

- **Alarm** – An alarm (*un système d'alarmes*) conforming to national standard (*norme française* or *NF*) P90-307, costing around €900. An alarm must be no more than 7m from any point in the pool; this means that one alarm positioned in the middle of one of the long sides of a 10m x 5m pool is adequate, but two alarms are required for an 11m x 6m (or larger) pool. No more than two alarms may be used. Bear in mind also that you must remember to switch an alarm off before you swim and on again afterwards, and, like a house or car alarm, it can easily be ignored!

- **Enclosure** – An enclosure or roof (*un abris*) conforming to national standard P90-309. There are various types of enclosure, all of which are expensive and most of them unsightly. Fixed enclosures, costing around €7,500 for a 10m x 5m pool, are also difficult to remove when you want to swim or clean the pool; 'telescopic' enclosures are easy to slide back, but cost around twice as much.

- **Fence** – A continuous barrier or fence (*une barrière de protection*) surrounding the pool no less than 0.5m from its edge and at least 1.1m high conforming to national standard P90-306. If you're letting the property, the fence must incorporate a self-closing (e.g. spring-loaded) gate. Fencing costs around €80 per linear metre (i.e. around €3,000 to fence a 10m x 5m pool). Although unsightly, fencing is generally recommended as the most practical system.

- **Safety Cover** – A safety cover (*une couverture de sécurité*) conforming to national standard P90-308. A safety cover, as opposed to an ordinary 'solar' cover, incorporates metal bars so that a child can walk on it without sinking into the pool; for this reason, it's heavy and difficult to roll up when you want to have a swim – for a 10m x 5m pool, two people are required! A safety cover costs around €1,800.

 Some letting agencies and even French insurers won't accept an alarm, enclosure or safety cover as the only safety system, as any of them can – inadvertently or otherwise – be left 'off'. Check before installing any of these systems.

Standards are set by the national standards agency, the Association Française de Normalisation (AFNOR, ☎ 01 41 62 76 44, 💻 www.afnor.fr), but only general information (in French) is available from them; the standards themselves cost around €67 each and are incomprehensible to anyone but an engineer! However, a reputable pool installation company should have details of the latest requirements.

Failure to comply with the regulations can lead to a fine of up to €45,000. If you haven't installed the required system and someone drowns in your pool, your third party liability insurance could be invalid and you could be sued for millions of euros!

Sanitation: If you wish to install a pool which will be shared by two or more dwellings, its sanitation system must meet more stringent regulations, as the pool will be classed as 'semi-commercial' (*demi-commercial*).

Extending the Season

Even in southern France, the swimming season is normally limited to little more than half the year (e.g. April to October). In northern parts, you may be lucky to have five months of swimming. There are several ways you can extend the swimming season, which may help you to let your property outside the summer, including the following:

● **Heating** – There are a number of ways to heat a pool to make it useable for a longer period or even all year round. Bear in mind, however, not only is heating extremely costly, it's unlikely that your clients will want to swim (even in a heated pool) when it's pouring with rain or in the depths of winter.

● **Indoor Pool** – An indoor pool heats up slightly more quickly and retains its heat for slightly longer. There's the added advantage that you can swim on days when you wouldn't want to swim outdoors, e.g. when it's raining or there's a high wind. A covered pool also needs less cleaning, and safety systems (see above) aren't required, provided the pool room can be (and is) locked when the pool isn't in use. Disadvantages include the extra cost of walls and a roof, possible unsightliness of the construction, and the fact that in summer the air temperature can reach 50°C or more.

● **Covered Pool** – It's possible to install a low removable roof, which doesn't require walls and provides some of the benefits of an indoor installation, but which obviously needs removing and replacing each time you want to use the pool.

● **Cover** – A 'solar' cover helps not only to keep a pool clean, but also to prevent heat gained during the day from being lost overnight.

For further information on installing, heating and maintaining a swimming pool, refer to *Renovating & Maintaining Your French Home* (Survival Books – see page 317).

Telephone

Most holidaymakers have mobile phones, but it's worth considering having a telephone installed in your property, especially if it's your own holiday home and you need it when you're there. In any case, the French mobile networks may not have good coverage in your area; and, if there's no nearby payphone, a fixed line telephone can be a useful facility for guests (and a boon to your privacy if they receive calls from home with news of sick relatives or failed exams). If you live on site and have only one telephone (your own), your guests may give it to all their friends and family, despite your pleas for it to be used for emergencies only!

If you have a separate line installed for clients, you can ask France Télécom to block usage apart from local, emergency and incoming calls (*service restreint*).

Guests can purchase a *Ticket Téléphone International* to make long-distance calls (to 75 countries) using a code number. These cards are available from France Télécom outlets, *tabacs* and newsagents', in denominations of €7.50 and €15.

Television

It's recommended to provide a television (TV): either French terrestrial TV or an English-language satellite system depending on your clientele. It's possible that having the latter will increase bookings, especially during major European sporting events. Cartoons to keep the kids quiet seem to work in any language!

Any digital satellite receiver can receive the BBC and other 'free-to-air' channels. If you want ITV channels, you need a Sky digibox and a Sky card, obtainable only if you have a UK address. A new Sky digibox costs £200 to £300, and a Sky card is currently £20. A useful website providing information about receiving British digital TV in France is 🖳 www.bigdish sat.com.

The six main French TV channels (TF1, France2, France3, Arté, France 5 and M6) can be received with a UHF roof aerial or with an analogue satellite receiver and dish, which is better in areas with poor reception. For Canal+ you need a subscription, a decoder and a VHF aerial. There are two digital satellite systems available in France: Canal Satellite and TPS. Canal Satellite carries the main terrestrial broadcasters except TF1, some films in English, Sky News and BBC World programmes. TPS has all the French terrestrial broadcasters, some films in English, and BBC Prime and BBC World programmes. A French digital decoder (*terminal numérique*) and dish (*parabole*) cost around €80 to €100. You then pay a subscription for the service, which varies according to the package you choose. Details are available on their websites (☐ www.tps.fr, ☐ www.canalsat.fr).

If you have French TV, give your guests a TV listings magazine for the week – most will be grateful for it and even those who don't watch TV may find the weather forecasts useful!

You must have a TV licence for each *gîte* that has a TV set; if you live on site, your licence covers only sets in your home. From 2005, a French television licence (*redevance audiovisuelle*) is to be charged as part of the *taxe d'habitation*. Your annual tax return now has a box to tick if you **don't** have a TV. The licence fee is €116 – €0.50 less than in 2004 (although it should be **much** less on account of the massive increase in revenue that will result from compulsory licensing!).

Other Facilities

Particularly if you wish to attract guests outside the summer season, when a swimming pool is less of a draw, you should consider offering extra facilities, such as a table tennis or pool table, table football and other indoor games, or a sauna, steam room and exercise equipment. Don't forget the potential appeal to business clients; you might convert a building into conference and meeting rooms, and offer (free) internet access, for example.

FURNISHINGS & UTENSILS

Furnishing a holiday cottage is a compromise between style and durability. If you fill it with precious family heirlooms, some clients will think it wonderful – 'just like a magazine!' – whereas others will complain that the place is full of second-hand furniture and want their money back; others will break things or, in very rare cases, steal them. Furnishings must be durable and in excellent condition. If you use antiques, make sure they're robust enough for use by people who possibly won't appreciate their value, e.g. brass beds but not intricately carved wooden beds (little Johnny might decide he could improve the carving with his penknife or colour in the designs with permanent markers). A holiday cottage isn't a place to dump all the furniture that you don't want in your own house; on the other hand it isn't worth spending a fortune on bespoke furnishings. A luxury or higher priced property must be furnished with quality fittings and equipment; a low-cost one must nevertheless be well equipped with good quality basics.

Bear in mind when purchasing furnishings and fittings that you're buying for others to use; they should be easy to clean and maintain. In the peak season (and hopefully other times of the year) you will have only a few hours between departing guests and new arrivals to restore the property to pristine condition. Although most contracts include a clause to the effect that clients should leave the property clean, there's always plenty of work to be done and little time in which to do it.

Those who let to British clients should be warned that, although their clients have booked a French country cottage, which traditionally has stone, tiled or wooden floors, many of them will expect to find fitted carpets throughout (their concept of a rural idyll often bears little relation to reality!).

Central heating is necessary if the property is to be let all year round. Otherwise, convection heaters that can be regulated are a good alternative. An open fire is an added attraction, especially in winter, but you should bear in mind that it will add to your cleaning time between lets.

Depending on the price and quality of a property, your guests may also expect a washing machine, dishwasher, microwave, covered parking area, a barbecue and garden furniture. Some owners provide bicycles and sports (e.g. badminton and table tennis) equipment.

Ensuite bathrooms are desirable, but not necessary (unless yours is a top-of-the-range property), but cottages sleeping more than six people should have more than one lavatory.

Decoration should be light and bright, with fresh colours, not gaudy or too individualistic. Some people like frills and flounces, others prefer clean modern lines, so keep a happy medium. It's best to keep walls white, as it's then easier to redecorate. Add colour with the soft furnishings and rugs, plenty of pictures and a selection of bits and pieces to make it more welcoming. Shops such as Gifi, Michigan and Casa sell attractive home décor that won't cost a fortune to replace if damaged or broken.

Keep all appliances well maintained, door and window fastenings working, tile grouting whitened, light fittings working, and above all keep everything **clean**!

If you use the property yourself, have a lockable area where you can store your possessions when it's let.

Lounge

You must provide sufficient comfortable seating for the maximum number of people for which your cottage caters. This might seem obvious, but it's often tempting to squeeze in extra bedrooms to increase the capacity (and consequently revenue) whilst not giving adequate consideration to the 'living' space.

Sofas and armchairs must be matching and have stain-resistant, washable covers. One spare set is essential, two is advisable. Add throws, which are easier to clean than loose covers. Three-piece suites are generally far cheaper and better designed in the UK than in France, so consider buying there or get them from IKEA (🖳 www.ikea.com or 🖳 www.ikea.fr). Provide plenty of cushions – particularly if you have typical French furniture with wooden arms. Many French sofas are *canapé-lits* or *clic-clacs* (sofa-beds), which can be an advantage if you're handling your own bookings; most agencies, however, won't consider them as extra capacity and you might sacrifice quality for this facility (some are also very heavy to move when cleaning).

If you let to British clients and the floors are tiled, as is usual in most parts of France, consider laying a large carpet covering the main part of the floor, or plenty of rugs. Have a bookshelf with a good selection of paperbacks in good condition and some toys, board games and jigsaws. French versions of well known games such as Cluedo and Monopoly are always popular – everyone knows the rules so it's fun to play in another language. (Scrabble and Trivial Pursuit are also available for those whose French is up to it!)

Dining Area

Provide a large enough table and sufficient sturdy dining chairs for the capacity of your *gîte*. Have a high chair available for small children.

Kitchen

The kitchen should be well equipped with utensils, crockery, appliances, glasses and cutlery. Make sure there are sufficient for the maximum number of people the property accommodates and that you have spares to hand. Some agencies and organisations require you to provide the exact quantity, others two of each (more if you have a dishwasher). All should be checked between visits and replaced or replenished as necessary. Make a careful compromise between quality and cost – choose crockery and cutlery that you can buy individually rather than in sets; teaspoons, for example, always go missing. Apply the same logic to cooking pans; it takes just one heavy-handed family to destroy the non-stick surfaces on a set of expensive pans.

If you're in a rural area, it's likely that you will have bottled gas for cooking. Ensure that there are instructions for lighting the oven and for changing the gas bottle (if you're on site, it's best to do this yourself; better still to check between lets that there's enough gas left for the period of rental). The connecting tube has a 'use-by' date – check that it hasn't passed.

French cookers don't usually have separate grills, so you might like to provide one, and a microwave oven is normally expected, along with all the usual equipment such as an electric kettle and toaster (often lacking in French-owned properties!). If you're with a French organisation (e.g. GdF), it will insist on certain items you may not have thought of, such as a pressure cooker and salad spinner, and not even mention an electric kettle!

Provide plenty of (mouse-proof) cupboard space for guests to store food and a large refrigerator with a freezer compartment. Check between lets that all food is removed.

Bedrooms

The number one requirement is solid beds with good mattresses. Give careful consideration to the number and type of beds in each room. Too many double beds limits the permutations of guests – if you have two large rooms, put a double bed in one and two singles in the other or, if there's room, a double and a single in each. If you have three bedrooms, make one a double and two twin-bedded rooms. If there are three or more rooms, you could put bunk beds in one of them for children. (Bunk beds should be used **only** by children.)

If you want to install antique beds from a *brocante*, measure the length before buying, as some older beds are too short for modern mattresses. The mattresses must not, under any circumstances, be of a similar vintage! While comfort is subjective and you cannot please all tastes (some like their beds hard, some soft, some in between), if the mattresses are new there's little that can be complained about. There's no shortage of good mattresses in France; every town has frequent visits from mattress-sellers – it's a national obsession.

Do use waterproof mattress and pillow protectors, as people dribble in their sleep (not to mention other accidents that can occur). Keep a spare set and clean them between lettings.

Supply a cot for young children, ideally the 'umbrella' type which folds down and can be stored in an unobtrusive place. It's normal for parents to bring their own cot bed linen, but keep a set just in case. A changing mat is also advisable – most parents bring their own, but it's cheaper to buy one than pay for extra cleaning of duvets and bedspreads.

Make sure you provide plenty of hanging space, with shelves or a separate chest of drawers (or a dressing table with drawers), a mirror, a wastebasket and somewhere for guests to store empty suitcases. Other furniture might include a small table and a couple of chairs, and perhaps a bookshelf. Have a bedside table and lamp for each person and non-slip rugs by each bed.

Linen

In the past, it was normal practice for guests to take their own linen (sheets, pillowcases, towels and tea towels) on self-catering holidays. Nowadays, there are three options regarding the provision of linen: You can ask clients to bring their own, you can hire it to them, or you can supply it, included in the rental price. Bear in mind that customers travelling by air won't be able to bring their own linen; if you're targeting this category of clients, it's therefore preferable to provide linen.

If you choose to hire linen, charge a set rate per person (between €12 and €15 per person per week is acceptable), which gives guests the choice of bringing their own. If you aren't on site or your caretaker isn't prepared to cope with laundry, you may decide to ask guests to bring their own, although this is a negative factor for many people.

If you don't provide linen, or guests choose to bring their own, check on their arrival that they've brought enough for the number of beds they're going to use. Be subtle: say that if they've left anything at home, you're happy to lend it to them (and make sure you have spare linen available). You should also ask them not to use duvets and pillows without covers.

Generally, including linen in the rental price is the best option – guests' first impression of a bedroom will be far better if the beds are made up; and the last thing they want to do after a tiring journey is to start wrestling with duvets! Providing linen also ensures that beds and bedding are protected, and duvet covers and pillowcases fit properly – if you provide square pillows, British visitors' pillowcases won't fit, and duvets come in a variety of sizes.

Buy good quality linen; cheap sheets and pillowcases soon become thin and tired-looking. Stick to white rather than colours and patterns – it's easier and cheaper to replace one item than to buy a whole new matching set. Cotton is best, but you may prefer polycotton for easier laundering. Pillows should have synthetic filling, as many people have allergies; you could keep some feather pillows in case guests request them.

Supply a bath towel and a hand towel for each person, plus bath mats, tea towels and a kitchen hand towel. Beach towels aren't normally included, but have a few available in case guests haven't brought their own.

Bathroom & WC

Ease of cleaning is the number one priority. WCs need a window or extractor fan. Shower cubicles with rigid sides are more expensive than those with curtains, but far easier to clean. Tile as much as you can. Provide plenty of shelving, a cabinet, and a mirror, clothes hooks and towel rails, a lidded waste bin and non-slip bath mats.

If you have a septic tank, supply the appropriate toilet paper and disposal bags for sanitary products. Make sure there's a clearly displayed notice that warns of the horrendous consequences of anything unsuitable being put down the lavatory. Provide plenty of cleaning materials!

GARDEN & GROUNDS

The garden should have a lawn where children can play, which must be kept mown (sometimes twice a week in the wet, warm areas of France!). If you have room, a play area with a swing, small slide, etc. is a valuable addition. If you provide any other outdoor equipment, try to limit the potential for damage and injury – badminton rackets and shuttlecocks are better than hard balls. Shrubs, trees and flowers should be fairly robust – children aren't always careful with plants, so keep fragile and rare specimens in your own area of garden, where you can tend and enjoy them. Avoid poisonous leaves and berries such as foxgloves, laburnum and yew.

Supply a good quality set of garden furniture – a big enough table and sufficient chairs for the capacity of your *gîte*. Cheap plastic ones are a false economy, as they will need replacing each year (or even more often), as they scratch easily and can even be blown away and broken in sudden summer storms. Guests appreciate a few loungers or deckchairs, a parasol and some outdoor lighting so that they can sit outside in the evening.

Gravel must be weed-free – use a long-term systemic herbicide such as Herbatak that doesn't leach into flowerbeds and lawns. Patios, terraces, etc. must be equally well maintained with the use of moss and algae removal products.

PRESENTATION

When you show visitors into your *gîte*, their first impressions are important. Beds should be made, soft furnishings and cushions arranged and towels folded neatly. Everything must be spotlessly clean and should smell pleasant – make sure the property is properly aired between lets. Put vases of fresh flowers in some of the rooms. Use house plants and ornaments to decorate and add accent colour. If it's after dusk, turn on all the lights and draw the curtains, close the shutters if it's cold and wet outside and light a fire or turn on the heating (your visitors will be coming in from a warm car). You should be dressed neatly – don't welcome your guests in an apron and your gardening boots! Making an effort and paying attention to detail creates an overall ambience enabling your guests to feel at home, and give them a positive impression from the start of their holiday.

SERVICING & MAINTENANCE

Between lets you (or a representative) must carry out some, or all, of the following tasks:

- **Bathroom & WC** – Clean, disinfect, remove old soap and toiletries, check bins, replenish cleaning products and toilet paper, polish tiles, taps and mirrors.

- **Bedrooms** – Remove used linen and towels, check that mattresses, pillows and protectors are clean, air and remake beds.

- **Bins** – Check that they're all empty, disinfect them and replace bags and liners.

- **Ceilings & Beams** – Dust, vacuum and remove cobwebs.

- **Electrics** – Check that all appliances and switches are working, and change broken light bulbs.

- **Floors** – Clean, bleach, vacuum as appropriate, check under beds.

- **Furniture** – Clean, polish, check for damage. Check that drawers and cupboards are empty.

- **Kitchen** – Clean surfaces, check fridge and icebox, clean oven, replenish cleaning materials, remove leftover food, check that cutlery, glasses, dishes, pans and utensils are all present and spotless. De-scale kettle.

- **Living Room** – Clean and check that loose covers, throws and cushions are clean; replace as necessary.

- **Outside** – Clean garden furniture and barbecue. Check lawn and drives for animal mess. Mow the grass, weed the borders and rake gravel. Carry out pool maintenance.

- **Safety Equipment** – Check that fire alarms, smoke alarms, fire blankets and fire extinguishers are functioning and in date. Check safety stickers on glass doors. Check that the gas bottle has enough gas in it for the next let and its hose is in date.

- **Visitors' Book & Information** – Check that all is in place for the next visitors.

- **Washing Machine & Dishwasher** – Check filters and run a load to test.

- **Windows** – Check fastenings and clean panes.

SURVIVAL TIP

Keep the property well aired in winter and leave minimum heating on even if there are no bookings.

Handling Your Own Changeovers

One person or a couple living on site might efficiently handle one or two *gîtes*, but if you have a greater number to run you must consider employing a cleaner and/or gardener. The amount of laundry can be overwhelming, so look into the cost of sending a weekly load to your local *blanchisserie* – but beware: these vary in quality as well as price, and some iron more creases in than they remove!

The obvious advantage of handling your own changeovers is that it saves you money. The personal touch also means a great deal to your guests. On the other hand, it means that you must be there every changeover day – and it's hard work!

Employing a Caretaker

If you aren't on site or cannot or don't want to carry out the above tasks, you must also ensure that you have someone to do so on your behalf, as well as carry out routine maintenance – gardening, pool maintenance, repairs, etc. – and to welcome guests to the property. Some owners simply arrange for key collection.

There are many and varied companies offering caretaking services, including large property management companies, estate agents who handle (usually longer-term) lettings and sometimes perform management tasks or employ people on your behalf, and 'management companies' that are in fact self-employed caretakers.

A property management company should be located in the same area as the property and provide a full package of services. These may include letting the property, as well as caretaking, welcoming clients and being on-call for emergencies, although such businesses are normally outside the budget of *gîte* owners and are more appropriate for the letting of luxury villas. At the other end of the scale is the 'lady down the road' who will do your changeovers.

 As the majority of routine tasks must be done on changeover day and the usual chageover day is a Saturday, it can be extremely difficult to find a caretaker on Saturdays in popular areas.

You should be realistic (even pessimistic) about your caretaking costs and bear in mind that a caretaker needs to be retained during the months when you have few or no lets. The amount you pay is obviously related to the extent of the services offered. If you have a luxury five-bedroom villa on the Côte d'Azur with gardens and swimming pool, it could cost at least €6,000 for an annual contract for a weekly caretaking visit. For a small rural *gîte* a weekly changeover should cost €50 to €70 (maintenance and grass cutting is extra). Generally, you should allow up to €15 per hour for each employee.

Welcoming Guests

It's an advantage if you can arrange for someone to be on hand to welcome your guests when they arrive, explain how things work, and deal with any special requests or minor problems. **It's essential to make your guests feel welcome.** You (or your caretaker) should obviously be at the property to greet them. If their arrival time is inconvenient, you can leave the keys in a concealed place or arrange for them to be collected from a third party, but this isn't recommended.

First impressions are important; a smiling, helpful owner is the best start to your guests' holiday, reassuring them you will be on hand to deal with enquiries and problems. Show them around the property as if you're selling it. Point out any important details such as how to regulate radiators, how the bathroom basin and bath plug operate, how window fastenings and door locks work (often different from those in the UK or other countries), give severe (but humorous) warnings about the misuse of septic tank drainage, etc. This avoids having to put notices everywhere. Tell guests how to contact you if there's anything they need to know, ask if they need anything (such as teabags, coffee and milk), point out the welcome pack, information folder and the tourist brochures, then leave them in peace to settle in. Call on them a day later to make sure that everything is satisfactory.

If you really want to impress your guests (in other words, if you want them back!), you may wish to arrange for fresh flowers, fruit, a bottle of wine and a grocery pack to greet them on their arrival (see **Extras** on page 62). It's little personal touches such as this that ensure repeat business and recommendations. If you 'go the extra mile', it will pay. Many people return to the same property each year and you should do an annual mail-shot to previous clients and send them some brochures. **Word-of-mouth advertising is the cheapest and always the best.**

Many people provide a visitor's book, in which guests can write their comments and recommendations regarding local restaurants and attractions, etc. Some owners also send out questionnaires.

Dealing with Problems

Major problems are unlikely to arise if you've described, equipped and furnished your *gîte* properly. If appliances fail during the guests' visit, do your best to sort the problem out, and assure the clients that you're doing so. If they know it isn't your fault (e.g. a washing machine failure, power cut or septic tank blockage), they're unlikely to complain as long as you deal with it quickly, sympathetically and professionally. If you feel that the problem is your fault, offer some compensation and ask for written assurance that they're happy with this. (It isn't unknown for clients to say they're happy, but make a major complaint on arrival home.)

Problems more often arise when the standard of the property doesn't meet the client's expectations. Your advertising and marketing **must** be a true representation of the accommodation. Under French law, if you misrepresent your property and make false advertising claims (e.g. 'near the sea' when it's 30km/18mi away) you will be liable to a very large fine.

If you've let the *gîte* through a third party (e.g. an agency or GdF), clients might complain upon their return. There are, unfortunately, far too many TV programmes featuring problem holidays, showing how easy it is to complain and get your money back, and there are a few unscrupulous people who put in spurious complaints with this in mind. Examine the agreement you have with the agency – there's probably a clause which states that any problems must be reported to you (or your caretaker) during the stay. If they cannot contact you, the clients should inform the agency's local representative and, failing that, its head office. If they haven't followed this procedure, they shouldn't be compensated. If the matter escalates, take legal advice.

There are, of course, problem guests! A certain amount of wear and tear is to be expected, but damage caused by guests' negligence and misuse can be deducted from their security deposit. Don't make a fuss about one or two broken glasses, but you're entitled to deduct the cost of more serious breakage and damage – that's what the deposit is for. It can be embarrassing having to inspect the *gîte* while the guests are waiting to depart, but it has to be done. Check it as quickly as possible, concentrating on potential problem areas (e.g. bathroom, oven, WC); if these are clean, the rest is likely to be in good condition. Check that nothing has been left behind (a reason to look inside the bedroom drawers and examine the bedclothes). Ask the guests if anything has been broken or isn't working properly.

One problem that frequently occurs in rural properties is invasion by animals and birds. Mice come in looking for food and sparrows, or even barn owls or other large birds, might nest in the eaves or roof space. Obviously, you should make sure that there are no mice living in the property, but the occasional incursion is difficult to prevent. You can ask guests not to leave open food (bread etc.) in the kitchen, and you can set traps, humane or otherwise, when there are no guests. Don't put down poison: children or pets might eat it, or poisoned mice might crawl off and die in inaccessible places, creating unpleasant smells!

Birds are easier to deal with, as their access can be blocked, but make sure you do this outside the nesting season; some species (e.g. barn owls) are protected. To deal with hornet and wasp nests, telephone the local fire brigade (*sapeurs-pompiers*), whose job it is to remove them. (Hornet stings, contrary to popular belief, are no more harmful than those of wasps.)

MARKETING

Effective marketing is key to the success of your business. Begin by asking yourself what your target market is; what type of customers do you hope to attract? "As many as possible! Everyone!" is the answer most owners initially give. But your marketing must be efficient in terms of time and money, and it isn't possible to promote your property to 'everyone'. Decide, for example, whether you want to attract families, young couples, older people, wealthy people? How do they prefer to communicate? What are they looking for? Which advertising medium are they most likely to read? You wouldn't advertise (nor let) a €4,000 per week apartment near Cannes to the same people as you would a €300 per week cottage in Brittany. Different sections of the population look for different criteria when booking a holiday. A family with two children on a low to medium income will opt for the €300 cottage, whereas the €4,000 apartment (for which a cleaning lady alone may cost you €300 per day!) will appeal to another socio-economic group. Your advertising must be targeted at your preferred customer profile. Ask yourself whether you can target more than one group? A property suitable for a family in the high season might attract older couples at other times of the year.

Make sure that all your documentation reflects your desired image and be consistent in your style of presentation – in letters, leaflets, advertisements, website, etc. (see **Literature** on page 85). You may wish to design (or have designed) a logo, incorporating the name of your establishment with a simple image.

Do you want mainly English-speaking visitors? This may be easier if your French isn't fluent. The Anglophone marketplace is much bigger (including all of the US and Canada, South Africa, Australia and New Zealand, for example, as well as the Netherlands!), its marketing techniques generally more effective and booking systems more efficient and the holiday season is less restricted.

There's no need to spend a fortune on advertising, but some advertising is almost inevitable; there are many ways of promoting your *gîte* cheaply, some of which are detailed below. Ask yourself whether your property has a 'unique selling point' (USP) and, if so, how you can best exploit it. This might be the nature of the property itself, or its location. Generally, the more marketing you do, the more income you're likely to earn. Bear in mind, however, that marketing takes time, which is in effect money.

A major decision you must take is whether to let your property yourself or use a letting agent or agents (see pages 100 and 95). If you don't have much spare time, you're better off using an agent, who takes care of your marketing and saves you the time and expense of advertising and finding clients.

You should monitor the effectiveness of your marketing by asking anyone who makes an enquiry how they found out about your property (although they will probably say "On the internet", which can be a less than useful answer!).

> **SURVIVAL TIP**
> Make sure your documentation (and especially a website) is regularly updated; there's nothing more off-putting than out-of-date information or a document that has been amended by hand.

Brochures & Internet Sites

There are numerous companies that produce printed and/or online directories of holiday properties for rent. These fall broadly into two categories: those that simply carry advertising, while properties are let directly by the owners (see **Advertising Sites** on page 89), and those that act as agents, handling bookings as well as advertising your property, usually on a commission basis (see **Using an Agency** on page 95 and the list of websites in **Appendix C**). Some agencies arrange a complete package for clients, including travel and accommodation. Note that Brittany Ferries offers a choice between an agency scheme (called Holiday Homes) and an advertising only arrangement (Owners in France).

Most people book their summer holidays in January and the deadline for an entry in printed brochures is typically the previous August. If your property renovation isn't yet completed, this can be a problem – concentrating on finishing the roof and facade and strategically positioning container plants to get an attractive photograph might be a solution! (Interior photographs can always be added to the related website at a later date.)

Tourist Office

Don't forget to contact regional and departmental tourist boards (*comités régionaux/départementaux de tourisme*). These maintain lists of holiday accommodation and publish widely distributed brochures, in which a listing may cost little (around €15). In recent years, however, regional tourist boards have become more stringent in respect of whose holiday accommodation they will promote; most advertise only premises which have been inspected and rated by their own representatives or those of Clévacances or Gîtes de France.

Networking, Promotion & Public Relations

Look for opportunities for joint promotions or 'tie-ins', such as promoting a local attraction, in return for which the attraction lists your establishment in its promotional material. The attraction may even offer your guests a discount on admission or products purchased there.

Contact companies that organise tours (e.g. wine, shopping, motorcycling) in your area and invite them to list your establishment in their documentation or even include your accommodation in their tours.

It also pays to work with other local people in the same business and send surplus guests to competitors (they will usually reciprocate).

Articles

The many magazines about France (see **Appendix A**) and even national newspapers are constantly looking for feature articles on unusual properties abroad – and properties in unusual locations. You could even write about the local area and include a mention of your establishment; they may not pay you for an article, but it could generate business.

Literature

Have a leaflet or brochure professionally designed (**recommended**) or, if you have the necessary skills, produce your own. If you need 100 or more, it's worth having them professionally printed – get several quotes for designing and printing. While you're having these printed, it may be cost-effective also to print some simply flyers (hand-outs) and business cards, which you should always keep in your wallet or handbag – you never know when you might run into potential clients!

Keep things simple if designing on your computer – just because you have 100 pretty fonts you don't have to use them all! A good rule of thumb is not to use more than two different typefaces on a page, and no more than two sizes. Don't get carried away with myriad colours, either.

A good format for a leaflet is a sheet of A4 (297mm x 210mm) folded into thirds. On the front, have the name and address of your property, any logos of organisations to which you belong (e.g. GdF) and a picture. Inside, include the following:

● Exterior and interior pictures.

● Important details.

● The exact location.

● Local attractions and details of how to get there (with a small map).

- The name, address and telephone number of your caretaker if applicable.

On the back page have your contact details: name, address, telephone and fax numbers, email and website addresses for more information.

It's necessary to make a home look as attractive as possible in a leaflet or brochure without distorting the facts or misrepresentation (you can be fined heavily for this). Advertise honestly and don't over-sell your property. You should enclose a stamped addressed envelope when sending out publicity material.

Signs

If you want to erect signs on a main road, your property must generally be within 5km (3mi) of it. If it's a national road (*route nationale*, prefixed by N), you must contact the Ministère des Transports, de l'Equipement, du Tourisme et de la Mer (🖥 www.equipement.gouv.fr); if it's a departmental (D) road, contact your local Direction Départementale de l'Equipement (DDE), which controls not only the roads themselves, but the land 3m on each side (unless private property); if it's a communal (C) road, ask at your local *mairie*.

One of the major benefits of GdF registration is that you're provided with signs: directional signs with arrows on for the road and circular signs for your gatepost or wall. Whether or not they're installed for you depends on how keen the regional, departmental or communal administration is to promote tourism, but it's as well to ask – if only to find out where they may and may not be sited. Clévacances also supplies signs, but these are less familiar to holidaymakers and consequently of less marketing value.

At the entrance to your property, the sign should be large and clear, visible to traffic passing in both directions. Test its position and visibility by driving past. Often, signs are just too small to be noticed, the lettering is too thin to be read from a moving car, or the sign doesn't actually say what it's advertising!

Advertising

Advertising can bring you success (if your advertising is effective) or failure (if you spend too much on ineffective advertising), and you should make your advertising strategy (and budget) one of your highest priorities.

Advertising doesn't just mean insertions in glossy magazines. You can advertise among friends and colleagues, in company and club magazines (which may even be free), and on notice boards in companies, shops and public places. It isn't necessary to advertise only locally or even to stick to your home country; you can extend your marketing abroad.

> **SURVIVAL TIP**
> The most expensive advertising is that
> which doesn't produce results!

Your Advertisement

A press or catalogue advertisement will be a limited size; it needs to be concentrated and effective. Think about what you look for when flicking through holiday advertisements – and, more importantly, what you see. Most people see the following in this order: 1. The picture; 2. The price; 3. The capacity of the accommodation; 4. The written description. All these aspects are important, but it's the picture that will sell your property. The location is obviously significant, but if people are looking for a holiday 'in France' they will browse all advertisements. You **should** include the price in your advertisement – that's the first thing people ask anyway (once they've seen the picture!). French advertisements often don't show prices, which is extremely irritating to people of most other nationalities.

Photographs: Some agencies take photographs, while others (including 'deal direct' companies) require you to submit your own. If you aren't confident of your ability as a photographer, or don't have a good enough camera (especially for interior shots), hire a professional. As stated above, the photograph is the most important element of your advertising, so don't skimp. If it's for print, you will normally need good 35mm prints or transparencies, but a high resolution digital image may be acceptable; ask the publisher what he requires. For internet advertisements, a lower resolution is adequate (and may even be required, in order to maximise upload speed).

The main photograph (of the front of your property) is the most important, as it must catch the eye of the magazine, catalogue or website browser and stand out from hundreds of others.

 Advertisements which don't display an exterior shot rarely attract bookings, as the impression given is that there's something unattractive about the property or its surroundings.

To get the best quality exterior shots:

● Choose a sunny day with a blue sky (a few fluffy white clouds are permissible!).

● Try unusual views and angles. If you can, erect a ladder and look down on the property or lie on the ground and look up.

- Choose the time of day when the sun is on the facade of the property. The quality and colour of light is usually better in the early morning or early evening than in the middle of the day.

- Dress your property. Even if you hate net curtains and wouldn't normally have them in your *gîte*, nevertheless hang some before taking photos, as they brighten the facade and avoid the 'empty eyes' effect.

- Introduce colour with pots of flowering plants and hanging baskets.

- Don't include people, cars or pets. The viewers must be able to see themselves staying in the property; if there are other people in the photograph, they will be subconsciously seen as intruders.

- Include pretty garden furniture – viewers can envisage themselves basking in the sun.

- Include the pool if you have one and the accompanying facade of the property is attractive.

For the best interior shots:

- Use a wide-angle or fisheye lens.

- Dress the rooms with big pots of fresh flowers and colourful accessories.

- Give your picture a focal point, e.g. an open fire (lit) or an antique bed.

- Let in as much natural light as possible and switch on all lights.

- Use a stepladder to find a good angle.

- Photograph the most attractive parts of the prettiest rooms!

Text: The text of your advertisement should describe the main selling points of your property – its location, proximity to tourist attractions, rural seclusion, wonderful restaurants nearby, sites of historical interest, facilities for walking, cycling and other sports – all the reasons why a holidaymaker would want to choose your *gîte* over all the others available. Mention the nearest important town or city, rather than a small town whose name is unknown outside the area.

If space allows, include a list of the facilities available and main appliances, information about the pool and garden, distances from the nearest towns and/or village shops, a breakdown of the accommodation (number of bedrooms, type of beds), and any special facilities such as disabled access or children's play equipment.

Newspapers & Magazines

There's a wide range of French and foreign newspapers and magazines in which you can advertise, e.g. newspapers such as the *Sunday Times* and the

Observer in the UK, although advertising a single property might be prohibitively expensive. You must experiment to find the best publications and days of the week or months to advertise.

You might have a particular special interest group in mind; for example, if your property is near Le Mans, you might want to target car and motorbike enthusiasts and advertise in their magazines. If you're in an area of outstanding natural beauty where there are good routes for hiking, aim your advertising at walkers. If you're near the D-Day Landing beaches or the WW1 battlefields, there's a huge amount of interest and properties in these areas will always let well. The same strategy applies if you're in an area with interesting wildlife and birds, Roman remains and other historical sites, outstanding sporting facilities, steam railways, gourmet restaurants or any other interest with a large number of devotees and dedicated publications. A glance at the shelves of any large newsagent will reveal a wide range of special interest magazines; an internet search will disclose even more!

The most obvious special interest group is those who love France! There are many magazines specifically catering for Francophiles, which are packed with holiday accommodation advertising (see **Appendix A**).

Guide Books

Although the internet has largely displaced guide books as the preferred medium for advertising properties to let, a few specialist publications remain in print, most notably Alastair Sawday's *Special Places to Stay – French Holiday Homes, Villas, Gîtes & Apartments* (UK ☎ 01275-464891, 💻 www.sawdays.co.uk), in which entries (for properties that meet the criteria) cost from €200.

Internet

Advertising on the internet is an increasingly popular choice for property owners. There are two options: take an entry on an advertising site (see below), or set up your own (see page 92); you can, of course, do both.

Advertising Sites: There's an endless list of websites offering 'deal direct' advertising, whereby the company simply lists your advertisement on its website (and sometimes in a catalogue or brochure) for a one-off or annual fee. Some are excellent; many are a complete waste of money. The potential holidaymaker contacts you directly and you handle the transaction, which gives you complete control over your bookings. There are advantages and disadvantages to using an advertising site; advantages may include the following:

- Exposure to a large number of potential clients.
- Flexibility as to how much you can charge and which weeks you can offer.
- The opportunity to vet clients – if you don't like the sound of someone making a telephone enquiry, you can choose not to accept their booking!

Disadvantages may include the following:

- The cost (although some sites offer free listings – see below).
- Time and effort producing an advertisement, which are much the same as those required for doing your own letting (see page 100).
- No guarantee of attracting bookings.

Every day someone sets up a new holiday accommodation site, and sites are so numerous that you cannot rely on clients stumbling across them when searching the web. Some sites will produce few or no bookings. Try a search engine (e.g. ⌨ www.google.com) with various related keywords and phrases and see which sites appear in the top ten. If a company is exclusively web-based, the search result is important – most people won't look further than the first page or two.

Some of market leaders in holiday property advertising may not appear high up in the results. However, their strengths lie in their strategy of consistent press marketing campaigns in conjunction with a well-organised, easily navigable, informative, well-maintained and user-friendly website – the essential factors which attract clients.

Look for sites where you can browse the properties, as many (particularly French) sites require you to enter the exact number of people, bedrooms, the area, the date and the precise length of stay before showing any properties, which won't attract any 'window-shoppers'. Some offer a free entry for a limited period (when they have a sufficient number of properties on their sites, they will start charging).

```
SURVIVAL TIP
Free is worth a try; cheap is a false economy.
```

The best companies are those with the greatest coverage (e.g. number of brochures distributed) and a known brand name, such as Chez Nous or Brittany Ferries, who also produce a glossy colour catalogue with wide distribution via travel agents and ferry ports and advertise in national newspapers. They're far more expensive to advertise with, but the returns are usually worth it.

You should bear in mind that catalogues and brochures are easier to browse than websites and choose a company that publishes these, as despite the meteoric increase in holidays booked via the internet, there are still many people who don't use computers, have no internet access, mistrust this method of making their holiday arrangements or simply prefer to do things the 'old-fashioned' way. There are still plenty of high street travel agents, and your property needs to be seen by their customers.

The major companies include the following:

- **Bonnes Vacances** (UK ☎ 0870-760 7073, 🖥 www.bvdirect.co.uk) – This company advertises in national newspapers, publishes a brochure, and offers travel discounts and an insurance service. Listing cost: from £200 per year.

- **Brittany Ferries Owners in France** (UK ☎ 0870-901 3400, 🖥 www.ownersinfrance.co.uk) – Has an easy-to-navigate site and a well distributed brochure, and offers ferry fare and other travel discounts. Listing cost: from £235 per year.

- **Chez Nous** (UK ☎ 0870-197 1000, 🖥 www.cheznous.com) – Has an easy-to-navigate site and a well distributed brochure listing over 4,000 properties. Listings can be on the website only or in the brochure as well. Listing cost: from £250.

- **France Direct** (🖥 www.francedirect.net) – A British company, also registered in France (95 per cent of advertisers are English-speaking) and the sister company of Gites Direct (see page 100). The website is easy to navigate (there's no brochure). Several levels of advertising. Listing cost: from €150 per year.

- **France One Call** (UK ☎ 0871-717 9092, 🖥 www.franceonecall.com) – Web-based advertising business with a referral system, whereby members refer enquirers to France One Call if they're unable to accommodate them. Listing cost: £180 per year for one property, £30 for each additional property.

- **French Connections** (🖥 www.frenchconnections.co.uk) – Has a fast, easy-to-search site including plenty of details. Listing cost: from £150 per year.

- **Guide Vacances** (🖥 www.guidevacances.com). French holiday listing site. Listing cost: Basic listing free, with several optional paid extras (e.g. €15 for a photograph).

- **Homelidays** (☎ 01 70 75 34 03, 🖥 www.homelidays.com) – The site is available in French, Spanish, German, Italian and Portuguese. Listing cost: €90 per year (you can choose to advertise for 1, 4, 8 or 12 months).

- **Vacation Rentals by Owner/VRBO** (🖳 www.vrbo.com) – The fast site provides comprehensive details of accommodation worldwide; France can be searched by region. Listing cost: US$148 per year (includes three photographs).

- **Visit France** (UK ☎ 0870-350 2808, 🖳 www.visitfrance.co.uk) – Has an easily navigated site (no brochure) listing over 500 properties, including *gîtes* and B&B. Listing cost: from £100.

The photograph is the most important feature of your advertisement. When potential holidaymakers view a brochure or website, the photographs are the main selling point (see **Your Advertisement** on page 87). Head your advertisement with a well known town, such as 'near Bayeux', or a description, e.g. 'Charente coast', and the name of your property. Highlight proximity to attractions in the area, with a brief description of the accommodation.

Your Own Site: Although more expensive to set up, your own website costs little to maintain thereafter. You can have it designed professionally (**recommended**) or do it yourself, although if you're a complete 'dummy', it's best to pay someone else to do it for you. Avoid asking your friend's 12-year-old daughter do it; she might be a whiz with computers, but probably knows little about design and marketing.

From the outset, bear in mind that you're selling a product and will be up against stiff competition; gear your efforts towards achieving bookings. You must include everything that the potential client needs to know in order to make a decision – this might seem obvious, but too many people design websites that don't include the essential information. However pretty and well designed, if you don't tell people what they **need** to know (what you're offering, where it is, how to get there and how much it costs), they will pass on to another, more informative website.

Even if your website isn't the main booking source, it can be useful for clients' reference – they can download pictures, information, directions, maps, etc. after having made the initial contact by telephone or email or having seen a magazine or internet advertisement.

Consider registering your own domain name (e.g. www.yourproperty name.net). This isn't essential and is an additional cost, but it's easier for people to remember and looks more professional than a long name provided by your internet service provider.

Although there are 'idiot-proof' website design packages (some of which are free), these often create more problems than they solve; to create a professional-looking site, you need to have at least a basic knowledge of HTML and to use more sophisticated design software. If you choose to create your own website, keep it simple. A good website should be easy to navigate (don't include complicated page links or indexes) and must include contact details, preferably via email. Flashing red text on a black background won't sell your property; a clean, simple, easy-to-navigate site with plenty of content will. Look at other owners' sites in order to evaluate what features and designs are the most effective; what would prompt you to make an enquiry to one owner but not another? Incorporate ideas (but don't copy them!) from sites you like.

Keep to standard font groups such as Verdana/Arial/Helvetica (sans-serif) and Times New Roman/Times (serif). You might have some exotic fonts on your system, but if the person viewing the site doesn't have the same fonts installed on his, he won't see them and your carefully arranged text might appear misaligned or even with words missing. In any case, fancy fonts are often difficult to read. Use a graphic for logos or any other items that you prefer to appear in a specific typeface.

Pictures speak louder than words, but photographs and logo graphics must be kept to a reasonable size – if people have to wait too long for a page to appear, they will lose patience and move on to the next property on their list. To make picture files smaller, use the resize option in your graphics program (specifying pixel dimensions in HTML won't reduce the file size!). Remember that many people don't yet have broadband access. If you want to include a lot of photographs, consider using thumbnail images, each of which can be clicked to link to a larger image. Include exterior and interior shots (see page 87).

Make sure you give each page an appropriate title – this is what shows in the bar at the top of the screen. 'Holiday Accommodation in Anyville, France' is preferable to 'Home Page' or 'Page 1'.

If you want a coloured background, choose a plain, light, neutral colour or a tiny tile in a subtle pattern that loads quickly and doesn't make the text difficult to read. Use dark text on a light background – you want people to read what you've written, not be dazzled.

You can include a downloadable booking form – a PDF file is best. If you don't have the necessary software to create PDF files, use RTF (rich text format) files, which can be opened with any word processing (e.g. Microsoft Word) or text program. Try to avoid using frames, as the inexperienced user might have difficulty in printing the page.

Do **not** use flashing or scrolling text, music, trailing mouse pointers or any other embellishments, as they serve only to make pages load more slowly, look tacky and are irritating to most users.

If possible, view your finished pages using several browsers (e.g. Internet Explorer, Netscape, Opera, Firefox) and at different screen resolutions. Not everyone has the same system or settings and this can cause huge variations in the way a page appears. Make sure each page appears in its entirety without the necessity for lateral scrolling (set widths as percentages rather than pixel dimensions). Many people have their screen resolution set at 640 x 480 because that's how it was set when they bought the computer.

Basic HTML for building your page can be found on ▣ www.davesite. com and a free HTML editor on ▣ www.arachnoid.com. For information about scanning and image manipulation, go to ▣ www.scantips.com. There are numerous books about website design, although some are incomprehensible by the novice.

Include comprehensive information about your property, with directions and maps that customers can print off and bring with them when they travel. If you receive repeated questions, add the information to your site.

The most important information should be on the first screen at the top of the first page. It shouldn't be a slow-loading photograph or graphic logo. You need to catch the attention of potential clients immediately, entice them to read and explore the rest of your site, absorb what they read and then encourage them to make a booking. This first paragraph is often what is found by search engines, so incorporate plenty of keywords.

SURVIVAL TIP
Have a good, but precise description of what you're selling, where it is and why people should want a holiday there.

Keep pages fairly short, with links to separate pages for details of the accommodation, its location, how to book, more information, maps, etc. Include a link back to the home page on each.

If you aren't confident of your writing and spelling abilities, hire the services of a copywriter or at least have someone with good language skills read through it carefully before uploading. Remember that you're projecting an impression of the product being sold – you don't want it to look shoddy and unprofessional. Professional doesn't mean impersonal – use 'we' and 'you' when extolling your accommodation.

Include plenty of text, which increases search engine visibility, as well as sells your property. You can provide information about flights, ferries, car rental, local attractions, days out, sports facilities and links to other useful websites (have external links set to open in a separate window; you don't want visitors to wander away from your site). It's also advisable to submit your website to all the popular search engines, such as Altavista, Google and Yahoo, although many use automated 'crawlers' to identify new sites, in which case telling them that you exist will make little or no difference to your visibility. What is more effective is to have your site 'search engine optimised' – an arcane process that can be carried out (for a fee) by a specialist in the field. Exchanging links with other websites is a free (although time-consuming) method of increasing your site's visibility. The following sites offer tips on how to make your site more easily found by search engines: 💻 www.spider-food.net, 💻 www.searchmechanics.com.

Google (💻 www.google.com) offers a 'pay-per-click' advertising system, whereby you write an advertisement and nominate various key words or phrases (e.g. 'gite', 'cottage', 'holiday', 'accommodation', 'France') that people might enter when searching for your type of product. Your advertisement appears at the right hand side of the search page each time someone searches on those terms. How often it appears depends on the amount you pay!

SURVIVAL TIP
The purpose of your website is to convey information and present your accommodation in the most attractive possible light, not to dazzle your potential customers.

Monitoring & Follow-up

Remember to keep track of your enquiries and bookings so that you know where your customers and potential customers are coming from and can adjust or focus your marketing effort accordingly.

Also make sure you obtain feedback from your customers. A visitors' book is all very well, but a confidential and comprehensive comment card will give you more useful information; it shouldn't take customers more than ten minutes or so to complete.

It's much easier (and much cheaper) to obtain repeat business than to constantly find new customers, so make previous (satisfied) clients your marketing priority. Contact them regularly, but without pestering them: send them a newsletter (by post or email) advising them of any improvements to the property, new attractions in the vicinity or special deals you have to offer. Maybe send them a Christmas card each year.

USING AN AGENCY

Apart from organisations such as Gîtes de France and Clévacances (see page 53), a number of companies operate as property letting agents, including French estate agents.

 The law relating to property agencies is currently under review and it's likely that only registered estate agents will be permitted to let property in the near future. You should therefore use only an agency whose staff have a *carte professionnelle*.

If you use an agency or tour operator, the agency may specify certain conditions of a contract or even supply you with a standard contract. For example, you may not be permitted to make certain supplementary charges (e.g. for electricity). If you offer longer lets (e.g. from one to six months) outside the high season, you need to ensure that you or your agent uses the appropriate contract, which is different from a holiday letting contract.

If you want your property to appear in an agent's catalogue, you must contact the agency the summer before the year in which you wish to let it (the deadline is usually August).

 Although self-catering holiday companies may fall over themselves to take on a luxury property on the Côte d'Azur, the top letting agents turn down as many as 90 per cent of the properties they're offered.

Advantages & Disadvantages

The advantages of using an agency may include the following:

- No advertising expenses.
- Large customer base.
- Brand loyalty – customers return to the same company year after year.
- Clients have the assurance of knowing that the property exists, that it conforms to the standards of a (hopefully) reputable agent and that they have back-up should any problems arise, rather than handing over hundreds of euros to a stranger in a foreign country, with the risk of arriving to find a building site or a non-existent property!
- Many holidaymakers prefer to book their holidays through an agency, making a one-step purchase rather than having to arrange accommodation, ferry crossings and insurance separately. (It's frequently cheaper, too.)
- Saves you time – you don't have to wait by the telephone or keep checking your email for enquiries.
- Support services (e.g. meeting and greeting clients, caretaking).
- No paperwork except when banking the cheque!

A good agency will find you far more bookings than you can hope to find yourself. Disadvantages can include:

- You cannot vet your clients.
- Exclusivity at certain times of year (including peak season), restricting your own use and any private bookings (e.g. family and friends).

- Third party intervention in disputes, although that can also be an advantage (see **Dealing with Problems** on page 81); for example, you might have to refund or compensate a client for reasons with which you don't agree.
- Fixed pricing structure.

Agencies normally set the rental prices for your property, although some (e.g. Gites Direct – see page 100) advertise your property and deal with the initial booking and deposit, thereafter passing the rest of the transaction on to you – they're neither an 'all-in' agency nor a simple advertising site and you're free to set your own rates. Others sell a whole holiday package to the customer, handling everything – the initial advertising, the first enquiry, the contracts and payment – up to the point of the visitors' arrival. Some may even be able to assist in locating caretaking services.

The question of whether you will earn more or less by using an agency has no simple answer. On the one hand, clients are often willing to pay more (sometimes considerably more) if they're booking through a reputable agency, as the product is better presented and they have the safeguard of being able to complain (and perhaps get money back) if the accommodation is unsatisfactory. Many have brand loyalty and use the same agency year after year. The premium paid by the client may or may not, however, be passed on to you, the owner. Agencies can sometimes offer owners a higher rate than they would be able to charge privately owing to the reductions the agency can negotiate with ferry and insurance companies, which subsidise the package they offer; it can even be cheaper for clients to book with an agency, particularly when ferry prices are high, because their package price includes discounted ferry fares, in which case everyone wins (except perhaps the ferry companies!): the client gets a better combined deal, and you earn more money than you would at private rates.

Of course, agencies take a commission; otherwise, they would soon cease trading! Some owners believe that agencies are simply taking profits that should rightly be theirs, while others appreciate the fact that agencies pay for expensive advertising and deal with all the paperwork, contracts and payments, thus saving you an enormous amount of time and effort. You might earn €75 less per week than you would for a private let in high season, but you have no advertising costs (which can run to several hundreds of euros to be effective) and the time you would spend on administration can be put to more profitable use.

SURVIVAL TIP
Regard any shortfall between your private
letting rate and that which you receive from an agent
as your advertising budget.

Choosing an Agency

Each agency has its particular requirements, but as a rule your accommodation must be available throughout the high season (July and August), although you may be able to block one or two weeks for your own use. Most agencies send a representative to inspect the property (some charge a deductible fee for this) and will do so each year to ensure that it continues to meet standards.

Take care when selecting a letting agent, as a number have gone bust in recent years owing customers thousands of euros. Make sure that your income is kept in an escrow account and paid regularly, or even better, choose an agent with a bonding scheme who pays you the rent **before** the arrival of guests (the better ones do). It's absolutely essential to employ an efficient, reliable and honest company, preferably long-established. Anyone can set up a holiday letting agency and there are many 'cowboy' operators. Ask for the names of satisfied owners and check with them. In particular, ask agents the following:

● Who they let to.

● Where they advertise.

● What information they send to potential clients.

● Whether they have contracts with other holiday and travel companies.

● What the payment arrangements are.

● What cancellation clauses are in their contracts with clients.

● What are the restrictions on your own use of the property.

You should also check the type of contract you will have with the agency: whether, for example, you receive a detailed analysis of income and expenditure and what notice you're required to give if you decide to terminate the agreement.

The larger companies market homes via newspapers, magazines, overseas agents, colour brochures and the internet, and have representatives in many countries. A good agency will do the following:

● Advertise in the national press.

● Produce a colour brochure.

● Have quality standards.

● Have an owners' helpline.

● Have regional representatives in France.

● Be registered in France, even if based elsewhere.

● Provide checklists for owners.

- Provide a level of publicity and marketing that a private owner cannot compete with.

- Have an online booking service where clients can book easily and pay using a credit or debit card.

- Obtain far more bookings than you could manage privately!

Leading Agencies

The main agencies include the following:

- **Allez France** (UK ☎ 0845-330 2056, 💻 www.allezfrance.com) – Over 300 properties.

- **Bowhills** (UK ☎ 01489-872727, 💻 www.bowhills.co.uk) – 350 properties. 30,000 copies of their colour brochure printed annually. Strongest in the Dordogne, Provence, Languedoc and Brittany. UK-based bilingual representatives, dedicated owners' telephone helpline. Looking for properties with pools or within 20 minutes of a beach or perhaps with a river frontage.

- **Brittany Ferries Holiday Homes** (UK ☎ 0870-536 0360, 💻 www.brittany ferries.com) – The official UK representative of Gîtes de France, with 850 *gîtes* and 450 cottages in its brochure, some villas with pools in southern France. Offers 15 per cent discount on Brittany Ferries fares.

- **Crystal France** (UK ☎ 0800-980 3381, 💻 www.crystalfrance.co.uk) – Nearly 300 mid to up-market properties, covering most French regions.

- **Easycottages** (UK ☎ UK 0870-197 2799, 💻 www.easycottages.com) – Part of the Holiday Cottages Group (see below), Easycottages offers a selection of cottages in the UK, Ireland and France.

- **French Affair** (UK ☎ 020-7381 8519, 💻 www.frenchaffair.com) – Operating in France since 1986. Villas in the Dordogne, Lot, Provence, Languedoc-Roussillon, Pays Basque, Atlantic Coast area and Corsica.

- **French Country Cottages** (UK ☎ 0870-078 1500, 💻 www.french-country-cottage.co.uk, www.countrycottagesinfrance.co.uk and www.cottages4you.co.uk) – Part of the Holiday Cottages Group (see below), with 900 French properties at the higher end of the market. 200,000 preview brochures sent to mailing list plus 200,000 main brochures to past and potential customers in November. Dedicated owner helpline, bilingual representatives in the UK. Annual inspections and regional representatives in France. Full back-up for owners. French Country Cottages pay up front any monies received (deposits and balance payments), which are non-refundable in the case of late cancellation by the client. 50 per cent of properties have pools.

- **French Life** (UK ☎ 0870-197 6675, 🖳 www.frenchlife.co.uk) – Part of the Holiday Cottages Group (see below), with 1,000 cottages and villas, priced between those of French Country Cottages and Welcome Cottages.

- **Gites Direct** (🖳 www.gitesdirect.com) – The same company as France Direct (see page 91), offering a booking service on a commission basis.

- **Holiday Cottages Group** – One of the largest companies in this field, incorporating Easycottages, French Country Cottages, French Life and Welcome Cottages (see this section) and Chez Nous (see page 89).

- **Individual France** (UK ☎ 0870-077 1771, 🖳 www.individualtravellers. com) – Formerly Vacances en Campagne. Around half of its 400 properties have pools. Prices include short Channel crossing or car hire. Properties to be submitted by May for inclusion in the following year's brochure, but can immediately go on the website.

- **Just France** (UK ☎ 020-8780 4480, 🖳 www.justfrance.co.uk). – Booking via the website and a glossy brochure.

- **VFB Holidays** (UK ☎ 01242-240340, 🖳 www.vfbholidays.co.uk) – Properties are mostly French-owned. Each property is inspected every year. Printed brochure. Cleaning included in holiday price.

- **Welcome Cottages** (UK ☎ 0870-197 6420, 🖳 www.welcomecottages. com) – Part of the Holiday Cottages Group (see above), offering less expensive cottages, villas and apartments across France.

Agency Fees

Agency fees vary greatly, but are usually a commission of between 20 and 40 per cent of gross rental income, although whether this means that you earn less than you would by marketing privately depends on a number of factors (see above).

DOING YOUR OWN LETTING

Doing your own letting is time-consuming, but allows you more control and flexibility over rates and who you let to and when, and enables you to use the property yourself whenever you choose. It also gives your clients the personal touch, which can be important. Possible disadvantages include the following:

- A lot of time, effort and paperwork.
- Telephone calls at unsociable hours (particularly from people in distant time zones).

- Advertising and other marketing costs.
- It can be embarrassing to handle cancellations and requests for reimbursement, if you've established a rapport with clients.

If you plan to let a home yourself, you must decide how to handle enquiries about flights and car rentals. It's easier to let clients make their own bookings, but you should be able to offer advice and put them in touch with airlines, ferry companies, travel agents and car rental companies. You must also decide whether you want to let to smokers or accept pets or young children (see **Other Considerations** on page 64).

Setting Rates

To get an idea of the rent you should charge, ring a few letting agencies and ask them what it would cost to rent a property such as yours at the time of year you plan to let. They're likely to quote the **highest** rent you can charge. You should also check the advertisements in newspapers and magazines and the many websites dealing in French holiday accommodation. Set a realistic rent, as there's a lot of competition. It's better to let 20 weeks at an average €400 than ten at €500 (see **Financial Considerations** on page 59).

Rental Periods

Many owners start out with flexible rental periods, but most find it's best to stick with Saturday as the changeover day; this is what holidaymakers are familiar with and it makes your life simpler. Some owners (especially French) prefer to have a minimum two-week rental period in July and August, but these weeks are the most likely to book anyway so such restrictions are usually unnecessary (although having two-week lets reduces the time you need to spend on changeovers and cleaning). If there are many French owners in your area, offering one week lets in high season gives you a USP.

There's a large market for short breaks (particularly in northern France), but as these are normally let from Friday to Monday, they will preclude you taking bookings for the whole week either side and you should therefore avoid them in high season. At other times of the year, they may bring in income that you wouldn't otherwise have.

Handling Enquiries

Make it as easy as possible for people to contact you, and **be available**. This may seem obvious, but if you don't answer the telephone or don't reply promptly to emails, your potential clients will pass on to the next property on their list. Email can be somewhat impersonal and some clients, especially in older age groups, may not have internet access. Telephoning abroad can also be off-putting, and your advertisements are likely to get more response when enquirers don't have to make an international call. If you have a UK property, you could rent an 0871 number and have it permanently diverted to your French address. These are available from (🖳 www.adcall.com/adcall0871/index.html) and are connected to your existing number, for a once-only cost of around £40.

It's necessary to have an answerphone and a fax machine. A computer is also essential, as many people book via websites and email. Once potential clients have seen your advertisement, or followed a recommendation, their first impression of you will reflect their expectations of your accommodation.

When sending emails, avoid over-enthusiastic spam filters at the recipient's end by using a distinctive subject line, e.g. the name of your property, in plain text and don't include any web links.

Telephone

Smile when you answer the telephone. Be friendly, but professional and efficient. Keep your calendar, tariff, a notebook and pen handy, so that you can answer questions about availability immediately. (There's nothing worse for a caller than hearing: 'Hang on a minute while I find a pen . . .') Don't allow small children to answer your calls – whereas some people might find it cute, others certainly won't. It doesn't give a professional impression and customers don't want to spend ten minutes on an international telephone call while a three-year-old chats or wanders off to find its mother! Be positive when you talk on the telephone, encourage the caller to make a booking by emphasising the benefits of coming to stay at your property. For instance, if they ask if it's near the sea, give the time it takes to drive there, or if you're a long way from the coast mention river bathing or nearby swimming facilities or your own pool. Remember that you're selling a product!

Email

Again, be friendly, but professional and clear. You convey an impression of your business in the way you respond. Use a spell-checker and punctuate correctly – don't use all upper case, this is interpreted as shouting; use upper and lower case letters where appropriate. Don't use abbreviations or 'chatty' language. When quoting prices, spell out the currency or use the standard abbreviations (e.g. GBP for pounds sterling, EUR for euros, USD for US dollars), as not all fonts support all currency symbols – you may be able to see them on your monitor, but the recipient might not. Likewise, don't use fancy fonts – if the recipient doesn't have the same font installed they won't see your pretty prose.

 Beware of email scams – messages from a large group offering to book all your accommodation for an extended stay are usually too good to be true. They might offer to overpay you by cheque or money order, requesting the surplus to be sent somewhere else and /or the payment may be counterfeit.

Check your emails frequently and respond promptly; don't miss the opportunity for a booking. Often people will make a list of all the properties in which they're interested and write to them all simultaneously – be the first to reply, as only one on that list will win the booking!

Contracts & Deposits

Following the initial enquiry, if the customer wants to book, you must have a simple agreement form that includes the dates of arrival and departure and approximate times. Note that if you plan to let to non-English speaking clients, you must have a letting agreement in the appropriate languages.

It's a legal requirement to have a written agreement for all rentals. Most people who let a property for holiday accommodation draw up a simple agreement form that includes a property description, the names of the clients, financial details, and the dates of arrival and departure. **You should check with a lawyer that your agreement is legal and contains all the necessary safeguards.** For example, it should specify the types of damage for which the client is responsible. All descriptions, contracts and payment terms must comply with French laws (see page 50).

Hold availability for one week, a non-refundable booking deposit to be paid within this time (see **Legal Considerations** on page 50). Request that the balance of payment be made at least eight weeks before the arrival date.

```
SURVIVAL TIP
Keep detailed records and ensure
that you never double book!
```

Methods of Payment

It's important to be able to offer your clients various methods of payment, although most of your bookings will be made in advance by post or online.

Cheque

If guests are British and you have a UK bank account, the easiest way for them to pay is with a sterling cheque. Ask French guests for a cheque in euros. Note, however, that although other European countries (except the UK) are in the euro currency zone, most French banks make a hefty charge for banking any cheques in euros from outside France – similar to the fee they would charge for a US or UK cheque.

Bank Transfer

A more frequent method of payment from one European country to another is a direct bank transfer. With this method you give the customer your IBAN and BIC codes (your bank will advise you of these if they aren't printed in the back of your chequebook) and they arrange a transfer, which takes just a few days. Make sure the customer pays the bank charge (or add it to the final bill). Ask your bank for details.

Online Payment

For payments from most countries across the world, PayPal is immediate and easy (🖳 www.paypal.com, 🖳 www.paypal.co.uk, 🖳 www.paypal.fr). This is an online payment method whereby clients can pay by credit card. You (the owner) must open an account, which is free. The fee structure varies according to where your account is based, and on the volume of payments received. For example, if you register with an address in the UK and have average monthly receipts of up to £1,500, you will pay 3.4 per cent plus £0.20 per transaction; for monthly receipts between £1,500 and £6,000 the fee is 2.9 percent plus £0.20 per transaction. Full details can be found on the above websites.

Western Union

If a client doesn't want to enter financial details online, another efficient method is a Western Union Money Transfer. Clients pay cash at their nearest Western Union agency, and you collect cash at your nearest main post office (after filling in a long form and providing proof of identity). A list of locations and further information can be found on the Western Union website (🖳 www.westernunion.com).

Credit Cards

If your business grows, you can apply for your own merchant account so that you can take credit card payments (Visa, MasterCard, etc.) directly. You must be registered as a business with the Chambre de Commerce and have a business account with your bank, which provides you with the card machine for a monthly fee and charge a small percentage of each transaction. You must be able to accept transactions when the customer isn't present (for deposits). This is called *vente à distance* and incurs an additional small monthly charge.

Chèques-vacances

Many French employers give their low-paid workers a form of holiday voucher called a *chèque-vacances*. Each voucher is worth €10 or €20 and can be used to pay for holiday accommodation, as well as leisure activities, restaurant meals and other holiday 'entertainment'. They're valid for two years from the date of issue. If you decide to accept these, you must register with the Agence Nationale pour les Chèques-Vacances (ANCV, 36 boulevard Henri Bergson, 95201 Sarcelles Cedex, ☎ 08 25 84 43 44, ⌨ www.ancv.com). Registration is free (details of how to register can be found on the website), but you're charged a 1 per cent fee on the redemption of vouchers, with a minimum of €2. You're paid the value of the vouchers (less the fee) by bank transfer within 21 days.

Information Packs

After accepting a booking, you should provide guests with a pre-arrival information pack containing the following:

- A map of the local area and instructions on how to find the property.
- Information about local attractions and the local area (available free from tourist offices).
- Emergency contact numbers in your home country (e.g. the UK) and France, if guests have problems or plan to arrive late.
- The keys or instructions on where to collect them on arrival.

Arrival & Departure Times

Specify the times when guests may arrive, for instance between 4 and 8pm, and ask them to notify you what time they expect to be with you, asking them to telephone if there's a change of plan. Be quite firm about this; you will have a lot to do on changeover day and won't want a car full of holidaymakers arriving at 2pm when you're frantically changing beds or unblocking the drains. Neither do you want to be waiting around until 11pm when they were expected at 5pm, but decided to stop for dinner without letting you know.

Departure time is usually 10am, but if you have no guests arriving the same day you can extend the deadline a little; departing guests might spend a little longer cleaning before they leave!

CASE STUDY 3

We arrived in France in 1992, from Sheffield, with a map of Normandy, a well thumbed copy of the magazine *Living France* and dreams of owning one of the ruins to renovate advertised therein. As it happens, we'd been unable to find any self-catering accommodation in the Suisse-Normande region, where we were hoping to buy, and this later influenced our decision to provide such facilities.

A friendly estate agent, in the pretty town of Thury-Harcourt, provided us with a *gîte* to stay in and showed us lots of properties within our budget of £10,000, but they were all in need of far too much work. The last one of the day, a large L-shaped barn near the town and the beautiful River Orne, had been up for sale for eight years because it lacked access to its small garden. However, this was amply compensated by the fact that it was in excellent condition, had lovely views over the surrounding Calvados countryside and, most importantly, was less than an hour's drive from the port of Caen. We therefore decided to purchase it, and subsequently solved the access problem by making a wooden balcony and staircase so you could get to the garden from upstairs – and we heaved the septic tank round and over the farmer's fences!

By 1996, the conversion of one half of the barn into a spacious four-bedroom apartment (which we called 'Le Grenier') was completed. We enlisted a graphic designer to give our brochure and booking form a professional look, and started distributing copies among our family, friends and acquaintances.

We contacted Brittany Ferries Holiday Homes, whose brochure we'd seen many times whilst crossing the Channel, and agreed to let them publicise and handle the administration for Le Grenier, in return for priority over all its peak season bookings of 1997. However, we were disappointed by the picture they had taken and the description of our property in the brochure and began researching alternatives.

We were introduced to Inghams, who were able to offer us a higher weekly rent for our 1998 season and whose contract had more flexible terms. By this time we were also filling our empty weeks through a basic advertisement in the Brittany Ferries Owners in France 'deal direct' brochure, costing us about £150 a year for a small advert. The substantial ferry discounts we qualified for subsidised this cost, but we soon realised that a photograph was essential to attract enquiries and upgraded the advert for the following year. We also became members of France One Call, who had initiated a telephone and internet service for clients seeking availability at the last minute.

In 1999, we heard about the sale of a small farmstead in the nearby Vire-Bocage region, which had been for sale for a couple of years. The owner, living in England, was desperate to sell the farmstead of five houses, two of which had been recently converted into living accommodation. He had already accepted a ridiculous offer, but the sale had fallen through; we immediately matched the previous offer (not thinking how we were going to finance it) and it was accepted. Luckily, the bank saw its potential too and agreed to give us a mortgage.

The farmhouse and cottage at the new site, Les Moueux, were updated and refurbished into gîtes ('La Valette' and 'Le Courty'), and were ready to let in 2000. We then discovered another agency, VFB, who put 'La Valette' on their books immediately, guaranteeing us a minimum fixed income, but disallowing any private bookings. However, we were again disappointed with their representation of our property in their brochure, and it stood empty for most of that year.

At this point, we had also finished converting our own home ('Le Poirier'), next door to 'Le Grenier' in Thury-Harcourt, and decided to let that too, so that we could move to Les Moueux. We had heard excellent reports, from holiday homeowners and clients alike, about French Country Cottages, and signed up 'Le Grenier' and 'Le Poirier' with them. We employed a local couple to clean and maintain the gîtes and to meet and greet our guests while we ran and developed Les Moueux.

However, running the two sites at the same time as bringing up a family required lots more help and much more expense, and in 2001 we sold 'Le Grenier' as a going concern, to concentrate on Les Moueux. We still live in Les Moueux, having renovated two of the three ruins and converted them into three gîtes. However, over the past few years, with the ever increasing number of gîtes available, it has become a lot harder to fill even the August weeks.

Another factor contributing to this decline is that people have changed the way they book their holidays, booking direct with owners via the internet offering cheaper and more exotic locations. We have therefore cancelled all our contracts with booking agencies for next year and arranged to let two of the gîtes long term to locals, which will save us the expense of providing for the ever more demanding expectations of clients, i.e. dishwashers, hi-fi, DVD, computer, pool. This also guarantees us a regular income with fewer running costs and less stress.

Hayley Shaw and Douglas Beal (☎ 02 31 66 00 17, 💻 www.les moueux.com)

CASE STUDY 4

We moved to France from the busy, overcrowded south-east of England in 1992 to find a quiet, low-stress lifestyle and better weather. Financing this lifestyle meant providing accommodation in which others could enjoy the same benefits, albeit only for a holiday. We decided to offer self-catering accommodation, as it seemed to involve less day-to-day work than bed and breakfast, although 12 years on I'm not sure that's how it has worked out.

House-hunting was fun, at first, but looking around endless decaying, smelly houses with crumbling barns did get a bit depressing even though the estate agents pointed out the potential at every turn. We decided to live in a part of France we wanted to live in and in a house we liked rather than research the market and buy something that was ideal for self-catering holidays. So, although there had to be potential for holiday accommodation and a swimming pool, our own needs were top of the list. With very little research and no business plan we chose the Dordogne and a house on the edge of a village. We've since come to appreciate the many advantages and conveniences of being part of a thriving community, and a lot of our visitors have come to us having spent their previous holiday isolated and miles from anywhere – literally up a goat track in some cases.

When we lived in England we had a house, garden and garage on the edge of a reasonable-size town, full-time jobs, no children and were in our mid-30s. We're now in our late 40s and during those 12 years we've gained a larger house, a larger garden, a swimming pool, two self-catering cottages, a large workshop/garage (all on the edge of a small village), have become self-employed and are raising two children. Sadly, two gîtes (or even the three we had for many years) didn't provide an income we could live on, and Charles has to work full-time, as well as helping with changeover chores during the summer months.

As soon as we arrived in France, we immediately started to renovate one half of the house (which had at some point been a separate house), as the plan was to start letting, and earning money, as soon as possible. We moved into the house in July, having already decided to advertise with Chez Nous and contacted them to get an idea of deadlines and costs. When we were house-hunting, we'd chatted to one of the agents, whose wife ran gîtes and a B&B, and over a cup of coffee she had said that she 'swore by Chez Nous', who were well established and very helpful and seemed professional. We decided to book space in their 1993 brochure and had to commit to this, and pay the money, in September 1992, which was quite scary. We got our first deposit cheque in early January 1993 when I was in hospital having our son and in our first season we were full from the end of May until early September. We were obviously novices: the place was only just ready and I'm sure our naiveté showed, but we were happy. We've advertised with Chez Nous ever since.

The money we grandly call our 'annual advertising budget' is around £1,000 and most of this goes to Chez Nous, but we have, over the years, sometimes used the Sunday papers to fill odd weeks and have used France One Call's late availability service for about five years. We've never been particularly impressed with the plethora of French lifestyle magazines, whose advertising sales staff pester us, nor the small companies offering 'deal direct' advertising and we avoid the host of website and internet services offered to us (almost weekly). We've built our own website, but most people find us through Chez Nous or France One Call and we're happy with the level of bookings. The season here seems to be limited to June, July and August, with only a few people interested in May or September.

We had three gîtes for several years, but have now shrunk to two, as the original has been incorporated back into our house to meet our changed domestic needs (growing children!) and because I'd become fed up with having guests so close. This year we've bought a part share in a rental property nearby, which should increase our income without impacting, further, on our privacy.

Privacy is a big issue. Basically, there's precious little. Most guests are pleasant and we enjoy a drink or a chat with them. And most of them are considerate; some want their privacy as much as we do and we respect each other's space. However, some guests are simply a pain in the neck and we cannot wait to see them leave. I console myself with the knowledge that I've got their money and I get to stay while they have to drive home!

As a sweeping generalisation, most visitors on a self-catering holiday want hot water, clean, practical accommodation, comfortable beds and sunshine – lots of it. If there's a pool, it must be clean, all the time. There are, of course, exceptions to every rule: one of our clients complained that it was too hot and that she wouldn't have come if she had known. At the time, in August, the temperatures were around the mid-20s rather than the usual low 30s (let alone the high 30s and more that we experienced in 2003). Running holiday accommodation is stressful, and taking responsibility for everything (including the weather) goes with the territory and means providing the same welcome and service to 'all sorts'.

Self-catering is probably easier than B&B (we do B&B occasionally if bookings are down), but still hard work. We do all the work ourselves, although when the children were very small I got a babysitter for changeover Saturdays and last year I was really spoilt and employed a friend to do the largest gîte while I did the second and the smallest. I also use a laundry service now for the large bath towels and double-bed linen – I still do the rest. I'm not sure that either of us trusts anyone enough to delegate the maintenance and cleaning completely, and it's difficult – in fact, impossible – to take even a few days away in the summer, which, I feel, is becoming a nuisance.

Audrey & Charles Fleming, Route de Boisseuilh, 24390 Cherveix Cubas (☎ 05 53 50 12 39, ✉ Audrey@LesFlamands.com)

TOP TEN TIPS FOR GITE OWNERS

- Be sure your property is marketable – a lot of time and effort can be wasted if it isn't in a good area for letting and doesn't photograph well.
- Aim to have a low-maintenance property.

- Be prepared to limit friends' and family's use – you will feel obliged to offer free or cheap stays, probably at a time of year when you could let for the going rate.
- Check with your insurer – in some cases insurance is void if the property is vacant for 30 days or more.
- Make sure you declare your rental income for tax purposes.
- Make your advertising strategy a priority.
- Focus on your target market.
- Do learn to speak, read and write French.
- Don't underestimate renovation costs and time.
- Don't overestimate the income.
- If you handle your own marketing, be professional, i.e. prompt and efficient.

3.

BED & BREAKFAST

Bed and breakfast accommodation – B&B, as it's known in the UK and US – wasn't familiar in France until relatively recently, the options for overnight accommodation being limited to hotels (small and large), *logis* (more like lodgings, where you would pay for breakfast separately), and a *pension* (board and lodging). The concept and the term *chambres d'hôtes*, along with regulations relating to B&B, were introduced in 1969 by the government organisation Gîtes de France (GdF), which was started in 1951 – initially for the promotion and marketing of self-catering cottages (*gîtes*). (*Chambres d'hôtes* literally – and confusingly – means either guests' rooms or hosts' rooms, and is also seen written *chambre d'hôte*, *chambre d'hôtes* and *chambres d'hôte*, even on official websites and road signs – sometimes all four variations in one place!)

Running a *chambres d'hôtes* is a particularly inviting option for those who buy large (especially rural) properties and wish (or need) to supplement their income by letting one or two rooms or even dedicating their entire house to a bed and breakfast business.

No authorisation is required to offer B&B accommodation, although if it's your principal source of income it must be registered as a commercial activity with the local Chambre de Commerce (see **Legal Considerations** on page 121).

As with *gîtes*, you can operate independently, with or without an official tourist board rating, or sign up with one of the recognised organisations – Gîtes de France or Clévacances (see **Registration** on page 124). The maximum number of rooms is five (six in some areas) with up to 15 guests; if you have more than this, you're considered to be running a hotel and must comply with far more stringent safety and hygiene regulations. Running a hotel is covered by this book's sister publication, *Making a Living in France* (see page 317).

THE MARKET

Gîtes de France (GdF)'s statistics for *chambres d'hôtes* registered with them show that this type of accommodation appeals mainly to couples aged between 35 and 64, without dependent children, most of them being city-dwellers and homeowners. In addition:

● 72 per cent are French, with Belgians the second-largest group.

● 49 per cent are middle management, senior executives or professional people.

● 26 per cent are retired.

● The average stay is three nights.

The following statistics apply to B&B businesses:

- There are currently around 25,000 rooms registered with GdF.
- 850 new addresses are added every year (around 2,500 rooms).
- The average investment is €10,000.
- The average annual occupancy is 14 weeks.
- The average charge is €46 per night for two people, including breakfast (prices ranging from €30 to €80).

These figures, of course, don't include the huge number of B&B businesses that aren't registered with GdF, many of which are run by non-French people.

The B&B market as a whole is divided into two main categories:

- Those who book accommodation in advance, for a day or two during a tour or for a whole holiday (usually a week or two).
- 'Passing trade', including local recommendations and tourist board referrals, who usually stay for just one night, but could end up staying longer if they like what you offer.

Satisfying the needs of both groups maximises your letting potential (see Where to Buy on page 116).

ADVANTAGES & DISADVANTAGES

Running a *chambres d'hôtes* with several rooms isn't a part-time activity, at least not in the summer; it's hard work – even harder than managing self-catering cottages. You are, in effect, 'on duty' 24 hours a day; you may have arrivals after midnight and then have to be on hand for people leaving at 6am. Work is also involved in attracting clients – you cannot simply put up a sign and wait for the visitors and money to roll in. The advantages of running a B&B include the following:

- The money!
- No formal qualifications or experience required (but see below).
- No formal registration if it isn't your main income.
- Little capital expenditure needed – you can start with one or two rooms and expand as time and money allow.
- Meeting interesting people.

There are also disadvantages, which may include the following:

- Having little free time, especially if offering evening meals.
- Having to share your home with strangers.

- Having to put up with people you don't like.

- Insufficient income to live on unless you let at least four or five rooms.

Running a B&B is hard work. Running a B&B is hard work. It bears repeating!

QUALIFICATIONS & EXPERIENCE

There are two essential 'qualifications' for running a B&B: you must enjoy meeting people and be able to get on with them, and you must be able to speak French. (A smattering of Italian, Spanish and German can come in handy, too!) These abilities are far more important than when letting a *gîte*, as you will have far more contact with your guests. Quite apart from communicating with guests, dealing with paperwork and officialdom is virtually impossible unless you have a working knowledge of the language. It's vital that at least one of the owners speaks good French; you won't be able to rely on English-speaking guests if you want to have a successful business.

 You may find that you cannot register with GdF unless at least one host can speak French, as this is becoming an increasingly common requirement.

A variety of other skills are required: you must act as chambermaids, cooks and bottle-washers, waiters, laundry workers and gardeners and perform routine property maintenance. If you're considering offering evening meals, but only have experience of providing family meals, it might be wise to sign up for a cookery course that's aimed at catering for larger numbers.

WHERE TO BUY

The criteria for the location of a B&B business are slightly different from those for *gîte* accommodation (see page 43), although location is perhaps even more crucial to the success of your business. In particular, you should consider the factors below. For further information on where to buy and a guide to the regions, refer to *The Best Places to Buy a Home in France* (Survival Books – see page 317).

Accessibility

It's an advantage if a property is served by public transport (e.g. local buses) or is situated in a town where a car is unnecessary. If a property is located in a town or development with a maze of streets, you should provide a detailed map. On the other hand, if it's in the country where signposts are all but non-existent, you must not only provide a detailed map with plenty of landmarks, but you may also need to erect signs (for which permission might be necessary). Holidaymakers who spend hours driving around trying to find their accommodation are unlikely to return or recommend it! Maps are also helpful for taxi drivers, who may be unfamiliar with the area.

Attractions

The property should be as close as possible to a major attraction (or more than one), e.g. a beach, theme park, area of scenic beauty or tourist town, although this depends on the sort of clientele you prefer. If you want to let to families, a property should be within easy distance of leisure activities such as theme parks, water parks, sports facilities (e.g. tennis, golf, horse riding and watersports) and nightlife. If you're planning to run a B&B in a rural area, it should be somewhere with good hiking possibilities, preferably near one of France's many natural parks. Proximity to one or more golf courses is also an advantage to many holidaymakers and is an added attraction outside the high season, particularly in northern France, where there may otherwise be little to attract visitors in the winter.

Climate

Properties in an area with a pleasant year-round climate, such as the Mediterranean coast and Corsica, have a greater letting potential, particularly outside the high season.

Market

Your chosen location depends largely on the type of guest you wish to attract (see **The Market** on page 114).

When buying a property with a view to offering B&B accommodation, make sure it's in a place where there will be demand and that it's easy to travel to and to find. To get your share of passing trade, you must be near enough to a main road to erect signs. Each department has its own rules about signing, but signs are normally allowed up to 5km (3mi) from a property. It's best to be fairly near a large town, especially a well-known one; you can then advertise at the local *Office du Tourisme* to attract visitors. Proximity to a major tourist town or attraction gives you good letting potential.

If you buy in a remote rural location, you will be reliant almost exclusively on clients who book their accommodation before leaving home, and will therefore be dependent on effective advance advertising. Some beautiful remote locations, excellent for *gîtes*, are too isolated for B&B. In years when the demand is low, places that are more accessible will have a better occupancy rate.

If you're targeting longer stays, choose an area that attracts the appropriate type of holidaymaker. Once you've chosen a region and area, consider the suitability of a property's location within that area. Many people prefer to target this group because it's less labour intensive. You can plan in advance and be prepared for your guests' arrival. You don't need to be 'on duty' 24 hours a day in anticipation of a car full of happy holidaymakers turning into your drive when you're looking forward to just **one** night off.

Although isolated locations aren't always the best for B&B, do make sure the location is peaceful; being near a road or railway line, nightclub restaurant or bar may be convenient for your guests, but they won't appreciate being unable to sleep for the noise.

If your property is in a popular winter sports area, you might choose to operate as a ski chalet. These can be self-catering and run on the same principles as a *gîte*, or you can cater for your guests. However, owners of catered chalets don't usually live in the same building, so it's not quite the same as running a *chambres d'hôtes*. The level of comfort can vary from rough-and-ready youth hostel type dormitory accommodation for younger guests to luxury hotel-standard rooms. You can attract skiers in the winter and walkers and nature-lovers in the summer, thus doubling your season.

Proximity to an Airport or Ferry Port

A property should be within easy travelling distance of a major airport or ferry port, as many holidaymakers won't consider travelling more than 45 minutes to their destination after arriving at the airport. This isn't as important for B&B as it is for *gîtes*, but is desirable if you're targeting longer stays. Make sure you choose an airport with frequent flights from your home country. It isn't wise to rely on an airport served only by budget airlines, as they may alter or cancel routes at short notice.

Type of Board

Another important consideration to be made when determining your location is whether or not you wish to offer evening meals. If you don't, or you don't intend to cook for guests every night, you **must** be within easy reach of one or more restaurants.

WHAT TO BUY

There are many factors to take into consideration when choosing your property. In general, the criteria that apply to properties to be used as *gîtes* (see **What to Buy** on page 119) also apply to properties to be used as B&B accommodation. The following points apply specifically to B&B properties.

The house must, of course, be large enough for the planned number of guest rooms and for your own accommodation. Aim for five guest bedrooms, possibly six (see **Legal Considerations** on page 121), ideally with room to install ensuite bathroom facilities. If you're planning on converting a property, keep this number as your target; you can always let one or two rooms to start with and renovate the others as you progress.

If it's a country property, you will probably have plenty of parking space; if it's in a village, make sure there's sufficient free parking nearby and no restrictions on loading and unloading.

Look for a house with an 'added value factor'. It may not be within your budget to buy and renovate a *château*, but a large country *manoir* or old farmhouse makes ideal *chambres d'hôtes* accommodation. Consider the surroundings, the views, whether there's a nearby lake or forest with attractive walks or any other feature that you can promote in your publicity and that will give you a competitive edge. Ask yourself: When people from overseas book holidays, what will attract them to this property rather than all the others they have to choose from?

Choose a house that photographs well. In printed advertising and on the internet, the first thing people see is the photograph. Try it yourself – look at a page of advertisements or an accommodation website and take note of which advertisements attract your attention.

Another important consideration is space for your own accommodation. Although the concept of *chambres d'hôtes* is having people stay in your house and however much fun it seems at first, you will soon find how much you value and need privacy. Try to have your own bathroom and living room, preferably with private access to the kitchen, or your own kitchen. (If you fancy a cup of tea in the middle of the night, you won't want to meet guests whilst trotting around in your pyjamas!) In any case, the kitchen must be of an adequate size for preparing meals, even if you decide only to provide breakfast.

BUYING AN EXISTING BUSINESS

You can of course buy an existing business, and there are advantages and disadvantages in doing so. The main disadvantage is, of course, the cost, as you're paying for the 'goodwill' of the business (*fonds de commerce*), as well as the building (*murs*). Assessing the value of a *fonds de commerce* is a difficult process, often involving more art than science, but it's **essential** to obtain at least one professional valuation and to check the value yourself. (French property agents may be able to give you a more accurate idea of the value of a *fonds* than a foreign agent.) A guide to assessing the value of a business can be found on the website of the magazine *ICF l'Argus des Commerces* (🖳 www. cession-commerce.fr). Click on '*Calculez la valeur de votre commerce*' and answer the questions. Whereas the value of the building is usually easily comparable with other buildings in the area, the value of the business may be impossible to relate to anything and you must make your own assessment of whether it's reasonable or not. If not, it may be worth negotiating rather than simply looking elsewhere. The cost of a *fonds de commerce* varies between around €300 and €2,000 per m² (€650–3,500 in Paris and up to €6,500 per m² in the most salubrious areas) according to a number of factors. Sometimes the building is included in the price, although rarely in Paris.

Another disadvantage of buying an existing B&B is that you won't have the freedom to style and decorate the accommodation as you would wish – unless you spend even more money refurbishing it. On the other hand, there are several advantages to buying an existing business, including the following:

- You won't have to spend time and money renovating or adapting buildings for use as *chambres d'hôtes*.

- You will (or should, if you buy a successful business) have guaranteed income from the word go, which reduces your marketing costs and lessens the risk.

- You won't be setting up in competition to existing B&Bs and so further diluting the market, but will in effect be buying a slice of the market.

Look for a going concern with room for expansion, e.g. a swimming pool, games room or outbuildings for conversion. Make sure the owners aren't exaggerating the existing profits or the potential. Do your research (particularly with regard to location and potential income) and find out why they're selling. In particular, ask the following:

- For detailed accounts for the past few years.

- Whether there are existing bookings for the coming season.

- How they market the property.

- Whether they're registered with GdF, Clévacances or the tourist board, and whether you will be able to continue the registration or must start anew.

- Whether they keep a database of past (happy) customers.
- Whether the price include the fixtures and fittings and any furniture. (If it does, ask yourself whether they're worth buying.)

If possible, buy a business in the autumn, to give yourself time to settle in, make any necessary alterations, do some marketing and (if necessary) improve your French before welcoming your first guests the following spring.

CONVERSION

If you want to install ensuite bathrooms (recommended), make sure that the layout of the house allows this. (Bear in mind also that rooms must be soundproofed, especially ensuite bathrooms.) You might need to take advice from an architect as to whether it's possible. If you cannot have a water supply and waste outlet in all the rooms, you could consider having two rooms share a bathroom and market it as a family suite; macerating lavatories aren't a good solution; they make far too much noise. On the other hand, if you're appealing to French clients, bear in mind that they generally prefer the WC to be separate from the bathroom (many French people are disgusted by the idea of having a lavatory in the same room as a bath or shower).

If you're on septic tank drainage (as is the case with most rural properties), check the size of the tank. If it's the original installation, it will be the right size for normal family usage with maybe just one WC. With several lavatories and bathrooms, you will need a much larger tank. Take advice on this before any unpleasant and expensive problems arise (sometimes literally!).

In an old property, the water heating system will also have been designed for a family and not for guests who want baths or showers daily. You must have sufficient hot water at all times for your guests and will probably need to install a larger tank and boiler.

LEGAL CONSIDERATIONS

French rules and regulations are a mystifying maze that most French people – let alone foreigners – find difficult to negotiate, particularly as they can change from one day to the next and from one office to the next. Two different official bodies may give you contradictory advice (if they don't know the answer, they're likely to give their opinion rather than find out!). Moreover, many regulations are formulated at departmental rather than national level; Gîtes de France, for example, is a national governmental organisation, yet each departmental office is run autonomously and their rules can be **very** different. It's therefore imperative to check the rules and regulations that apply in your commune.

To this end, your first port of call (**even before you purchase a property**) should be the local *mairie*. If the *maire* is in favour, he will point you in the right direction and even help with the process. If your *maire* isn't in favour of any more tourists, B&Bs or foreign-owned businesses on his patch, you won't find it easy. There's no reason why you should meet opposition unless there's a surfeit of French-owned (or other) *chambres d'hôtes* in the commune, but if this were the case there would be little point in continuing anyway.

The most widespread and relevant regulations for B&B accommodation are those of Gîtes de France. Although these aren't national law, many departments are now requiring *chambres d'hôtes* businesses to be inspected by GdF or the tourist office and rated before opening. The government is considering drawing up standard national regulations for B&Bs; until such rules are drafted, your only legal requirements are those detailed below and, if the earnings of your B&B are to be your sole or main income, registration with the Registre des Commerces et des Sociétés (see page 124).

Number of Rooms

There's no legal definition of *chambres d'hôtes*, but the phrase is understood to mean a room or rooms in the owner's house for tourists staying one or more nights, including breakfast. Five is the normal maximum for the number of rooms. In some departments it's six, and in yet others you may have six, but the sixth must have disabled access. If you offer more rooms than this, your business won't be defined as a *chambres d'hôtes* by GdF, Clévacances or the tourist board and must comply with stringent fire and safety regulations in line with those for hotels, in accordance with the rules governing *Établissements Recevant du Public*.

Tariffs

In line with the law of 18th October 1998, the price of accommodation and meals must be displayed outside the premises and inside – in the reception area and on the door of each bedroom. If there are different prices according to the size or quality of the rooms, all of these must be on the list outside and in the reception area, along with the prices of meals if applicable.

Invoices

An invoice must be given to each client on demand or if the total amount charged is more than €15.23. Invoices must be in duplicate, with one copy given to the client, the other kept by the owner for a year and filed in date order. Invoices must include the date, name and address of the person paying, name of the client (if different), the date and place of payment, a detailed breakdown of items charged for and the price of each and the total to be paid. **If this procedure isn't followed, you can be fined €1,500!**

Foreign Visitors

Since 1999, foreign visitors (including EU nationals) must fill in and sign a 'police card' (*fiche de police*) – obtainable from the *préfecture* – with the following information: their name and surname, date and place of birth, nationality, and the address of their normal residence. In theory, these cards must be handed in on the day of arrival to the local police or *gendarmerie*; in practice, you might be met with a look of bemusement! If this happens, ask if it's necessary to do this; you may be allowed simply to keep the cards on file.

Table d'Hôtes

Table d'hôtes is the term for the evening meal in a *chambres d'hôtes*. Legally (to protect the interests of restaurant proprietors), a B&B must provide *table d'hôtes* only to overnight guests; otherwise it must be registered as a restaurant. The menu must be fixed, the meal is to be served at one table, and the seating must not exceed the number of guests staying overnight. **If these rules aren't followed, you're liable to a heavy fine.** For further details, see page 142. You must also adhere to strict hygiene regulations (see page 146).

Help & Advice

The Comité Départemental du Tourisme can help you in the following ways to establish your business:

- Analyse your project and advise on adjustments to meet local regulations and requirements.
- Provide information and advice on accommodation grading systems and standards.
- Provide information about B&B organisations and their requirements (see page 124).
- Provide information and advice on standards and equipment for adapting your accommodation for disabled use.
- Provide information on financial assistance, e.g. grants (see page 132).

- Provide data from the departmental tourist office.
- Help to direct your questions to the appropriate organisations.

REGISTRATION

Registering as a Business

If running a B&B isn't your principal activity, it can be declared on your tax forms as additional income under *Bénéfices Industriels et Commerciaux (BIC)* and is allowed as supplementary income without further registration. If the earnings of your B&B are to be your sole or main income, however, you must register with the Registre des Commerces et des Sociétés (RCS) and pay contributions (*cotisations* – roughly equivalent to UK national insurance contributions) amounting to around €2,500 in the first year and €3,500 in the second year; in subsequent years you pay a percentage of your income. Registration is made at the Centre de Formalités des Entreprises (CFE), which is part of the Chambre de Commerce et Industrie (CCI). Otherwise, no registration is required; the following types of registration are optional.

Tourist Board

If you choose to register with the tourist board (or if registration is compulsory in your department), you must apply for an inspection, and you will be awarded a star rating. (The inspector might be a GdF or Clévacances representative, but there's no obligation to become a member of either organisation – see below.) You should check with your local *préfecture* whether an inspection is required.

B&B Organisations

There's no obligation to register with any of the recognised B&B organisations, but depending on your target clientele it may be to your advantage to do so. The two main B&B organisations are Gîtes de France and Clévacances (see below). Gîtes de France is the clear market leader with over 25,000 *chambres d'hôtes* on its books compared with Clévacances' 5,000, as well as a much higher public profile, but only Clévacances handles B&Bs in urban areas. Both are official government organisations, linked to and working closely with the Comité Régional du Tourisme and the Comité Départemental du Tourisme. Other organisations include Fleurs de Soleil (see page 128), Accueil Paysan and Bienvenue à La Ferme (see **Appendix A**), but the last two, as yet, have few members and are largely unknown, especially to overseas clients.

GdF and Clévacances have a range of quality standards and grade your accommodation according to the following:

- The appearance of the building's exterior.
- The quality of the materials in its construction (principally walls, floors and ceilings).
- The standard of decoration.
- The quality of the breakfast.
- The quality of bedding, bathroom facilities, etc.

Great emphasis is also put on the participation and attitude of the hosts, although this doesn't appear in the official list of criteria. You don't have to register with any B&B organisations, but if you want to maximise your income from letting, registration has a lot of advantages, certainly far more than with a *gîte* business (especially if you're relying on passing trade), although there may be disadvantages as well (see below).

SURVIVAL TIP
To attract passing trade and French customers,
it's essential to register with an official organisation;
otherwise, it's unlikely you will get enough business.

Advantages & Disadvantages

The advantages of registration include the following:

- You're 'buying into' a recognised brand name, which appears on your publicity material and signs. (According to a poll carried out by the Institut Français d'Opinion Publique on the reputation of tourism businesses, the brand name Gîtes de France appeared third, below only Club Méditerranée and Nouvelles Frontières.)
- You benefit from the organisation's promotional and publicity material (catalogues, internet site, etc.).
- Your accommodation will be known to meet certain recognised standards, which reassures clients.
- You will attract a greater number of French visitors (who constitute 80 per cent of GdF's clientele).
- You may not be able to advertise your B&B with the local tourist board unless it's registered.
- You might be eligible for a grant (see page 132).
- You can use the organisation's booking system.

- You're supplied with documentation (e.g. contract forms).
- You can obtain free advice (e.g. on setting up your business).
- You have access to financial and legal assistance.

Disadvantages of registering with an officially recognised organisation may include the following:

- The cost of registration (see below).
- The cost of adapting your premises to meet their standards.
- If you take advantage of a set-up grant from Gîtes de France (see page 132), you're tied to the organisation's booking system for a considerable time – up to ten years – and these systems are often less than 'user-friendly'; for example, to book accommodation via Gîtes de France's site, you must input the name of the department (not just the region) you're interested in, how many people will be holidaying and what dates you're interested in, and go through half a dozen screens before you can even **see** any properties!
- Clientele are on average 80 per cent French, and the French are 'conservative' in their choice of holiday periods, which may limit the number of weeks you can sell.
- Marketing is mainly aimed at the French, although the major organisations have increased their overseas marketing in recent years.
- Pricing is structured around French holidays, so that high season is limited to around six weeks in the summer.
- Rents are often lower than can be obtained by direct marketing focused on British and other overseas clients. (GdF quotes the average price of a three-*épi* room as €45; for UK-marketed properties the average is closer to €60.)

Gîtes de France

By far the best known French accommodation 'label', Gîtes de France (GdF), as its name suggests, was set up to regulate *gîtes*, but added B&B to its operations in 1969; its green, yellow and white '*Chambres d'Hôtes*' signs are a familiar sight throughout the country (see **Signs** on page 148).

Under the GdF system, the rooms you let must usually be part of your own house; in exceptional circumstances, they may be in an adjoining building. Other requirements vary from department to department, but are generally as follows:

- Five or six rooms is the maximum (the sixth may have to have disabled access), accommodating a maximum of 15 guests.

- The price per room must include breakfast.
- Each room must have a minimum area of 12m² excluding the bathroom.
- If there's no ensuite bathroom, every room must have at least a basin and there must be a WC and bathroom on the same floor.
- Rooms must be cleaned daily by the owner, and sheets and towels must be supplied.
- Meals must be freshly prepared, using local ingredients wherever possible.
- In some departments, your property must be located in a commune of fewer than 1,500 inhabitants.

The classification, like the *gîte* system, is by *épis* (corn ears): B&Bs are awarded between one and four.

GdF publishes the following guides (a total of 2 million copies are printed annually), in which your accommodation is listed as appropriate:

- Departmental guides – One for each department.
- Regional guides – One for each of the following regions: Auvergne, Corsica, Normandy (Upper and Lower combined) and Midi-Pyrénées.
- National guides – For the following types of accommodation: near a ski resort (*Séjours à la Neige*); in the mountains (*Vivez la Montagne Autrement*); near fishing water (*Séjours Pêche*); 'charming' properties (*Chambres d'Hôtes de Charme*); accommodation offering evening meals (*Chambres et Tables d'Hôtes*).

Clévacances

Clévacances was set up in 1997 to promote self-catering and B&B accommodation. It has around 3,000 *chambres d'hôtes* properties registered in 80 departments, covering a broader variety of property types than those of GdF, including seaside and mountain properties, villas, apartments and character properties, many of them in urban areas. Accommodation is graded with key (*clé* – hence the name of the organisation) symbols – one to four – according to the following criteria:

- The environment, i.e. the quality of the building, the site and its surroundings and absence of nuisances such as noise and smells.
- The quality of the interior, i.e. comfort, furnishings, decoration, facilities, and the arrangement and function of rooms.
- The welcome and assistance offered by the owner.

For a visit from a Clévacances representative, you must apply to the departmental office or your tourist office. After an initial visit in the presence of the owner or caretaker (and possibly an inspector from the tourism office), a report is prepared. This report is submitted to the department's *préfecture* for assessment and a star grading according to the ministerial decree for standards in tourist accommodation. If these steps are completed successfully, you receive accreditation from Clévacances and a grading of one to four *clés* (keys).

Successful owners receive a sign to fix to the exterior of their property, a certificate stating the number of keys awarded, and documentation (invoices, contracts, etc.) to use. A Clévacances representative visits at least every three years, more often in certain cases (e.g. if you request advice, carry out alterations to your property or have problems with a client). The fees charged for inspection, registration and the yearly subscription vary by department; ask at your Comité Départemental du Tourisme. Further information is available from the Clévacances website (⌨ www.clevacances.com).

Fleurs de Soleil

Fleurs de Soleil is a not-for-profit organisation formed in 1997, under the auspices of the association Les Maisons d'Amis en France, to promote quality *chambres d'hôtes*. Fleurs stipulates the following:

- The property should be in a region with cultural, historical and other tourism interest.
- The accommodation must be in a detached house that isn't part of a housing estate.
- If the property is in a village, there must be no noise from passing traffic, trains or neighbours.
- The house must have character or charm, be well decorated, and have an attractive garden.
- The owner cannot run any other business on the same premises.
- Members can let up to five rooms, for a maximum of 12 guests.
- The guest rooms must be in the hosts' own house or in an annexe, and there should be a communal room where guests can have their breakfast, talk, read, listen to music or watch television (TV).
- Rooms must have private bathrooms.
- If further facilities (such as a pool or tennis court) are offered, their use must be included in the price of the room.

- Breakfast must comprise tea, coffee or chocolate, a selection of breads and jams, butter and, if requested, cereals, eggs or yoghurt, and must be included in the price of a night's accommodation.

Great emphasis is put on the quality of welcome from the owners. There are further, lengthy regulations regarding furnishings, facilities, size of beds etc., some of which are included in **Appendix F** and which can be obtained by contacting the organisation's departmental office, via the head office: Fleurs de Soleil, Domaine du Frère, Les Milles, 1382 Aix-en-Provence Cedex 3 (☎ 08 26 62 03 22). Details can also be found on the website (🖥 www.fleurs desoleil.fr). Fleurs de Soleil publishes a 212-page accommodation catalogue.

FINANCIAL CONSIDERATIONS

If you already have a main occupation and/or income, your initial outlay need not be large; you could start by converting, decorating and letting one or two rooms, then expand as time and finances allow. If, however, you intend to rely on a B&B business for your main or sole income, you must 'hit the track running', which can require a considerable capital investment – well in advance of your first earnings. You must therefore budget carefully, balancing set-up costs (see below), taxes and social security contributions, and the cost of simply staying alive with your projected receipts, which could take years to reach their potential.

Set-up Costs

Your initial expenses may include the following:

- Renovation (including the installation of bathrooms and WCs) and decoration.
- Beds and other furniture.
- Soft furnishings.
- Bed linen and towels.
- Kitchen equipment, including a dishwasher, or even two (essential), crockery, cutlery, pots and pans, and table linen.
- Books, board games and other leisure equipment.
- Swimming pool.
- Registration with a B&B organisation (see page 124).
- Advertising and publicity.
- Printing of brochures, headed paper, business cards, invoices, etc.

Your set-up costs will obviously depend on the number of rooms you equip for letting, the quality of furnishings and equipment you choose, whether you install a dedicated kitchen for preparing guests' meals, and a number of other factors.

Running Costs

Your budget must also allow for running costs, which include the following:

- Laundry and cleaning.
- Food for breakfasts and possibly evening meals.
- Fuel for the daily trip to the *boulangerie*.
- Advertising, publicity and printing.
- Extra electricity, gas, heating fuel, water consumption and possibly waste charges.
- Maintenance contracts for appliances (you cannot afford to have a broken down washing machine or dishwasher).
- Redecoration of rooms as needed.
- Renewal of worn furniture, fabrics and fittings.
- New clothes (you must look smart when dealing with guests!).
- Swimming pool maintenance (if you have one).
- Insurance.
- Taxes and social security charges (see **Chapter 6**).

Viability

The principles of calculating the viability (or not) of your B&B business are essentially the same as those for a *gîte* business (see **Viability** on page 60). If you cannot achieve 40 per cent occupancy (see below), your business is unlikely to be viable and even then, much depends on the number of rooms you have to let and what other income you can generate (e.g. by offering meals, courses or local tours).

 You won't earn enough to live on unless you let four or five rooms, offer facilities that enable you to extend the season and carry out effective marketing.

Occupancy

Occupancy rates vary according to several factors:

- The type and quality of accommodation you offer.
- Its location.
- The time of year.
- Your pricing and marketing.

Calculate the amount you would receive with full occupancy over ten weeks (the average summer season). For example, four rooms at €60 per night would generate €16,800 at 100 per cent occupancy. With good, registered accommodation, the correct location and efficient marketing you should be able to achieve between 40 and 60 per cent of full occupancy within two years.

Taking the figures above as an example: at 40 per cent occupancy, your gross income would be €6,720 and at 60 per cent it would be €10,080. Out-of-season occupancy is a bonus.

The Agence Pour la Création d'Entreprises estimates the average occupancy rate across France to be 37 per cent, although this figure includes B&Bs run as a supplement to a main income, sometimes with only two rooms (in which case, if a cancellation is made, occupancy drops to 50 per cent).

Another factor to consider when estimating your occupancy is that bookings are unlikely to dovetail conveniently – unlike those for *gîtes*, which are normally booked for a week at a time with a regular changeover day.

Letting Rates

A *chambres d'hôtes* business is more restricted than *gîte* accommodation in terms of pricing, as local competition has a far larger influence on what you can charge. As you must display your tariff outside the premises, prospective clients can see your prices. If they're higher than those of the B&B down the road, they will probably go there instead, unless there are other means of comparison. Rather than have a simple price list, therefore, consider a covered notice board with photographs of the rooms, garden and any other 'unique selling points'.

Additional income can be generated by offering evening meals, but these must be costed very carefully in order to offset the time required to prepare them and make a significant profit without overcharging (see **Table d'Hôtes** on page 123). In your calculations, don't rely on all guests taking advantage of the service; depending on your proximity to affordable restaurants, you will find that a quarter to half of your guests will book evening meals.

Letting rates vary considerably according to the time of year, the area, and the quality of accommodation. You're free to charge whatever you choose, but don't price yourself out of the local market. Do some research in your area and find out what similar establishments are charging. Look at advertisements in newspapers and magazines and on the internet.

The standard room rate quoted is usually for a room with ensuite facilities, accommodating two people for one night including breakfast. Whereas registering with GdF greatly increases your occupancy rate, its charges are generally lower than you would be able to charge foreign (particularly British) clients booking direct. GdF quotes the average price of a three-*épi* room as €45; for UK-marketed properties the average is closer to €60.

For rooms which accommodate more than two guests you must work out a suitable tariff – for instance a room which is €60 for two people could be priced at €45 for a single occupant and at €75 for three people. You can have a lower rate for children sharing with their parents (e.g. €12 on top of the two-person price), but charge the normal rate if they're in a separate room. Consider discounting the price for stays of more than two nights, tempting guests to stay longer and cutting down on the piles of laundry and cleaning time!

For *gîtes*, most people who let year round have low, medium and high season rates, but this isn't as common for B&B, one reason being that heating costs are higher in mid and low season and these must be covered. If you choose to have different rates, high season generally includes the months of July and August and possibly the first two weeks of September, mid-season usually comprises June, September and October (and possibly Easter and Christmas/New Year), and the rest of the year is low season.

When setting your rates and comparing them against those of other owners, take into account the level of comfort, the market in your area, your geographical location, and whether you offer any additional facilities such as a pool. Set a realistic rent, as there's a lot of competition. **You must make a profit without pricing yourself out of the market!**

Grants

Grants may be available for conversion of a property to B&B use, from the Conseil Général, the Conseil Régional, and even the European Union. Certain conditions usually apply:

- Applicants must be permanent residents of the department.
- The rooms must be in an existing building (not newly built) and in a house (not a flat).
- The property must be in a rural location.
- The rooms must graded at least at level three (*épis*, *clés* or *étoiles*) with one of the recognised organisations when completed.

Work that can be taken into account for a grant includes the following:

- Building work.
- Interior alterations.
- Improvements to the fixtures and fittings (not furnishings and decoration).

The first step is to contact the departmental office of Gîtes de France, which handles all grant applications irrespective of where the funds originate. There's a catch – or rather, several – the biggest of which is that once you've accepted a grant you're obliged to register with GdF, usually for ten years, and must use its booking service for some or all of this period (the exact periods vary by department). If you sell the property, your business fails, or you simply decide to cease operating during this period, the grant received must be paid back in full or part. **Grants are counted as income and are therefore taxable.**

In addition to this, you must comply with GdF standards and have the work carried out by registered artisans, submitting the bills before the grant is paid. In some cases, it's acceptable to do the work yourself, submitting the invoices for materials, but ask first! Work must not start until it has been approved by GdF. **Note that the money might not be forthcoming until long after work is completed.**

The amount awarded varies considerably. In many departments, there's no provision for grants whatsoever, whereas in other areas, especially those that are seeking to extend their tourist appeal, you may receive from €7,500 to €10,500 per room. Generally, grants are available in areas designated as *Zones de Développement Régionales* (*ZDR*). Sometimes these are simply poor areas looking for money from tourism, and if you're in one of these areas (or considering buying property in one) you must do your homework – if there's a lack of tourist accommodation, it could be because no one wants to visit the area!

The award depends not only on your location, what budget for grants is available in your area and whether any more tourist accommodation is needed, but also on your financial contribution to the work; generally, the more you invest, the bigger the grant you're eligible for. There are usually further amounts allowed for buildings 'of character' and facilities for disabled clients.

SURVIVAL TIP
A grant isn't an easy way of paying for renovations.
Carefully weigh up the pros and cons of obtaining
a grant before committing yourself.

Taxation

An important consideration for anyone running a B&B in France is taxation, which includes income tax, property tax and other local taxes. **Bear in mind that you must pay tax in France on all income from property letting.** Before buying a property for letting, you should obtain expert advice regarding French taxes. This will (hopefully) ensure that you take maximum advantage of your current tax status and that you don't make any mistakes that you will regret later.

If you run a B&B, you're also normally liable for *taxe professionelle* (see page 217), although you may be granted exemption if you let for less than half the year and/or the property is your principal residence. Under certain circumstances you could be required to register for value added tax (VAT) (see page 218), and the local authority may charge you a *taxe de séjour* for each paying guest (see page 218).

OTHER CONSIDERATIONS

Insurance

You must notify your insurance company that you're letting your property and obtain appropriate cover. It's a legal requirement to have adequate third-party liability (*responsabilité civile*) and fire insurance. You should also have comprehensive household insurance (*assurance multi-risques habitations*) and should check that this includes theft cover. Policies vary between insurance companies, so discuss with your insurer your particular circumstances and needs. In particular, it's essential to have cover against food poisoning (*le risque d'intoxication alimentaire*), and extra insurance is required for swimming pools – consult your insurance company. Further information about insurance can be found in *Buying a Home in France* (Survival Books – see page 317) and from the Centre de Documentation et d'Information de l'Assurance (CDIA), 26 boulevard Haussmann, 75311 Paris Cedex 09 (🖳 www.ffsa.fr).

Smoking

You must decide whether to allow smoking or not. You might attract clients who prefer a non-smoking environment, or put off others – French people are generally less accustomed than Britons and Americans, for example, to restrictions on their freedom to smoke. You could have some areas where smoking is allowed, such as the lounge or outdoor sitting areas, but forbid smoking in the dining room and bedrooms.

Animals

Allowing animals should be seriously considered. Since the introduction of 'pet passports', it has become easy for travellers from the UK to take their dogs and cats on holiday with them. There are several disadvantages, not least that they might mess indoors, bark at night, or decide that your own dog or cat is their worst enemy (or best friend – you must keep an eye on bitches at certain times of the year!). They may leave hairs, causing allergy reactions in other guests. You can ask that dogs be kept on leads when not in their owners' rooms, and ask owners to bring a rug or their animal's bed. Animals shouldn't be allowed to climb on beds or other furniture or cause annoyance to other guests. Check with your insurance company if you decide to allow pets.

Children

Not allowing children drastically reduces your letting potential. However, your property might simply be unsuitable. You might have beautifully landscaped gardens or fragile antique furnishings unsuitable for children's play, the property may not be fenced, or you might not want to risk the possibility of babies crying in the night and disturbing other guests. Some people don't allow children under five years of age because of the risk of bed-wetting. If you prefer not to cater for children, make it clear in your advertising, promoting your property as a peaceful adult environment.

In general, however, you should do your best to make your accommodation child-friendly by providing extra facilities for babies, such as a cot, highchair, potty, changing facilities, enclosed garden, protected electric sockets and stair gates, and for older children outdoor play equipment such as swings and a climbing frame, and even a games room with table tennis, TV, computer games and books.

It's usually expected that you will charge less for children if they share a room with their parents (see **Letting Rates** on page 131). If they occupy a separate room, you may choose to charge full price – after all, they're occupying the same accommodation that could otherwise be let to adults.

Access

Keep the entrance to your property well maintained – a weed-infested drive, overhanging hedges and rickety gates won't attract custom, however smart the house itself.

If your property has disabled access, including wide doors, and no steps to at least one bedroom and bathroom, this can be a good selling point. Most agencies have provision for emphasising this in their advertisements, and there are some that specialise in this area, e.g. Access Travel (UK ☎ 01942-888844, 🖥 www.access-travel.co.uk).

Specialist Holidays

To maximise your bookings, particularly out of season, exploit your location. For example, there may be a large annual 'antiques' fair or a Christmas market nearby. You could offer 'apple picking' or 'grape harvesting' holidays. If there are interesting walks in your area, photocopy some local maps, have them laminated and offer them to your guests (and then provide somewhere for them to leave their muddy boots!). This can also be done for a tourist route by car, or itineraries for a day's sightseeing, mountain biking, horse riding, golf or bird watching – a one-off effort on your part which can lead to repeat bookings and recommendations.

To add to the appeal of your B&B, you might offer accommodation as part of a themed or special interest holiday: painting, cookery, wine tasting, business training, and writing and language courses – the possibilities are endless. If your property is in an area with historical interest (e.g. the D-Day landing beaches, World War One/WW1 battlefields, Roman sites), you could arrange guided tours. All these extend your season, as you won't be relying solely on the family summer holiday visitors. If you have particular skills or qualifications, you could consider running speciality holidays based on your own knowledge and interests. Otherwise, for holidays including tuition (e.g. painting, writing, cookery) you must factor in the cost of hiring instructors and a specialised advertising budget targeting your prospective clientele in the relevant magazines.

FACILITIES

The facilities listed below can add value to your accommodation.

Telephone

A telephone for guests' use is a valuable facility. Although most people now have mobile phones, reception, especially in the more rural parts of France, can be patchy and calls from a fixed line are often cheaper. Guests can purchase a *Ticket Téléphone International* to make long-distance calls from your fixed line (by keying in a code). Alternatively, you can provide a separate payphone or invoice them at the end of their stay by consulting your France Telecom account online.

Internet Access

So many people now depend on internet access for their business and personal needs that it's a huge advantage to offer this facility. Even if they don't rely on the internet for business, it's now part of everyday life and many feel bereft without a connection. At the very least, many guests will ask if they can check their email; it's a big plus to be able to offer them a dedicated computer for their use. If you have an unlimited use contract or broadband access, there's no extra cost involved (you could nevertheless charge by the minute); with dial-up access you can easily monitor time spent online and charge accordingly. A relatively inexpensive computer system and a telephone socket in the guests' lounge are all that's needed.

Swimming Pool

A swimming pool is desirable, particularly in warmer regions, as properties with pools are much easier to let than those without (unless a property is situated near a beach, lake or river). You can also charge a higher rent for a property with a pool, and you may be able to extend the season by installing a heated or indoor pool. Note that there are new safety regulations regarding pools used by the public, which include pools at private homes that are let for holidays. Make sure that you understand the regulations before installing a pool. For further information about swimming pools, see page 68).

Keys

Guests must have a key to their room and possibly to the front door if they're out late at night. You might prefer to have the front door key available on request; if there's a fire, you must know how many people are in the building.

Additional Facilities

Additional facilities can give you a competitive edge. They should give extra value either in monetary terms (for instance bicycle hire) or by improving the level of comfort and service, which will earn you recommendations to guests' friends, relatives and colleagues. If you have enough room outside, a children's play area with swings and maybe a slide is a valuable addition (but check your insurance). You could provide sports equipment – a few badminton rackets and shuttlecocks and other lawn games – and offer other equipment for hire, e.g. bicycles or fishing tackle.

FURNISHINGS & EQUIPMENT

Many people prefer B&Bs to the anonymity of hotel rooms. In furnishing and equipping your rooms, as in the service you provide, you must strike a balance between being professional and providing a personal and individual service – the personal touch. Make your accommodation welcoming and comfortable, but avoid making guests feel that they're intruders in your home. For example, many owners name their rooms, thus avoiding an impersonal numbering system; you could choose a colour or theme for each (e.g. local flowers, towns or artists).

When letting rooms, don't fill them with expensive furnishings or valuable belongings. While theft is rare, items will be damaged or broken eventually. Bear in mind when purchasing furnishings and fittings that you're buying for others to use; they should be easy to clean and maintain in good condition. In the peak season (and hopefully other times of the year) you have only a few hours between departing guests and the new arrivals to do all that's necessary to restore the accommodation to pristine condition.

When furnishing a room that you plan to let, choose durable furniture and furnishings and hard-wearing, neutral-coloured carpets that won't show the stains. Shops such as Casa, Gifi and Michigan sell inexpensive home décor that won't cost a fortune to replace if damaged or broken. Decoration should be light and bright, with fresh colours, but not gaudy or too individualistic. Some people like frills and flounces, others clean modern lines, so keep a happy medium. It's best to keep walls white, as it's then easier to redecorate. Add colour with soft furnishings and rugs, plenty of pictures and a selection of bits and pieces to make the rooms more welcoming.

Central heating is necessary if the property is to be let all year round. Otherwise, convection heaters that can be regulated are usually adequate. Depending on the price and quality of a property, your guests may also expect a TV with satellite channels, tea/coffee-making facilities, and covered parking.

Bedrooms

Ideally, all bedrooms should have ensuite bathroom facilities, which are expected by the majority of clients nowadays. Sometimes the layout of the house doesn't permit the necessary plumbing for the water supply and waste outlets, in which case you could have two rooms sharing one bathroom, perhaps marketing them as a family suite. Don't install macerating lavatories, as they're far too noisy.

You should also supply a bedside table and a reading lamp for each guest and a water jug (or a bottle of water) and drinking glasses. A full length mirror is always appreciated, and there should be an electrical socket nearby for hair dryers and other styling appliances. Optional extras include an alarm clock (ensuring that guests are up in time for breakfast!), a hairdryer, and a small safe for valuables. Think carefully before installing clock radios, a TV or any other item that might disturb other guests.

Some owners provide a tray with a kettle and cups, teabags, coffee, milk, etc., although this is more appropriate for a hotel room. French clients don't expect this facility. You could compromise by putting them in the dining room so that people can make a hot drink whenever they choose.

Furniture

You need solid beds with good mattresses. Give careful consideration to the number and type of beds in each room. Too many double beds limit the permutations of guests. If you have only one room, provide twin beds; if you have just two rooms, make one a double and the other a twin. If the rooms are large enough, you could have a double and a single in each, which allows for various permutations (a couple, separate people or a couple with a child). If there are three or more rooms, you could put bunk beds in one of them for children. (Bunk beds should be used **only** by children.). If you have a small room, consider a single bed; if there's enough space, use a 120cm (4ft) bed – luxurious as a single bed and adequate for a couple provided they know in advance that it's a small double. Have a cot available – the collapsible type is the best, as it can be easily stored when not in use.

Provide plenty of hanging space and a chest of drawers (or a French wardrobe with hanging space and shelves), plus a small table and chair with an electrical socket nearby for guests to use for writing or to plug in a laptop.

If you want to provide antique beds, measure their length before buying, as some older beds are too short for modern mattresses. (Mattresses must not, under any circumstances, be of a similar vintage!) Normandy beds and *bâteau-lits* with wooden sides are quaint and typically French, but enormously difficult to make tidily (and your guests are likely to bruise themselves getting into and out of them!). While comfort is subjective and you cannot please all tastes (some like their beds hard, some soft, some in between), if the mattresses are new there's little that can be complained about. There's no shortage of good mattresses in France; every town has frequent visits from itinerant mattress-sellers, although it may be preferable to buy from an established local business.

Linen

It's generally a good idea to use white bed linen (whether real linen, cotton or polycotton). It looks clean and fresh and you can replace it piece by piece if one item is damaged or worn, rather than having to buy a whole new set. Colour can be added with quilts, bedspreads or throws. Always use good quality fabrics. Cheap sheets and pillowcases are a false economy, as they wear thin very quickly and can be difficult to iron. The larger supermarkets have sales and promotions for household linens in January, so that's a good time to buy. Mail order catalogues such as *La Redoute* and *Trois Suisses* are also good sources.

When deciding on what to buy, bear in mind how easy or difficult it will be to make the beds. Do you want to wrestle with double duvet covers? You could have sheets and blankets, or instead of putting a duvet in a cover use it like an eiderdown with sheets under it and a bedspread on top – much easier to change (do use a protector, though).

Antique pure linen monogrammed and embroidered sheets can sometimes be found at bargain prices in France. Nothing beats the comfort and quality of real linen, it improves with age, and it's the perfect complement to antique furniture – also an added-value point for your publicity.

Provide two pillows for each person, or a pillow and a bolster (*traversin*). Your guests have chosen to come to France, and typical French items such as square pillows and bolsters are all part of the experience (although you might keep a few British-style pillows handy in case of violent objections!). Use waterproof mattress and pillow protectors, as people dribble in their sleep (not to mention other 'accidents' that can occur). Keep a spare set and clean them between lettings.

Supply a bath towel and a hand towel for each guest. For guests staying a week or more, you must change bed linen every five days and towels every three days (they might need drying in between). Have some beach towels available on request, as people often forget to bring them and you won't want your bath towels taken to the seaside. Provide a towel rail to avoid wet towels being draped over your furniture and windowsills.

Bathrooms

Shower cubicles take up less room than bath tubs, and showers use less water than baths. Make sure when installing a shower that you minimise the danger of overflowing water (sliding doors are preferable to a curtain and easier to clean). Fit impermeable flooring – guests won't always take as much care as they would at home. Tile as many surfaces as possible, which makes them far easier to clean. Fit a long mirror so that people of all heights can use it easily, with a light above it and a shaver point nearby.

You might like to keep a selection of small soaps, shower gels, shampoos and toothpastes, as well as shower caps and disposable razors for guests who have omitted to bring their own.

Dining Room

You need a dining room, even if not providing evening meals (unless you have an exceptionally large kitchen!). Whatever you do, don't put carpet in the dining room (a tiled floor is ideal); French bread and croissants generate a huge quantity of crumbs. French guests can be particularly messy, preferring bowls without saucers for their morning *café au lait* or *chocolat*, and they often put plates aside, breaking their bread on the table. Provide plenty of napkins – paper serviettes are acceptable for breakfast, although it's better to use cloth ones for dinner. You could also use a vinyl, paper or authentic waxed (*ciré*) tablecloth at breakfast time.

Under *table d'hôtes* regulations (see page 123), you must have just one 'table' for dinners, but consider having two or three small tables that can be separately laid for breakfast and pushed together for the evening meal according to how many are staying. Use sturdy chairs; many people have the annoying habit of swinging their chairs and when they're adult paying guests it's embarrassing to have to tell them to stop!

You can also provide tea and coffee-making facilities and a small fridge/freezer for guests' own cold drinks, snacks and ice blocks. If you don't provide a freezing compartment, you will find your own freezer permanently full of blue blocks!

Lounge

A guest lounge should have comfortable seating, a small table and chairs for writing, and something to keep children amused on wet evenings. If you don't have a separate lounge, make sure that guests have somewhere to sit and read or write postcards in their rooms.

There should be a TV in the lounge, preferably with a UK satellite system, as it's possible that this will increase bookings, especially during major European sporting events. Cartoons to keep the kids quiet seem to work in any language! Have a video and/or DVD player and a supply of films. Although it's technically not legal to receive UK programmes outside the UK, it's a very grey area and unlikely to cause any problems. Any digital satellite receiver can receive the BBC and other "Free-to-Air" channels. If you want ITV channels, you need a Sky digibox and a Sky card, obtainable only if you have a UK address. Check out forums on the internet, as the details are constantly changing. A good site with specific information for France in its fact sheets is (🖳 www.bigdishsat.com).

You must have a TV licence, but one licence covers all TV sets in a property. From 2005, a French television licence (*redevance audiovisuelle*) is to be charged as part of the *taxe d'habitation*. Your annual tax return now has a box to tick if you **don't** have a TV. The licence fee is €116 – €0.50 less than in

2004 (although it should be **much** less on account of the massive increase in revenue that will result from compulsory licensing!).

 The Société des Auteurs, Compositeurs et Éditeurs de Musique is currently pressing for performing rights payments to be made by owners of *chambres d'hôtes* that have a TV for guests' use, so check for the latest legislation – or you could face a hefty fine.

Have a bookshelf with a generous selection of paperbacks in good condition (French and English) and some toys, board games and jigsaws. French versions of well known games such as Monopoly and Cluedo are always popular – everyone knows the rules, so it's fun to play in another language.

Guests will appreciate a range of maps, guide books, local interest books and a large selection of brochures – check regularly to make sure they're up-to-date, and put stickers on ones you want to keep, to discourage guests from taking them home.

MEALS

Breakfasts **must** be included in the price of the accommodation. The provision of other meals is optional, but can be a useful supplement to your income, as well as attracting more bookings; many clients prefer to eat on the premises rather than travel to a restaurant. Many French people stay only in *chambres d'hôtes* that offer *table d'hôtes* (see **Evening Meal** below), and many British and American visitors to a remote area might not want to battle with restaurant menus that don't have an English translation, especially on their first night when they arrive tired and hungry. Guests can have a drink with their meal without worrying about driving home, and young children can be put to bed, leaving parents free to enjoy their evening.

On the other hand, providing meals is time consuming: fresh produce must be bought regularly (French guests in particular won't accept frozen meals), which may entail a long round trip to the shops (and the cost of transport), meals must be prepared and cooked, the table laid and cleared, and cutlery and crockery washed, dried and put away. Imagine catering for a large family group twice a day, every day and you will have some idea of what is entailed (except that you cannot ask your paying guests to 'help themselves'!)

Breakfast

You should restrict the hours at which you serve breakfast – some guests will proudly announce that they get up at 6am every day, but not actually surface until 11am. You must then wait while they eat their breakfast, return to their rooms, wash, dress and finally go out at one o'clock, severely limiting the time you have to clear up, clean, make beds and begin preparations for the evening meal, not to mention prepare lunch if you decide to do so. Set a limit according to your needs and preferred routine, for instance between 7.30 and 9am.

The standard breakfast is fresh *croissants* and bread or *brioches* (which must be bought or delivered first thing every morning) with butter and a selection of jams, honey, etc. Serve a choice of coffee, tea, *tisanes* or hot chocolate and a range of fruit juices. You can also provide a selection of yoghurts, cereals and crispbreads. Some nationalities might request a different menu – the British like their eggs and bacon, the Dutch and Germans eat cold meats and sausage for breakfast. If you choose to offer a cooked breakfast at a supplementary cost, or provide extras, bear in mind the extra work, and calculate whether or not you will make a profit.

If you register with Gîtes de France or Clévacances, your breakfasts are inspected in addition to the rooms.

Lunch

Lunch isn't normally offered, although you might like to offer packed lunches as an additional service. If you do so, make it clear (especially to French guests) that it's a light meal, as many French people eat their main meal in the middle of the day and expect a packed lunch to contain starter, main course, cheese and dessert – plus wine and aperitifs!

Evening Meal

The provision of an evening meal in a *chambres d'hôtes* is known as *table d'hôtes*, which literally means 'hosts' table' and implies that your guests eat with you, sharing your table. It isn't a restaurant service and you mustn't offer a choice of dishes for each course, but a set menu (see **Legal Considerations** on page 121). You might think that you cannot compete with local restaurants offering three-course menus with alternatives for €12, but in fact you aren't competing with them; you're offering a different service – dinner *en famille* – and your guests are free to go out to eat if they prefer. In any case, by the time all the extras have been added (aperitif, wine, coffee, etc.) the restaurant meal will add up to far more then €12.

The requirement that you eat with your guests poses a problem: who's going to cook and serve the food? Menus with dishes that can be prepared earlier in the day can help overcome this; you can then nip out to the kitchen to add the finishing touches as the meal progresses and clear up as you go, perhaps joining your guests at the table for one or two courses and coffee at the end of the meal. It's unlikely you would want to eat a four-course dinner every night anyway, but it can, in good company, be a very enjoyable way of spending an evening.

Consider also the following:

- Although main ingredients **must** be fresh (see **Menu** below), some elements can be prepared in advance for use over two to three days (e.g. stocks and sauce bases), and the cheese board can be carried forward each day (with additions).

- You're more likely to make a reasonable profit if you provide dinners on a regular basis, as it's cheaper to buy catering packs of staple ingredients and larger quantities of others.

- It often isn't worth cooking a four-course meal for one or two guests, so you might choose to stipulate that evening meals are available only if there are four or more adults booking together.

- Make sure that guests (particularly British and American) know what to expect if they book dinner: some visitors to France aren't familiar with the concept of a meal being a whole evening's activity. "Can we have our tea at six? The kids have to be in bed by seven?" is a difficult request to answer when you would normally gather for aperitifs at 7.30 to eat at 8, work your way through four courses and finish with a coffee and *digestif* at around 11pm!

- Some people request just a main course for a reduced price, or smaller portions for children. You can either accommodate their wishes (perhaps losing money), or you can gently and apologetically explain that you're obliged to offer a set menu at a set price.

- It's easy to put on a lot of weight if you eat a full meal every night!

Ask guests when they book a meal whether they have any food allergies or strong dislikes and cater accordingly (see also **Catering for Vegetarians** below) – it's too late if they're already sitting at the table.

SURVIVAL TIP
Budget very carefully: sometimes you will make only
enough profit to cover the cost of your own dinner.

Menu

All food should be home cooked using fresh ingredients and should include regional dishes (a requirement if you're registered with GdF). Dinner in France normally has four courses. The starter (*entrée*) can be soup, a salad, pâté or cold meats (known as an *assiette anglaise*), prepared in advance. For the main course, work out roughly seven basic dishes that can be prepared in the time allotted and within your budget. You can of course vary these (especially when you want to eat something different!), but having standard menus increases efficiency. Cooking for guests **isn't** the time to start experimenting and on many days, time will be short.

The cheese course is served before the dessert; serve three to five cheeses, including local varieties, a goat's cheese and a blue cheese. For *le dessert*, again use tried and trusted dishes. Desserts such as chocolate mousse, *crème caramel*, apple tart (there's probably a local version) and *crème brûlée* can largely be prepared earlier in the day. Finish with coffee.

Catering for Vegetarians

Vegetarian catering is a useful service to offer and can be a valuable marketing opportunity. Vegetarianism is unusual in France, so it's very difficult for non-meat-eaters to eat in restaurants unless they eat fish – an endless diet of omelettes soon palls! Strictly, however, under *table d'hôtes* regulations, you aren't allowed to offer alternative menus, so you could do one of the following:

● Cater only for vegetarians.

● Offer a vegetarian menu on certain nights of the week.

● Offer all-vegetarian menus to groups who book together.

Make sure it's clearly stated in your advertising if you provide **exclusively** vegetarian food and note that vegetarian meals won't appeal to many French guests, as most French people feel cheated without a chunk of meat as part of their dinner.

Drinks Licences

If operating a B&B, you must obtain a drinks licence, even if you don't provide evening meals. This doesn't mean you're expected to serve wine with breakfast! A licence is required for any drinks served with a meal, including coffee, tea and fruit juice. Drinks are classified into five categories, but only the first two are readily obtainable:

● **First Category** – Mineral water, fruit and vegetable juices, lemonade, fruit syrups, milk, tea, coffee and chocolate.

● **Second Category** – Fermented, but not distilled, drinks, including wine, champagne, beer, cider, Perry (*poiré*), and alcoholic syrups (e.g. *crème de cassis*) with up to three degrees of alcohol (if you can find them!).

If you wish to serve spirits (e.g. as a *digestif*), you must offer them free (or 'lose' the cost in the overall meal price).

You need a *licence à consommer sur place du premier groupe* to serve first category drinks (i.e. if you're serving breakfast only). If you provide evening meals and must therefore serve wine (or other drinks in the second category), you need a *petite licence restaurant*.

You must obtain an application form at the *mairie* and the licence itself at the local customs office (*douanes*). If the *mairie* has no knowledge of such a licence, you must go to your departmental *préfecture* for an application form. The licence is free.

Drinks may be served only on the premises, to B&B clients, and with meals. You cannot sell alcoholic drinks without meals; this requires a quite different class of licence that's strictly controlled.

Hygiene Regulations

The preparation and provision of meals as *table d'hôtes* are subject to the law of 9th May 1995, which regulates food preparation, kitchen cleanliness, avoidance of food contamination and other matters relating to hygiene. For more information and the full regulations in your area, or advice, contact the Direction Départementale des Services Vétérinaires, whose contact details can be found on 🖳 http://lesservices.service-public.fr/local/index.htm. Alternatively, as with many procedures, contact your local *mairie*.

MAINTENANCE

There's a great deal of everyday maintenance involved in running a *chambres d'hôtes* business, much of which is made up of repetitive household chores. You must clean the rooms and make the beds every day. On a changeover day, allow an hour per room for cleaning and changing the bed linen. Time must be allocated for cleaning the dining room and guests' lounge, tidying outside areas, garden and pool maintenance, etc.

Washing and ironing can occupy a huge part of the day; you need a robust washing machine (probably two), a large tumble dryer for wet days and a **huge** ironing surface – a table covered with old blankets and a sheet is suitable. Rotary irons are good for items that can be folded flat. It may be worth sending your washing out to the local commercial laundry (*blanchisserie*). If you do this you must buy a much larger quantity of linen to compensate for turn around time, allowing also for weekend and public holiday delays, which will also reduce your profit margin. If you have more than one commercial laundry within a reasonable distance, ask for quotes and find out whether they collect and deliver. You should also send a test load to see whether the standard is satisfactory, as laundries sometimes iron in more creases than they remove! If you use precious antique linen or embroidered sheets, it's best to launder them yourself. Nothing beats the smell of sun-dried bed linen . . .

If you're offering evening meals, take into account the time required for daily shopping (fresh ingredients are essential). Preparation and cooking may take another two or three hours, then there's the clearing, cleaning, washing up and laying the table for the following morning's breakfasts. **It's a long day!**

MARKETING

As with any business, effective marketing is crucial to your success – and marketing doesn't just mean advertising. Start by asking yourself: What is my target market? What type of customer do I hope to attract? When marketing a B&B, you must throw your net wide and catch customers from every possible source. Unlike a *gîte*, you aren't marketing a relatively small quantity of discrete units (weeks), but a variable product – you're chasing goals as diverse as a fortnight's family holiday and a one-night stopover for a businessman.

Nevertheless, you can narrow your target market in some respects. For example, do you mainly want to attract families, young couples, older people or wealthy people? Having decided this, ask yourself: How do they prefer to communicate? What are they looking for? Which advertising medium are they most likely to use? You wouldn't advertise, nor let, a €300 per night suite in a chateau to the same people as you would a €50 per night room in a cottage. Different sections of the population look for different criteria when booking a holiday. Your advertising must be targeted at your preferred customer profile, without excluding the wider market. Don't limit yourself to a single customer type: a property suitable for a family in the high season might attract older couples at other times of the year.

A key decision is whether to target mainly English-speaking or French people. It can be easier to look to the English-speaking world, especially if your French isn't fluent, but you will have fewer guests. The Anglophone marketplace is much bigger (including all of the US and Canada, South Africa, Australia and New Zealand, for example, as well as the Netherlands!), its marketing techniques generally more effective and booking systems more efficient and the holiday season is less restricted, but the French and other Europeans make frequent use of *chambres d'hôtes*, especially those that are registered with Gîtes de France. Advertising through UK publications and websites will attract visitors from the US, Australia, Canada and other Anglophone countries. Advertising with Gîtes de France or Clévacances will attract mostly French visitors, but also a number of other (mainly) Europeans.

Monitor the effectiveness of your marketing by asking anyone who makes an enquiry where it was they found information about your property, although they may say, "On the internet", which can be a less than useful answer! Also make sure you obtain feedback from your customers. A visitors' book (*livre d'or*) should always be provided for guests' comments – even though some of them may make unpleasant reading!

SURVIVAL TIP
Remember to monitor your enquiries and bookings so that you know where your customers and potential customers are coming from and can adjust or focus your marketing effort accordingly.

There's no need to spend a fortune on advertising, although some advertising is almost inevitable (see below); there are many ways of promoting your B&B cheaply. Does your property have a 'unique selling point' (USP) and, if so, how can you best exploit it? Generally, the more effort you put into marketing, the more income you're likely to earn. Bear in mind, however, that marketing takes time, which is in effect money.

Business Name

You need a name for the signboard outside the property and for your letterheads and publicity material. In rural areas, several properties may share an address, the postman distinguishing between them by the names of the occupants. Choose a name with the help of an intelligent French person; you don't want something that sounds peculiar to French people. Don't choose an English name that means something quite different in French; in fact, it's best not to use an English name at all. Don't choose a name that could be mistaken for another type of business, e.g. *La Boulangerie* for a property converted from an old bake house – clients looking for your B&B will be directed to the nearest baker's! It should be easy to pronounce by people of all nationalities, and kept short to stand out on signs (see below).

Signs

If you're catering to passing trade and there's strong competition in your area, you must find a way to entice guests to stay at your establishment rather than passing on to the next one down the road. Signs are the first step. If you want to erect signs on a main road, your property must generally be within 5km (3mi) of it. If it's a national road (*route nationale*, prefixed by N), you must contact the Ministère des Transports, de l'Equipement, du Tourisme et de la Mer (💻 www.equipement.gouv.fr); if it's a departmental (D) road, contact your local Direction Départementale de l'Equipement (DDE), which controls not only the roads themselves, but the land 3m on each side (unless private property); if it's a communal (C) road, ask at your local *mairie*.

One of the major benefits of GdF registration is that you're provided with signs: directional signs with arrows on for the road and circular signs for your gatepost or wall. Whether or not they're installed for you depends on how keen the regional, departmental or communal administration is to promote tourism, but it's as well to ask – if only to find out where they may and may not be sited. Clévacances also supplies signs, but these are less familiar to holidaymakers and consequently of less marketing value.

At the entrance to your property the sign should be large and clear, visible to traffic passing in both directions. Test its position and visibility by driving past. Often, signs are just too small to be noticed, the lettering is too thin to be read from a moving car, or the sign doesn't actually say what it's advertising! Once people have arrived at your entrance, they will see your price tariff, which must, by law, be displayed there. Use this as a marketing opportunity by having a display board with photographs of your rooms and facilities and a description of the accommodation in French and English (and any other language relevant in your area).

Publicity & Public Relations

Look for opportunities for free publicity (in terms of money, not necessarily time!), such as spreading the word via friends and family, putting up cards in local supermarkets and petrol stations, and contacting local estate agents (people who are on house-hunting trips may be looking for somewhere to stay).

The many magazines about France (see **Appendix B**) and even national newspapers are constantly looking for feature articles on unusual properties abroad – and properties in unusual locations. You could even write about the local area and include a mention of your establishment; they may not pay you for an article, but it could generate business.

Look for opportunities for joint promotions or 'tie-ins', such as promoting local attractions, restaurants, supermarkets, etc. in return for a listing in their promotional material. The promoted business may even offer your guests a discount on admission or products purchased there.

Contact companies that organise tours (e.g. wine, shopping, motorcycling) in your area and invite them to list your establishment in their documentation or even include the cost of accommodation in their tour prices. It also pays to work with other local people in the same business and send surplus guests to competitors (they will usually reciprocate).

Advertising

The success of your business depends largely on your advertising and it's essential to make your advertising budget one of your highest priorities. It need not be astronomical; effectiveness is the key. You can advertise among friends and colleagues, in company and club magazines (which may even be free), and on notice boards in companies, shops and public places. It isn't necessary to just advertise locally or stick to your home country; you can extend your marketing abroad.

There's a wide range of French and foreign newspapers and magazines in which you can advertise, e.g. *Daltons Weekly* and newspapers such as the *Sunday Times* in the UK, although advertising a single property may be prohibitively expensive. Most of the English-language newspapers and magazines listed in **Appendix B** include advertisements from property owners. You must experiment to find the best publications and days of the week or months to advertise.

Your Advertisement

For general information on how to produce an attractive and effective advertisement, see page 87. The details below are those that differ from those for a *gîte* advertisement.

Photographs: For the most part, the criteria for good photographs of your B&B are the same as for *gîtes* (see page 87), but there are a few significant differences, as follows:

● Include people in exterior shots (this is an advantage for a B&B, but not for a *gîte*, as guests will expect to mix with others), but make sure they're the right sort of people!

● In interior shots, create a mood in keeping with your chosen image – whether you're selling a romantic getaway or a fun family holiday, try to convey that impression in the photographs.

● Include a shot of your dining table laid with a delicious meal, lighted candles, and glasses of wine ready for drinking.

Tourist Board Literature

Don't forget to contact regional and departmental tourist boards. These maintain lists of holiday accommodation and publish widely distributed brochures, in which a listing may cost as little as €15. The costs vary by department. In recent years, the regional tourist offices have become more stringent in respect of whose holiday accommodation they promote; most advertise only premises which have been inspected and rated by their own representatives or those of Clévacances or Gîtes de France. Ask your local Comité Départemental du Tourisme whether or not you must be graded to qualify for entry and for details of other requirements. Most people book their summer holidays in January, and the deadline for an entry in printed brochures is typically the previous August.

Guidebooks

Entries in guidebooks are one of the most effective methods of advertising B&B businesses, as many people use a guidebook to plan their holiday itinerary. The disadvantage is that there are so many titles that it's difficult to choose which ones to advertise in. Also, you must plan your advertising well in advance – you must normally prepare and place your advertisement at least a year in advance for the following season's edition, and it takes some time after that to fully reap the rewards, as even the most fervent guide book user won't buy a new copy every year. Popular English-language B&B guidebooks include the following (there are also several published in French):

- **AA Bed & Breakfast in France** – This guide, which has over 3,000 entries, is a joint promotion with Gîtes de France, incorporating GdF properties with a grading of three *épis* and above. Arranged by region, it includes contact details, prices, and local facilities and attractions.

- **Karen Brown France Charming Bed & Breakfasts** – A prestigious US-published guide. Listings are free, but by invitation only once the property has been visited by their research team/author. (🖳 www.karen brown.com)

- **Alastair Sawday's Special Places to Stay – French Bed & Breakfast** – A popular UK-published guide. Entries cost from €200. (UK ☎ 01275-464891, 🖳 www.sawdays.co.uk).

Internet

Advertising on the internet is an increasingly popular option for *chambres d'hôtes* owners. There are two options: place an advertisement on a holiday accommodation listings site, or set up your own site. (You can, of course, do both.) Look for websites where you can browse the properties, as many (particularly French) sites require you to enter the exact number of people and bedrooms, the area, the date and the precise length of stay before showing any properties, which isn't going to attract any 'window-shoppers'!

Your Own Site: General information on setting up your own website can be found on page 92. In particular, for a B&B business, note the following:

- The first (home) page should contain an overview of the property, the accommodation available and its main selling points – e.g. near the sea, tourist attractions or airports, friendly welcome by fluent French-speakers. This page should contain links to all the other pages, plus contact information, and the best photograph you have.

- The next page could be a general information page with exterior pictures of the house and garden. Describe the facilities available – garden, terrace, play equipment, guest lounge, swimming pool, etc. If you want to display more than two or three photographs, use small (but visible) thumbnails that link to a larger version.

- Provide a page for each room, describing it in glowing terms with details of exactly how many people it sleeps and whether a cot is available; if it has stunning views, include photographs of them, as well as of the room itself.

- If you offer evening meals, have a page with a photograph of your beautifully laid dining table and describe your delicious meals, maybe including a typical menu.

- Provide information about the area, the nearest tourist attractions, sports and leisure facilities and any other USPs that will attract people to book with you rather than with another establishment.

- Include a contact page with your address, telephone number and email address (or an email form). It **is** wise to include your telephone number, but also include a table comparing time zones in a selection of countries, as you won't want telephone calls from the US in the middle of the night. If you speak to a potential client, you immediately establish a relationship and will be better positioned to convert the enquiry into a sale. Email is more convenient, but impersonal; the person browsing holiday accommodation sites will probably fire off identical emails to several addresses – only one will get the booking, so do your utmost to make sure it's yours!

- Include maps showing the exact location – one of France as a whole, one more detailed showing the nearest airports or ferry ports, and a local map with precise directions for finding your property. Don't simply copy from books or websites, as there are particularly heavy penalties for infringement of copyright on maps. Draw your own (or have someone draw them for you). Alternatively you can link your website to mapping websites (such as ▣ http://uk.multimap.com) for the larger-scale maps and prepare a simple sketch map for the local details.

- It's important to include a tariff; the first question people ask is the price, so you might as well put the details on your site.

- Use bulleted lists (like this one!) – they're easier to read than long blocks of text, and easier on the eye when reading on a computer monitor.

- Each page should have links to all other areas of the site.

Advertising Sites: There's an endless list of websites offering 'deal direct' advertising, whereby the company simply lists your advertisement on its website (and sometimes in a catalogue or brochure) for a one-off or annual fee (see page 89 for details). The major sites for B&Bs in France include the following:

- **Bonnes Vacances** (UK ☎ 0870-760 7073, 🖥 www.bvdirect.co.uk). This company advertises in national newspapers, publishes a brochure, and offers travel discounts and an insurance service. Listing cost: from £200 per year.

- **Chez Nous** (UK ☎ 0870-197 1000 or 01282-445158, 🖥 www.cheznous. com). Has an easy-to-navigate site and a well distributed brochure listing over 4,000 properties. Advertises in the UK national press. Listing cost: from £225.

- **French Connections** (🖥 www.frenchconnections.co.uk). Has a fast, easy-to-search site including plenty of details. Listing cost: from £150 per year.

- **Guide Vacances** (🖥 www.guidevacances.com). French holiday listing site. Listing cost: Basic listing free, with several optional paid extras (e.g. €15 for a photograph).

- **Homelidays** (☎ 01 70 75 34 03, 🖥 www.homelidays.com). The site is available in French, Spanish, German, Italian and Portuguese. Listing cost: €90 per year (you can choose to advertise for 1, 4, 8 or 12 months).

- **Le Petit Futé** (☎ 01 53 69 65 35, 🖥 www.lepetitfute.com). A well known French guide (website only). Listing cost: €120 including a photograph.

- **Vacation Rentals by Owner/VRBO** (🖥 www.vrbo.com). The fast site provides comprehensive details of accommodation worldwide; France can be searched by region. Listing cost: US$148 per year (includes three photographs).

- **Visit France** (UK ☎ 0870-350 2808, 🖥 www.visitfrance.co.uk). Has an easily navigated site (no brochure) listing over 500 properties, including *gîtes* and B&B. Listing cost: from £100.

It's now possible to produce downloadable (and even emailable) virtual tours of your property, which are rather more impressive (if also rather more costly) than the standard printed leaflet (see below). One company offering these is Visites360 (🖳 www.visites360.com), which is based in Aude and run by an English-speaker.

Literature

Make sure all your printed material (brochures, leaflets, flyers, etc.) reflects your desired image and be consistent in your style of presentation in printed matter as well as in signs, letterhead, advertisements, your website, etc. For further information, see page 85.

Special Offers

Apart from offering discounts for families or stays of more than two nights (see page 131), you could make special offers in low season – once you've discovered which times of year are low on bookings. If you're near a ferry port, tie your offers in with their fare structures: ferry companies often offer five-day return tickets, so you could arrange five nights' stay for the price of three or four nights to fit in with these. You could also offer money off on repeat bookings out of season or a percentage discount for friends or family booking on a client's recommendation.

Monitoring & Follow-up

As with running *gîtes*, monitoring the effectiveness of your marketing and contacting previous (satisfied) customers should be an essential part of your sales strategy (see page 95). In addition, keep a record of any dietary or other foibles your clients have so that, if they book again, you can anticipate them (your guests will also be impressed that you've remembered!).

HANDLING ENQUIRIES

General information about handling enquiries can be found on page 101; the following details apply specifically to a B&B business.

As many B&B bookings are received at short notice, carry a cordless telephone with you at all times so that you don't miss any, and perhaps even have calls diverted to your mobile telephone when you're out.

Decide how to handle enquiries about flights and car rentals. It's easier to let clients make their own bookings, but you should be able to offer advice and put them in touch with airlines, ferry companies, travel agents and car rental companies.

When sending emails, avoid over-enthusiastic spam filters at the recipient's end by using a distinctive subject line, e.g. the name of your property, in plain text, and don't include any web links.

BOOKINGS

Following the initial enquiry, if the customer wants to book, you must have a simple agreement form that includes the dates of arrival and departure and approximate times, a description of the rooms and beds required, the price and your terms and conditions (see below). You can send this by post, email it or have it as a downloadable document on your website. Clients should return the form to you with their non-refundable deposit; there's no fixed amount, but 25 per cent of the price of the stay is usual. You might choose to ask for the total price in advance, especially during peak season. Hold a provisional booking for a week or ten days, and require the deposit to be paid within this time.

Cancellations

Some cancellations are inevitable and, if the booking was made within a week or so of the intended stay, you won't even have a deposit to bank. This can be avoided to some extent if you take credit cards (see below) – if clients have already parted with their money, they're less likely to cancel. Make it clear that the deposit isn't refundable; if cancellation is due to illness, the clients' insurance should cover them.

Methods of Payment

When running a B&B, it's important to be able to offer various methods of payment. Bear in mind that you will have a lot of small transactions to handle – far more than if you're running *gîtes*.

Cheque

If guests are British and you have a UK bank account, the easiest way for them to pay is with a sterling cheque. Ask French guests for a cheque in euros. Note, however, that although other European countries (except the UK) are in the euro currency zone, most French banks make a hefty charge for banking any cheques in euros from outside France – similar to the fee they would charge for a US or UK cheque.

Bank Transfer

A more frequent method of payment from one European country to another is a direct bank transfer. With this method you give the customer your IBAN and BIC codes (your bank will advise you of these if they aren't printed in the back of your chequebook) and they arrange a transfer, which takes just a few days. Make sure the customer pays the bank charge (or add it to the final bill). Ask your bank for details.

Online Payment

For payments from most countries across the world, PayPal is immediate and easy (⌨ www.paypal.com, www.paypal.co.uk, www.paypal.fr). This is an online payment method whereby clients can pay by credit card. You (the owner) must open an account, which is free. The fee structure varies according to where your account is based, and on the volume of payments received. For example, if you register with an address in the UK and have average monthly receipts of up to £1,500, you pay 3.4 per cent plus £0.20 per transaction; for monthly receipts between £1,500 and £6,000 the fee is 2.9 percent plus £0.20 per transaction. Full details can be found on the above websites.

Western Union

If the client doesn't want to enter financial details online, another efficient method is a Western Union Money Transfer. The clients pay cash at their nearest Western Union agency, and you pick up cash at your nearest main post office (after filling in a long form and providing proof of identity). From some countries funds can be sent online. A list of locations and further information can be found on the Western Union website (⌨ www.western union.com).

Credit Cards

If your business grows, you can apply for your own merchant account so that you can take credit card payments (Visa, MasterCard, etc.) directly. You must be registered as a business with the Chambre de Commerce and have a business account with your bank, which provides you with the card machine for a monthly fee and charge a small percentage of each transaction. You must be able to accept transactions when the customer isn't present (for deposits). This is called *vente à distance* and incurs an additional small monthly charge.

Chèques-vacances

Many French employers give their low-paid workers a form of holiday voucher called a *chèque-vacances*. Each voucher is worth €10 or €20 and can be used to pay for holiday accommodation, as well as leisure activities, restaurant meals and other holiday 'entertainment'. They're valid for two years from the date of issue. If you decide to accept these, you must register with the Agence Nationale pour les Chèques-Vacances (ANCV, 36 boulevard Henri Bergson, 95201 Sarcelles Cedex, ☎ 08 25 84 43 44, 🖥 www. ancv.com). Registration is free (details of how to register can be found on the website), but you're charged a 1 per cent fee on the redemption of vouchers, with a minimum of €2. You're paid the value of the vouchers (less the fee) by bank transfer within 21 days.

Information Packs

After accepting a booking (possibly for a longer stay only), you can provide guests with a pre-arrival information pack containing the following:

● A map of the local area and instructions how to find the property.

● Information about local attractions and the local area (available free from tourist offices).

● Emergency contact numbers in your home country (e.g. the UK) and France if guests have problems or plan to arrive late.

Arrival & Departure Times

Specify the times when guests may arrive, for instance between 4 and 8pm, and ask them to notify you what time they expect to be with you, asking them to telephone if there's a change of plan. Be quite firm about this; you have a lot to do on changeover day and won't want a car full of holidaymakers arriving at 2pm when you're frantically changing beds or unblocking the drains. Neither do you want to be waiting around until 11pm when they were expected at 5pm, but decided to stop for dinner without letting you know. Also specify a departure time, e.g. 10am; you should be flexible, but it's best to state a time so that guests aren't tempted to linger.

CASE STUDY 5

We moved from Newcastle-upon-Tyne in the UK to the Dordogne, where we now run a B&B. The house was bought in 1983, but we didn't start running it as a B&B until 1989. My father had restored the house but, owing to unforeseen circumstances, never ran it as a B&B himself. We had holidayed in the area for many years before we came and knew it well.

We didn't hate the UK, our jobs or lives, but we had the opportunity to do something different and our children were young enough (four and seven) to adapt to a new life. They fitted into the village school within the first six months and made their ways through the local schools. They're now both at university in Bordeaux.

B&B is ideal for those who aren't fluent in French to begin life in France and make some money at the same time. We had no mortgage, as the property was cheaper than the one we'd sold in the UK, and we had plenty of free time in the winter to learn to be passable at DIY – we weren't very good when we arrived!

The house has plenty of space and there are five bedrooms with a large dining room. The garden was small but, when we bought the house next door (in 1989), we were able to combine the gardens into one large one. This was important, as guests like to enjoy the sun and outdoor life when they come to France. Having the house next door meant that we could keep our guests separate from our growing children and also have some privacy for ourselves.

The house is in a hamlet in the countryside, 2km from the nearest village. This hasn't proved a problem for us, although it might not suit many guests. But we don't hide the fact in our publicity that we're remote, and most guests like the idea of a country holiday.

We've had a few unforeseen problems. One of the areas outside the B&B has no proper access. The *notaire* or estate agent should obviously have pointed it out when the house was bought and we assumed (wrongly) that there was no problem. The neighbours are OK about it, but get ratty if our guests casually park cars on their land.

When we started, we advertised in the Sunday newspapers, at great cost and without great response. We also targeted some advertising at the vegetarian market, which was more successful (we aren't vegetarian, but knew that they find France difficult). Later we got into some guides (published in the UK and abroad, e.g. Holland). This was mostly by recommendation, and they've been the best form of advertising and at a reasonable price – or even free.

Our guests are broken down thus: 75 per cent Anglophone (British, Canadian, South African, etc.); 20 per cent Dutch and Belgian; 5 per cent French – mostly wanting accommodation for weddings, celebrations or summer festivals.

We used to advertise with the *Syndicat d'Initiative* in the nearest town but, because we're so remote, few people made it, so we dropped that. We've been lazy about developing the French market. Our website might be the way forward. It works well, but probably because it's linked to the guides. 95 per cent of our enquiries and bookings are made by email.

We're always stony broke, especially in the winter months. There's no significant winter season round here. Social contributions always hit us hard.

Our guests are always unbelievably good and we've had no serious problems, but in the summer season we stay up late and party a bit too much. Sometimes we work non-stop for weeks on end without free time. We haven't employed staff – we cannot afford to and couldn't really justify it. The kind of B&B we run demands our presence – we couldn't really ask someone to do it for us.

We both enjoy it still. The winter gives us time to recover, although I could do without the financial hardship. We used to worry too much about what people would think, but now we believe you should be honest and offer what you feel to be the right service; if people don't like it, the worst that can happen is that they won't come back.

Jane and John Edwards

CASE STUDY 6

We're migrants from Southampton in the south of England to Aude in the south of France. While in Southampton, we'd been a host family for the Southampton English Language Centre (an organisation that provides English tuition to foreigners) and had always liked having people to stay with us for two main reasons: you meet many very nice people and you learn a lot of things about other cultures. We'd often thought about running a B&B and, as we wanted to start a new life in France, it seemed sensible to try to combine the two.

We searched different regions and areas within regions in France for a long time and finally decided to buy a plot in the village of Granes in Aude, then to design and build the house that would be our new home and hopefully provide an income. We chose this area for its stunning landscape (it's in the foothills of the Pyrenees), varied attractions for holidaymakers and ease of access from the three airports nearby. We designed the house with B&B accommodation in mind and included a small, two-person gîte, aimed at couples who wanted good quality accommodation for holidays or house hunting. We decided to advertise to a specific market – mainly vegetarian. The reason for this was that we realised how difficult it is for vegetarians to get good quality, varied meals in a mainly carnivorous country.

While the house was being built, we sold our house in Southampton, rented accommodation in Eastleigh and kept our jobs for a year to help finance the project. This turned out to be a good move, as it enabled us to design our brochures and website, spend time on word-of-mouth promotion among friends and work colleagues and take advance advertising space in two specialist magazines. Buying advertising space cost us around £200, but didn't produce a single enquiry; it just generated a lot of interest from other companies trying to sell us much more expensive advertising space with no guarantee of results.

This year of preparation also gave us the chance to visit the area several times to oversee the construction of the house and to stay in various types of B&B to get a feel for what we liked and didn't like, so that we could focus on providing top quality accommodation for our guests. Once we'd moved into our house in France, there was a flurry of activity lasting many months to get the house ready for guests. 2004 was to be our first year of operation.

Our breakthrough came with advertising in the Aude Tourist Board brochure, a full-colour publication available from all the tourist offices. Each advertisement costs €25 and entitles you to two photographs plus supporting text. We took two advertising spaces, one for the B&B and one for the gîte, at a total cost for the year of €50 and the results so far have been very encouraging – in a year when everyone told us that tourism in the area was down by around 30 per cent. Enquiries came from France, Germany and Denmark, and all the enquirers subsequently booked with us. In our small village of around 120 inhabitants, there's also a gîte equestre, which offers horse riding holidays. Having visited us to see what we offer, they often use us for overspill accommodation.

For the B&B, we have one twin-bedded room with full ensuite (shower, WC, washbasin) and one double-bedded room with shower, washbasin and separate WC. Our small, self contained gîte has a lounge/dining room, bedroom with double bed, ensuite shower and toilet and fully fitted kitchen; gîte users have their own entrance and a private area of the terrace with table and chairs. All visitors benefit from fully non-smoking, no pets accommodation, this being remarked upon by most guests as a very important factor in their choice of accommodation.

If they wish, guests can eat with us on an 'en famille' basis and we have already achieved quite a reputation for being able to meet most dietary needs. Perhaps it's a little easier for us, as Suzie has a life-threatening nut and nutmeg allergy, which means that we must be ultra-careful about what we buy and what we eat – especially in an area that uses nuts, nut oils and nutmeg in many foods!

We provide a book for visitor comments plus a handbook for the gîte. We are encouraged by the comments that guests write, so we thought it would be a good idea to translate the handbook from English into French and German, thus covering most people's needs. What we didn't realise was that computer translation programmes don't always 'understand' the nuances of English. Given our limited French and even more limited German, it looked reasonable to us; the reality, though, provokes much hilarity and has led us to wonder if we should change it or leave it as a talking point!

Looking back over our first year, we have met many lovely people, have benefited from interesting and varied conversations, have found that people genuinely appreciate the standard of accommodation that we set out to achieve, but haven't yet made our fortune – nor are we likely to.

Mike and Suzie Broderick, Les Tamaris, Chemin du Moulin, 11500 Granes, France (☎ 04 68 20 72 53, ✉ aude@connxns.demon.co.uk, 🖥 www.audexperience.com)

TOP TEN TIPS FOR BED & BREAKFAST

- Don't even think about running a B&B unless you enjoy meeting people and are happy about having strangers in your home.
- You must be prepared to work long hours at tasks which can become repetitive and boring.
- You must speak French if you're to attract the maximum number of clients.
- Think carefully whether the layout of your property is suitable for a B&B.
- Make sure your electricity and drainage system will cope with the extra load.

- Consider registering with Gîtes de France or another recognised organisation.
- If in a remote location, you must provide evening meals.
- Make a business plan and budget carefully.
- Check the rules and regulations that apply in your department, as they can vary considerably from one to another.
- Think of ways to give added value, as there's a lot of competition.

4.

LONG-TERM LETTING

L etting unfurnished property should be seen as a long-term investment, but you should be aware of market trends. In the '60s, a greater proportion of French people rented than owned their homes; today, 57 per cent of French people own their own dwellings, whilst 38 per cent rent (what the remaining 5 per cent do isn't mentioned in the statistics!), and this trend is continuing. Nevertheless, this 38 per cent represents over 9.3 million properties, an increasing proportion of which are rented privately. Currently, 45 per cent of rented accommodation is 'social housing', i.e. owned and let by the government (and commonly known as *habitation à loyer modéré/HLM*, although this term confusingly also means 'block of flats'). Between 1992 and 2002 the number of rentals in the private sector increased by 17 per cent and it continues to grow. Moreover, since 2001, rents in the private sector have increased at a higher rate than the cost of living index. In 2004, rental rates rose at 2.2 per cent above inflation.

A major factor to take into account when considering long-term letting is that it's subject to stringent legislation (detailed in this chapter). Long-term lets are normally unfurnished, but there's a growing market for furnished properties (especially luxury apartments) – particularly in Paris and other cities and large towns – and these are less bound by red tape. Apart from this, many landlords prefer to let properties furnished, as the property looks better and they can charge a higher rent.

 Very different legislation applies to different forms of letting according to whether a property is furnished or unfurnished, and the length of the lease.

Very different tax rules also apply to furnished and unfurnished letting (see **Chapter 6**).

Property letting is subject to the regulations in the *Code Civil* (Articles 1708 – 1762), which can be found on ▢ www.legifrance.gouv.fr (click on the Union Jack next to '*Les codes*' to find the English translation). The *Code Civil* defines three categories of letting:

- Long-term unfurnished letting – normally for a minimum of three years, but under certain circumstances for as little as one year (see **Unfurnished Property** on page 169).

- Long-term furnished letting – normally for more than three months; different rules apply to letting for less than three months (see **Furnished Property** page 179).

- Short-term (holiday) furnished letting (see **Chapter 2**).

Other laws apply according to the type and duration of lease, notably, for unfurnished long-term lets, the *Loi Mermaz* (Nos. 99 – 462) of 6th July 1989 (see **Unfurnished Property** on page 169). In general, the legislation regarding furnished letting is far less stringent than that which applies to unfurnished accommodation.

Note also that, if you let a property in France, but live elsewhere, you're required to pay tax on your rental income in France, irrespective of any double-taxation or other agreements (see page 212).

This chapter also considers the implications of letting commercial property and the leaseback scheme. Further information can be obtained from a variety of sources, including the following:

- Century 21 (💻 www.century21france.fr).
- Fédération Nationale de l'Immobilier (💻 www.fnaim.fr).
- L'Immobilier – monthly magazine listing properties to rent (and buy) region by region and its website (💻 www.lesiteimmobilier.com).
- Immobilier.fr (💻 www.immobilier.fr).
- Le Nouvel Observateur (💻 http://annonces.nouvelobs.com – click on 'Immobilier').
- De Particulier à Particulier – Leading property magazine sold weekly at newsagents and its website (💻 www.pap.fr).
- Le Site Immobilier (💻 www.lesiteimmobilier.com).

WHERE TO BUY

The criteria for the location of accommodation for long-term letting are quite different from those intended for holiday accommodation. Generally speaking, long-term unfurnished lets are viable in all regions and areas, as there's continuing demand for residential accommodation. Residential furnished lets are in demand in cities and towns – for business people and for students who want to be near a college/university. More than 60 per cent of the residential rental market is in towns and cities with more than 100,000 inhabitants. Within cities, the best location for a property is within easy reach of the main workplaces. Further out, and in the provinces, it's best to buy near transport links (e.g. a railway station). In particular, there's a vibrant market for Paris apartments, which are popular with visiting Americans, although on a relatively short-term basis (a few months at a time).

The following table shows the number of long-term unfurnished rentals (subject to the Loi Mermaz) in the whole of France, separated into Ile-de-France (the Paris region) and the rest of the country (Source: Institut National de la Statistique et des Etudes/INSEE).

Area	No. of Rental Properties	Percentage of Total
Ile-de-France		
Outer region	189,328	4%
Paris suburbs	355,461	7%
Paris	387,288	8%
Total Ile-de-France	**932,077**	**19%**
Rest of France		
Pop. up to 2,000	650,945	13%
2,000 – 20,000	699,800	14%
20,000 – 50,000	41,943	7%
50,000 – 100,000	347,374	7%
100,000 – 200,000	364,408	8%
Over 200,000	1,493,063	31%
Total Rest of France	**3,897,533**	**81%**
Total	4,829,610	100%

The following list shows the number of unfurnished rentals in each department:

- **Over 400,000** – Paris.
- **200,000 – 400,000** – Bouches-du-Rhône.
- **100,000 – 200,000** – Alpes-Maritimes, Bas-Rhin, Gironde, Haute-Garonne, Hauts-de-Seine, Hérault, Nord, Rhône, Seine-et-Marne, Seine-Maritime, Seine-St-Denis, Val-de-Marne, Var and Yvelines.
- **50,000 – 100,000** – Calvados, Finistère, Gard, Haut-Rhin, Haute-Savoie, Ille-et-Villaine, Isère, Loire, Loire-Atlantique, Maine-et-Loire, Meurthe-et-Moselle, Morbihan, Moselle, Pas-de-Calais, Puy-de-Dôme, Pyrénées-Atlantiques, Val-d'Oise and Vaucluse.
- **20,000 – 50,000** – Ain, Aisne, Allier, Ardèche, Ardennes, Aude, Aveyron, Charente, Charente-Maritime, Cher, Corrèze, Côtes-d'Armor, Côte-d'Or, Deux-Sèvres, Dordogne, Doubs, Drôme, Eure, Eure-et-Loir, Haute-Vienne, Indre-et-Loire, Jura, Landes, Loir-et-Cher, Loire, Lot-et-Garonne, Manche, Marne, Mayenne, Oise, Orne, Pyrénées-Orientales, Saône-et-Loire, Sarthe, Somme, Tarn, Vendée, Vienne, Vosges and Yonne.
- **10,000 – 20,000** – Alpes-de-Haute-Provence, Ariège, Aube, Cantal, Corse, Gers, Haute-Marne, Haute-Loire, Hautes-Pyrénées, Hautes-Alpes,

Haute-Saône, Indre, Lot, Meuse, Nièvre, Territoire-de-Belfort and Tarn-et-Garonne.

● **Under 10,000** – Creuse and Lozère.

Yields vary considerably with the region or city and the type of property, and you should carefully balance the cost of the property against the demand for rentals in the chosen area.

General information about finding a property to buy can be found in *Buying a Home in France* (Survival Books – see page 317). If you're thinking of buying to let in Paris, a useful property search service is provided by the Paris Property Ladder (☎ 01 45 44 66 00, 🖳 www.parispropertyladder.com), which is run by an English-speaker.

WHAT TO BUY

General advice as to what makes a good (and bad) property for investment, and notes on renovating a property for letting, can be found on pages 18 and 26 respectively. The type of property you buy depends on the target market in your chosen area. Smaller properties, e.g. apartments, in towns and cities will let to business people and professional couples – the typical profile of people who rent their principal residence. Single people make up 39 per cent of this group, couples without children being the next largest group at 11 per cent. In university towns, smaller apartments are in demand for student accommodation. In other areas, three or four-bedroom houses on the outskirts of towns appeal to families, but this a small sector of the rental market; couples with two or three children represent only 16 per cent of the total. Rural farmhouses and cottages are less likely to be in great demand, as most French people prefer to live within easy travelling distance of their workplaces and schools, often preferring to go home for lunch. If this is the type of property you're considering buying, you may be better advised to consider holiday letting (see **Chapter 2**), where higher rents can be charged for a shorter season.

SURVIVAL TIP
Bear in mind that, in the last resort,
you may have to sell if you cannot find a tenant,
so you should also buy with a view to selling.

UNFURNISHED PROPERTY

In general, the French prefer to rent property unfurnished – or, at least, they're more accustomed to renting unfurnished. There are advantages and disadvantages to letting unfurnished, as opposed to furnished. There's obviously no need to buy or replace furniture, but it's more difficult to make an empty property attractive and its location becomes paramount. The main disadvantage of unfurnished letting, however, is the extensive legislation governing it, which is outlined below. **Ensure that you're fully aware of the rules and regulations before deciding to let unfurnished.**

The Law

The letting of unfurnished property is strictly regulated, and several laws and amendments apply, principally the *Loi Mermaz*, which came into force on 6th July 1989 to regulate unfurnished letting, which must normally be for a minimum of three years, although you may let for as little as a year under certain circumstances (see **Short-term Lets** on page 178). The law applies mainly to residential tenancies, but also to mixed use – partly residential and partly commercial, along with garages, parking bays, gardens and other buildings let with the premises by the same landlord. The *Loi Mermaz* was supplemented by the so-called *SRU* (*Solidarité et Renouvellement Urbains*) law, passed on 13th December 2000, which states that the premises must meet 'normal' standards of comfort and habitability (i.e. it must not pose a risk to the occupier's safety or health), and a further decree (*décret*) of 30th January 2002, which stipulates minimum areas and heights (e.g. the main room must be at least 9m^2 and 2.2m high), equipment, standards and comfort. These regulations do **not** cover business lets (see **Commercial Property** on page 181), holiday lets (see **Chapter 2**), or furnished lets (see page 179).

The *Loi Mermaz* states that the right to housing is fundamental, and it's weighted in favour of the tenant rather than the landlord, so if you consider letting a property unfurnished you must be aware of its stipulations, the most important of which are detailed below.

Some types of unfurnished rental property are wholly or partially exempt from the *Loi Mermaz*, but these are generally not properties that foreigners might invest in; they include those with regulated rents and those financed by state loans under urban renewal schemes, which are subject to various other laws and conditions.

The full text of the *Loi Mermaz* and the *SRU* law can be downloaded from the LegiFrance website (🖳 www.legifrance.gouv.fr).

Contract

The rental contract must be in writing, and include the following:

● The name and address of the landlord or his agent.

- The start date and duration of the rental.

- A description of the type of property.

- A description of the premises and equipment for the exclusive and, if applicable, communal use of the tenant.

- The intended use of the premises – i.e. residential or a combination of residential and commercial.

- The amount of rent, method of payment and any conditions under which the rent may be increased (as stipulated in the *Loi Mermaz* – see page 172).

- The amount of the deposit (see below).

The contract must **not** include any clauses that:

- Require the tenant to pay the rent by direct debit or by bank drafts signed in advance.

- Allow the landlord to deduct the rent from the tenant's wages at source.

- Include any estimate of expenses for deterioration of communal areas.

- Commit the tenant in advance to the cost of repairs based solely on the landlord's estimate.

- Contain any clause for the cancellation of the contract for any other reason than non-payment of rent, service charges, deposit or insurance.

- Allow the landlord to alter the conditions of the contract.

- Allow the landlord to stipulate penalties in advance if the conditions of the contract are infringed.

- Prevent the tenant practising any political, union, denominational or society activity.

- Require the tenant to take out insurance with a specified company.

- Allow viewings on public holidays or for more than two hours on working days (if the property is to be re-let or sold).

If the tenant leaves the premises or dies, the contract can be passed to his spouse or partner, his dependants or descendants, his parents or grandparents, if they've lived there with him for a least a year.

Blank rental contracts are published by Editions Tissot, BP 109, 74941 Annecy-le-Vieux Cedex (☎ 08 25 07 71 11, 💻 www.editions-tissot.fr).

Lease

The lease for an unfurnished rental is for a fixed period: three years if the property is owned by a private individual or a family *société civile immobilière* (*SCI* – see page 216); six years if the property is owned by a company. Unless the tenancy is ended by either party in accordance with the law (see page 176), the lease is automatically renewed for a further three or six years, as appropriate.

Deposit

Tenants must pay a deposit, which cannot exceed two months' rent and should be held by you or your agent, or (preferably) by a *notaire* or *huissier*.

Rent

Until 1997, the fixing of rent at the start of a tenancy was subject to regulation. This no longer applies, and you may freely fix the rent of unfurnished premises (for information about setting an appropriate rent, see page 172). However, restrictions apply to increasing the rent (see below).

Increases

Leases normally carry an indexation clause whereby the rent is linked to the cost of construction index (*ICC*). In this case, the rent may be increased annually by the appropriate amount on a date specified in the contract. Apart from this annual indexed increase, you may not increase the rent until the lease renewal becomes due, unless you make improvements to the property. You may offer a tenant a rent increase in exchange for improvements. If he agrees, you must both sign a new clause in the lease. If he declines, you may not increase the rent. If improvement work lasts more than 40 days, the tenant can demand a reduction in rent, either by agreement or via a tribunal.

If you wish to increase the rent at the end of the lease period, you must send the tenant written notice at least six months before the expiry of the lease, delivered by registered letter or by *huissier*. The proposal must include the amount of the new rent and a list of neighbouring premises whose rents are at a similar level (giving exact address, condition, etc.).

The tenant has two months to accept or refuse the rent increase. In the case of refusal or no response from the tenant, the matter can be taken to the *commission départementale de conciliation* (a committee of representatives of owners and tenants, sitting at the *préfecture*). They will call together the two parties, with relevant documentation, and try to reach an agreement. They must give their decision within two months. If there's still a dispute, you can go to a tribunal, which will fix a new rent in accordance with the advice of the commission. In all cases, agreement must be reached or the dispute process started before the end of the current lease; otherwise the lease is automatically renewed, at the existing rent.

The rent increase is applied once only, but is spread over the period of the lease as follows:

- If the increase is less than 10 per cent, it's spread over the duration of the new lease. For example, if you obtain an increase of 9 per cent and the new lease is for three years, the rise will be 3 per cent per year; if the new lease is for six years, the rise will be 1.5 per cent per year.

- If the increase is more than 10 per cent, it's applied by a sixth per year for the duration of the new lease, even if the new lease is only for three years.

The annual revision in conjunction with the *ICC* applies each year along with any rent increase.

Inventory

Article 1730 of the *Code Civil* states that the tenant must leave the premises in the same condition as they were let. In order to establish whether or not this is the case, you must draw up an *état des lieux* (*EdL*), which, literally translated, means 'state of the place' and is both an inventory and a description of the property's condition. **It's very important to draft the *EdL* properly.** It can be drafted on plain paper or on a prepared form, but should describe in detail the condition and equipment of each room, and it must be revised at the start and at the end of the lease period. A comparison between the two versions enables you to ensure that your tenant has fulfilled his obligations regarding repairs and maintenance. If all is well, you must return the tenant's deposit in full; otherwise, you can deduct repair and maintenance costs for damage and wear caused by the tenant.

You (or your agent) and the tenant should draw up the *EdL* together, in agreement, just before the keys are handed over at the beginning of the let and again when the premises are vacant at the end of the tenancy. It must be dated and signed with a copy for each of the people concerned.

If you and the tenant disagree over the *EdL*, either of you may call on the services of a *huissier* (a public servant, roughly equivalent to a bailiff, although a *huissier* has a wider range of functions) to prepare the *EdL*. The *huissier* must announce his visit at least seven days in advance, by registered letter.

When an *EdL* is drawn up between the owner and tenant, there are no fees. If it's drawn up by a *huissier*, there's a set fee (currently €114.65), which is shared equally between you and the tenant.

If there's no *EdL*, Article 1731 of the *Code Civil* states that, without proof to the contrary, the premises are assumed to have been let in good condition. If the owner refuses to have an *EdL* prepared, it's up to him to prove that any damage at the end of the lease is due to the tenant's neglect, which of course is virtually impossible.

Landlord's Obligations

As landlord of unfurnished rental premises, you're bound by certain obligations, including the following:

- To provide and maintain the premises in good condition.
- To ensure that the tenant enjoys peaceful occupation of the premises.
- To use the premises for their intended purpose, as specified in the contract, and to make all necessary repairs (other than those the tenant is responsible for – see below).
- To allow the tenant to make improvements, provided they don't 'transform' the premises.

Tenant's Obligations

Although the law is weighted in favour of the tenant, he also has certain obligations, including the following:

- To pay the rent and service charges (see page 175), as specified in the contract.
- To use the premises peacefully according to their intended use.
- To repair any damage unless it has been caused by *force majeure*, the landlord or a third party (e.g. vandalism).
- To be responsible for routine maintenance and minor repairs of the premises and equipment as in the contract (see **Maintenance & Repairs** on page 174).
- To allow repairs or improvements to be made by other tenants in the same building.
- Not to 'transform' the premises or equipment without written permission of the owner.
- To have comprehensive insurance (i.e. a *multi-risques* household policy – see page 186).
- Not to transfer the rental nor sublet without written permission from the landlord.

Maintenance & Repairs

Responsibility for maintenance and repairs is divided between you and the tenant. The following expenses are your responsibility:

- Maintenance and upkeep of the property – major repairs and building work, e.g. roofing, creation of gardens, resurfacing, replacement of equipment (heating system, lifts, etc.).

- Fees applying to the management and administration of the building (e.g. insurance).

- Installation of new equipment such as fire doors or security systems.

- Legal inspections relating to the standard of lifts, fire-fighting equipment, etc.

- Security and caretaking (to assure the tenant's right to peaceful enjoyment of the property).

- Repairs due to vandalism by third parties not introduced to the premises by the tenant.

- Repairs to old or malfunctioning equipment (e.g. heating system, lifts).

The tenant's expenses fall broadly into three categories:

- Consumables – i.e. water, gas, electricity and heating fuel, cleaning products, etc.

- Cleaning of and minor repairs to communal areas, and a percentage of the maintenance cost of any equipment mentioned in the lease (washing machine, boiler, lifts, etc.) and of concierge's wages.

- Taxes for services such as street sweeping and rubbish disposal from which the tenant benefits directly.

The tenant must also carry out a certain amount of maintenance and repair work in his home and any outside areas that are for his use only. However, the tenant cannot be held responsible for repairs when they result from *force majeure* (e.g. a storm) or a fault in the building or a malfunction of an installation (e.g. flooding due to bad drainage) or when they reflect normal usage of the furnishings and decoration. For example, the tenant cannot be asked to replace flooring after ten years of occupation. If the carpet or wallpaper is simply soiled, the owner must pay for renewing them; if they're soiled and damaged the costs must be shared by the tenant.

You can make a monthly or quarterly service charge to the tenant to cover the expenses for which he's liable and adjust the amount charged once a year to reflect the actual costs. If the service charge changes during the course of a year, the landlord must provide evidence of how the new amount has been calculated. All charges must be detailed, and you must produce utility bills, etc. if asked.

You must pay for all repair and work that isn't chargeable to the tenant, but if there's damage due to neglect by the tenant, you aren't obliged to pay for repair or replacement.

There's often disagreement between landlords and tenants over whose responsibility certain maintenance and repairs are, especially at the end of a tenancy, and the law isn't always clear on the matter (6,471 cases were brought before a tribunal in 2004), which is why it's essential to make a detailed *EdL* (see page 173).

The tenant cannot be held responsible for repairs when they're necessitated by a fault in the building (e.g. flood damage due to inadequate drainage), when they result from normal usage or 'wear and tear' (e.g. the replacement of flooring after ten years of occupation), or when the damage is a result of *force majeure* (e.g. a storm). On the other hand, if damage is due to neglect by the tenant, the owner isn't legally obliged to pay for repair or replacement. However, it's often difficult to ascertain precisely the nature or cause of 'damage'. For example, if a carpet is soiled or damaged, is this due to normal use or neglect? In such cases, it's often advisable to share the cost of replacement with the tenant.

If the owner doesn't fulfil his obligations, the tenant may ask a *tribunal d'instance* (small claims court) for authorisation to carry out maintenance or repair work himself and for the cost be deducted from his future rent.

Ending a Tenancy

A tenancy can be terminated by either party, but whereas a tenant can cancel his lease at any moment without having to give reasons (see page 177), a landlord can cancel only under certain circumstances, detailed below. Generally, unless a tenant has failed to meet his obligations (see page 174), you cannot evict him until his lease has expired.

Termination by Landlord

It's very difficult to evict tenants. You may terminate the tenancy in order to repossess the property – to turn it into commercial premises, to sell it or to live in it yourself (see below) – but only in the most stringent circumstances. You may also terminate the tenancy if the tenant has failed to fulfil his obligations or broken the terms of his contract, e.g. by irregular or late payment of rent (see below), unauthorised sub-letting, or disturbing his neighbours.

Repossession to Sell: You must give at least six months' notice if you decide to sell the premises. The tenant, however, has a right of first refusal (under certain conditions) unless you're selling to your parents, grandparents or great-grandparents (in which case they must subsequently live in the property for at least two years). If the tenant wishes to buy, he must make an offer within two months and must sign the *compromis de vente* within two months of your acceptance of the offer (or four months if he's applying for a loan). The lease is extended to the date of sale. If the sale doesn't take place within the period specified in the sale contract, it's rendered null and void, unless it's the owner's fault. If the premises are subsequently offered to a third party at a lower price than that detailed in the original offer, the tenant has a further right of refusal and has one month to make a further offer; the other conditions of the sale are the same as before. If the owner is unable to sell after the tenant has left, he has the right to re-let the property. There's no minimum period that must elapse before you re-let, but the tenant may bring a court case if he feels that he has in effect been evicted.

Repossession to Occupy: You must give six months' notice if you wish to make the property your principal residence or that of your parents. The notification must give the name and address of the future resident(s).

Non-payment: If the tenant fails to pay his rent at the appointed time, you must have a demand for payment drawn up by a *huissier*; the tenant then has two months to pay the amount due. He may ask for an extension, but this must be authorised by a judge. If the tenant still doesn't pay or obtain an extension of payment, you can begin legal proceedings, but these can be long, complicated and expensive, so it's essential to obtain expert legal advice.

Protected Tenancy: If the tenant is over 70 and his income is less than one and a half times the minimum wage (*SMIC*), you cannot terminate the lease without offering him alternative accommodation. This must correspond to the needs and financial position of the tenant and be situated in the same area (generally within 5km).

Termination by Tenant

The tenant can cancel his lease at any time without having to give reasons. He must give written notice three months (to the day) before the date he wishes to vacate the premises, and the notice must be delivered by a *huissier* or sent by registered post. Once he has done this, he may not change his mind. If he stays in the property after the expiry of the notice, he may be legally evicted. The period of notice can be reduced to one month in certain cases, including the following:

● When the tenant loses his job, e.g. is made redundant. This excludes voluntary change of occupation, retirement or resignation. It never applies to unsalaried people who cease their activity.

● When the tenant's job is transferred.

● When the tenant has lost his job or been unemployed and finds work.

● When the tenant is receiving *RMI* (unemployment benefit).

● When the tenant is over 60 and he must move for health reasons.

In the case of married tenants or *PACS*ed partners (*pacte civil de solidarité* – a legal agreement between an unmarried couple that gives them certain rights), it's sufficient for one of the partners to meet any of the above conditions.

The tenant must continue to pay the rent until the end of the notice period even if he leaves before that date. The deposit cannot be in lieu of payment of the last two months' rent.

Return of Deposit

The tenant's deposit should be repaid within two months of the keys being returned. You may deduct any charges for repair and cleaning which should have been carried out by the tenant, and for any unpaid rent. If you don't repay the deposit within two months, it gains interest at 2.05 per cent (2005 figure) in his favour. You may demand proof of payment of *taxe d'habitation* before refunding a deposit.

Landlord's Visiting Rights

To find a new tenant, you must naturally have right of access to the property. This is limited by law to two hours per day, excepting Sundays and public holidays. You must have permission from the tenant to enter when he's absent.

Disputes

In general, disputes over residential leases can be taken to a tribunal. The plaintiff drafts a writ, which must be delivered by a *huissier* to the defendant at least 15 days before the hearing. A copy must be submitted to the office of the clerk of the court at least eight days in advance of the hearing. Before the hearing, the judge may ask for additional information or even take the tribunal to the premises. It isn't mandatory to have legal representation, but it's advisable to take legal advice (possibly from a *huissier*). If the amount disputed is more than the rent and service charges due plus the deposit, the case must be taken to the *commission départementale de conciliation*. There follows a long and complicated series of hearings, for which it's necessary to take legal advice.

Short-term Lets

Article 11 of the *Loi Mermaz* makes provision for the possibility of letting an unfurnished property for between one and three years, under several conditions (unfurnished lets of less than a year aren't permitted under any circumstances). First, the landlord must be a private individual or a family *SCI*, whose capital is held solely by parents and relatives. Second, he must need to let the property short term as a result of a particular event (which must be specified in the lease), e.g. marriage, redundancy, leaving a job or retirement.

Two months before the event stated as justification for the short-term lease (see above), you must give notice to the tenant. If the event doesn't take place, the lease is automatically extended to three years. If the event is postponed, you may propose a postponement of the expiry date, but the tenant may refuse. If he accepts it, you must then confirm the event two months before the new expiry date. The law allows only one postponement; if the event is again rescheduled, the lease is automatically extended to three years.

FURNISHED PROPERTY

A furnished let is defined in law as a property containing furniture and household items at the time of letting, into which the tenant can move and live, bringing personal effects only. There must be an inventory. If these conditions aren't met, the tenant can take you to a tribunal and have the premises redefined as unfurnished. You would then be subject to the far stricter regulations imposed on that type of accommodation, with the tenant entitled to a let of at least three years.

For furnished lettings you're free to set the rental duration, as well as the rental charge, but different regulations apply according to whether the lease is for more or less than three months. If the rental is for less than three months, it counts as holiday letting (see **Chapter 2**). If you want to let for longer than three months, stricter rules apply (see below).

Rules & Regulations

Tenants renting for between three months and a year must have their principal residence elsewhere; those whose principal residence is the property rented are entitled to a minimum lease of a year. (Until January 2005, this applied only to properties let by landlords who habitually let four or more properties; now it applies to all cases.) The lease is automatically renewable for the same period and under the same conditions, and there are stringent regulations, similar to those for unfurnished letting (see page 170), restricting the landlord's right to reclaim the property.

If you wish to terminate a lease, you must give the tenant three months' notice; if the tenant wants to end it, he has to give only one month's notice. Letting contracts must be in French.

It's essential to take legal advice and use the services of a *notaire* if you're planning to let furnished premises as someone's principal residence.

Professional Activity

Letting furnished property isn't considered a professional activity if you earn €23,000 or less per year from it or if your earnings are less than 50 per cent of your total income. If the income is below this figure you're considered to be a non-professional landlord (*loueur en meublé non-professionnel/ LMNP*). You may, in this case, choose to make a business registration if it suits your circumstances, but it isn't obligatory. If you're classed as an *LMNP*, there are two tax disadvantages; any capital gains on selling the property are taxed under private capital gains tax rules, and you cannot offset any losses against your main income, although they can be carried forward for five years against future rental income.

If your income is above this figure or your earnings are more than 50 per cent of your total income, you're deemed to be a professional landlord (*loueur en meublé professionel/LMP*) and you **must** register with the local Chambre de Commerces. You will pay higher social security payments (see page 220), but you can offset any losses against your total income (provided the losses don't result from depreciation) and you may be exempt from capital gains tax (your earnings must be under a certain limit and you must have been letting for at least five years).

Furnishings & Decor

Furnishings must be 'sufficient' (i.e. allow a tenant to live in the premises) and should obviously be appropriate to your target tenants, e.g. students, single professionals or a family. The following guidelines apply to most furnished property:

- The property should be light, spacious and perfectly decorated in neutral colours (white, cream, etc.), with modern, hard-wearing furniture.
- You should provide quality appliances, but shouldn't go overboard with chic design or kitchen gadgets.
- Carpets should be dark and made of resilient materials and must be regularly cleaned.
- Sofas and armchairs should have machine-washable covers (two sets).
- Don't install cheap or coloured bathroom suites (white is best) and don't carpet bathroom floors.

- There should be no clutter and only a few pictures and ornaments, as most tenants will want to provide their own. In particular, don't clutter the kitchen, but keep spare electrical items handy such as a kettle or toaster.

- Don't buy second-hand furniture unless you're letting to students (if you do, make sure that it meets fire regulations).

- Avoid cheap handles, knobs, curtain rails and other items that will get a lot of hard use.

- Only use workmen (electricians, plumbers, etc.) who have been highly recommended and who are registered *artisans*.

- The furniture and decor must be spotless and in excellent condition each time a property is let. Replace bedding and mattresses (which should be turned between tenants) frequently and discard appliances that are well past their best.

Depending on the price and quality of a property, your guests may also expect central heating, a washing machine, dishwasher and microwave, covered parking and a telephone (you could install a telephone on the *service restreint* tariff that receives incoming calls, but allows outgoing local and emergency calls only).

If you want to let a property at the top end of the market, it must be beautifully, even luxuriously, furnished and equipped. This includes top-of-the-range finishes, bed linen, deluxe fully-equipped kitchen (dishwasher, microwave, etc.), television, DVD player, cable or satellite TV, power shower, off-road parking and resident concierge, caretaker, porter, gardener or maid, as appropriate.

You will need an inventory (see page 173) for a furnished property, which must be taken before each tenant moves in and when he leaves. An inventory should list all removable items.

COMMERCIAL PROPERTY

If you let all or part of a property for business purposes (e.g. for someone to set up an art studio or a chocolate shop), you must normally use a nine-year lease, which is subject to the law of 30th September 1953. The law is heavily weighted in favour of the tenant, who requires some measure of security if he's to operate a successful and stable business in the premises. You cannot evict the tenant at any time during this nine-year lease, unless he breaks the terms of the contract (see **Renewal & Termination** below). The tenant can sell the business, along with the right to the lease.

Another type of commercial lease is known as *bail précaire* (literally, 'precarious lease'), whereby a commercial premises may be let for a period not exceeding 23 months. This isn't renewable and isn't subject to the regulations of a normal commercial lease, but if the tenant is still present after 24 months the lease is automatically extended to a regular nine-year lease.

 The laws relating to commercial leases are extraordinarily extensive and complex, and it's essential to take legal advice should you wish to embark upon commercial letting.

Rent Reviews

Most commercial letting contracts include an annual indexed rent increase. In addition, the landlord or the tenant can request a rent review at the end of each three-year period. If you wish to increase the rent, you must give notice at least six months before the end of the three-year period; this should be served by a *huissier*. If the tenant doesn't wish to accept the new rent, he can quit the premises or stay in the premises whilst paying the previous rent and you or he can take the matter to a tribunal, which examines the case, taking into account any changes in the local business environment (whether detrimental or beneficial), and appoints and instructs an independent specialist to draw up a report, which is generally binding upon both parties. Any change set by the tribunal is backdated to the renewal date.

Renewal & Termination

The tenant has the right to remain in the premises for the full nine years and to renew the lease for a further nine years, although a rent increase may be applied for the renewed lease (see above). **The renewal procedure is very formal and failure to comply with its precise provisions can have expensive consequences for the party concerned.** Both the format of the documents and the time frame are crucial, the whole process possibly being rendered null and void if these aren't in accordance with the law. When the tenant seeks renewal, he should do so using a *huissier* to serve the relevant documents. If you agree to renew at the same rent or don't respond, the lease is renewed for a further nine years.

Often, the terms and conditions of a lease include a clause to the effect that it's valid only for a particular type of business. If the tenant wants to change the nature of his business, he can inform you and you can reach a private agreement, but neither you nor the tenant can alter the terms and conditions of a renewed lease.

Renewal disputes can be taken to tribunal only if they concern the rent; other terms and conditions of a lease aren't subject to such arbitration. Any disputes must be heard within two years.

Termination by Landlord

If during the course of the nine-year lease, the tenant hasn't complied with the terms of the lease, e.g. he hasn't paid the rent, you may serve notice to quit without an offer to renew the lease at the end of the term. However, if the tenant takes the matter to a tribunal and it finds in his favour, you may have to pay substantial compensation: e.g. 90 per cent of one year's turnover (based on the average of three or four years' turnover) or the equivalent of two years' profit. The amount depends on the formula used by the expert witness and can vary greatly according to the nature of the business. This process can take years, and the tenant is entitled to stay in the premises during that time.

If you wish to end a tenancy because you wish to undertake construction, rebuilding or demolition or to occupy the premises yourself, you may be allowed to do so without paying compensation – but don't count on it! In any case, you must give notice at least six months before end of the nine-year term; again, this should be served by a *huissier*.

Termination by Tenant

Every three years, the tenant has the right to terminate the lease. Notice of this intention must be delivered by a *huissier*, or he may find himself bound to another three-year period.

FINANCIAL CONSIDERATIONS

Mortgages

'Buy-to-let' mortgages as such aren't a familiar concept in France, with the exception of leaseback schemes (see page 190). Mortgages are normally only granted for residential properties, which can include second homes. Letting property is permitted by French lenders, but letting income is usually only taken into consideration if the property is rented on long-term contracts, after submission and assessment of the viability of your business plan. It may then be considered a business loan rather than a mortgage, and you should take specialist legal and financial advice to ensure that this is the best option for your circumstances. All applications must be supported by proof of income; self-certification isn't accepted.

Mortgage providers in the UK cannot use French property as equity. However, if you're resident in the UK or elsewhere, there are several mortgage brokers who will arrange mortgages with French providers, e.g. Conti Financial Services Ltd (💻 www.mortgagesoverseas.com) and

PropertyFinance4Less (⌨ www.propertyfinance4less.com). The latter has a useful mortgage calculator on its website. As would be the case if you're resident in France, you must furnish proof of income.

Further information on French mortgages can be found via the internet (e.g. ⌨ www.europelaw.com, www.french-mortgage.com and www.french entree.com).

Yield

The yield on a property is the profit on your capital investment (after the deduction of expenses, but before tax), which varies according to how much you pay for a property, the rent you charge and your expenses in equipping and maintaining it; the resulting figure can be used to compare the efficacy of your property investment with alternatives such as savings accounts, stocks and shares.

Generally, the cheaper the property, the higher the yield. For example, if you buy a property for €100,000 and let it for €700 per month (gross income €8,400 per year), your gross yield is 8.4 per cent (8,400 divided by 100,000 = 0.084, multiplied by 100). If you buy a property for €200,000, you're unlikely to be able to let it for €1,400 per month to achieve the same yield; you might only be able to charge €1,200 per month (€14,400 per year), in which case your gross yield will be 7.2 per cent.

Expenses can include purchase costs, furniture and furnishings, service charges, ground rent, insurance, agent's fees, cleaning, maintenance and (re)decorating, repairs, marketing, etc. – but not your mortgage payments. Void periods (when the property is unoccupied, between lets) also count as expenses. These must be deducted from your gross income in order to calculate your net income and net yield. For example, if you buy a €200,000 property, earn €15,000 per year in rent and have annual expenses of €5,000, you've a net income of €10,000. Your net yield is therefore €10,000 divided by €200,000 = 0.05, multiplied by x 100 = 5 per cent – but bear in mind that you still have to pay tax on your net income (although you can deduct mortgage repayments and costs). Note that you should always use the current market value of a property to calculate the yield.

SURVIVAL TIP
It's important that you know the yield you can expect to earn before embarking on a buy-to-let scheme.

In general, your rental income should cover your mortgage repayments plus another 25 to 50 per cent. Buying to let isn't a good idea if your maximum rent will barely cover your mortgage and you've little other disposable income.

Letting Rates & Deposits

The rent you can charge varies considerably according to the area, as well as the size and quality of the property, local demand and the competition. You must set a realistic rent that compares with similar properties in the area and gives you a reasonable return on your investment.

You can check the rents of similar properties in local newspapers or via the internet. For example, the website of *Le Nouvel Observateur* (💻 http://permanent.nouvelobs.com) has a useful facility (add to the address /php/loyer/index.php) that allows you to enter a detailed description of a property – e.g. nearest town, location, environment, floor area, garden and grounds, construction material, number of rooms and facilities – and gives you the likely monthly rental you can charge.

If you use a letting agent (see page 187), he will suggest an appropriate rental. However, you must be prepared to lower the rent (particularly for a long-term tenant) or pay higher fees to an agent when prospective tenants are thin on the ground.

If you have a desirable property in a good area and you're letting for at least 12 months at a time, you may be able to budget for 45 to 50 weeks' income a year. In an area that's saturated with rental properties, however, or if you're offering only short-term (furnished) lets, you may have to make do with 40 weeks or less. It's often better to lower the rent than have a property empty for a number of weeks. For example, if your rent is €800 per month and a property is empty for two months, you earn €8,000; if you had reduced the rent to €700 per month for a quick let, you would have earned €8,400 in 12 months – and you would have spared yourself the agony of not having a tenant! A void of one month is equivalent to a loss of 8.3 per cent of one year's rent.

Tenants pay one month's rent in advance plus a deposit, which cannot exceed two months' rent. Tenants also usually pay separately for utility services such as gas, electricity, water and telephone, as well as for their TV licence and cable TV service (if applicable) and *taxe d'habitation*.

Taxation

Income tax is payable in France on rental income (*revenu foncier* for unfurnished property), even if you live abroad and the money is paid there. All rental income must be declared to the French tax authorities, whether you let a property for a few weeks to a friend or 52 weeks a year on a commercial basis. Letting furnished accommodation is a commercial activity for tax purposes and **must** be declared under the *bénéfices industriels et commerciaux* section of your annual tax declaration. You must also pay *taxe foncière* on the property. For details of taxes payable, see **Chapter 6**.

Insurance

You must notify your insurance company that you're letting accommodation and obtain appropriate cover. Under French law, long-term tenants must have their own comprehensive household insurance policy (*multi-risques habitation*). Nevertheless, whether you're letting furnished or unfurnished, you must have adequate third-party public liability (*responsabilité civile*) and fire insurance for your property. Ensure that it includes a guarantee for *recours de locataires contre le propriétaire*, which applies when a client causes water or fire damage.

Further information about French insurance is available from insurance companies or from the Centre de Documentation et d'Information de l'Assurance (CDIA, 🖥 www.ffsa.fr).

OTHER CONSIDERATIONS

Security

Your insurance company will advise you what security measures are required (in order for its cover to be valid), which depends largely on its location (e.g. central Paris or rural Auvergne) and may include the following:

- Locking grilles on patio and other doors.
- Lockable shutters.
- Alarm.
- Closed circuit television (CCTV).

If these aren't required by your insurer, you may consider installing them anyway, depending on the type of clients you're letting to.

Safety

You should have the following equipment:

- **Fire Extinguishers & Fire Blankets** – Check between lets that they haven't been used and that the 'use-by' date hasn't passed.
- **Smoke Alarms** – Check batteries and test alarms between lets.

Other safety measures (e.g. child safety gates) depend on the location, nature and facilities of your property. If necessary, ask advice from your insurance company.

USING AN AGENT

If you're letting a property long-term, the most important decision is whether to let it yourself or to use a letting agent (or agents). If you don't have much spare time, you're better off using an agent, who will take care of everything and save you the time and expense of advertising and finding clients. An agent charges commission, although some of this can be recouped through higher rents.

Estate Agents

The role of estate agents in France isn't simply that of selling houses; they also deal with rentals and are qualified to advise on and deal with the legal side of long-term letting, provide contracts, rental agreements and so on. Some even manage your letting business for you. Obviously, their charges vary according to the extent of their involvement. Agents' fees are around 10 to 12 per cent of the rental price; they may also charge an introduction fee. Any management fees on top of this obviously depend on the nature and extent of the work necessary. Agents' fees are tax deductible.

If you use an agent, you can be confident that all dealings and agreements will be in compliance with the law, giving you full protection and peace of mind. All French estate agents must be registered, and they're affiliated to the Fédération Nationale de l'Immobilier (FNAIM, 🖥 www.fnaim.fr), Union Nationale de la Propriété Immobilière (UNPI, 🖥 www.unpi.org), or Syndicat National des Professionels Immobiliers (SNPI, 🖥 www.snpi.org).

You should nevertheless take care when selecting a letting agent, as a number have gone bust in recent years owing customers thousands of euros. Obtain recommendations, and make sure that your income is kept in an escrow account and paid regularly. It's absolutely essential to employ an efficient, reliable and honest company, preferably long-established. Ask for the names of satisfied customers and check with them. It's also worthwhile inspecting properties managed by an agency to see whether they're well looked after.

Other things to ask a letting agent include the following:

- Who they let to.
- Where they advertise.
- What arrangements/agreements apply to maintenance of the property (e.g. obtaining your approval for expenditure above a certain sum or charging the lessee).

You should also check the type of contract you will have with the agency: whether, for example, you will receive a detailed analysis of income and expenditure and what notice you're required to give if you decide to terminate the agreement. You can place a property with more than one agent when looking for a tenant.

A good agent should do some or all of the following:

● Inspect your property and tell you what you need to do in order to let it for the highest possible rent.

● Advise you on market trends and suggest a rental rate.

● Market the property (the larger companies market homes via newspapers, magazines, overseas agents, colour brochures and the internet, and have representatives in many countries).

● Arrange viewings and vet clients, e.g. by checking their references (you can reserve the right to approve them).

● Compile an inventory.

● Prepare the tenancy agreement.

● Collect and hold the deposit.

● Notify service companies (electricity, gas, water, telephone, etc.) of changes of tenant.

If you use an agent, make sure that you have a contingency fund (say €1,000) to cover any problems and you give him a telephone number where you can be contacted. **Agents' employees work mostly on commission and they can be pushy in trying to get your business.**

DOING YOUR OWN LETTING

Some owners prefer to let a property themselves, without involving an agent, marketing a property and vetting clients themselves, although this is easier with short-term and holiday rather than long-term lets. An agent may be marketing a glut of properties in your area, whereas by advertising privately you won't be competing with all the other properties on the agent's books. You must have somewhere to advertise and time to show clients around. You must do a good selling job, promoting local transport services, restaurants, supermarkets and other shops, sports facilities, etc.

If you would prefer to find tenants yourself, the administrative procedures (e.g. drawing up contracts and leases) can be handled by a *notaire* or a *huissier*, which is recommended.

The first things you need to confirm with a prospective tenant are his identity, where he works, whether he has sufficient income to pay the rent (you need to see proof) and his previous address. **It's vital to check a prospective tenant's references carefully.** References usually include one from a bank or accountant to establish a prospective tenant's financial standing, an employer's reference and a character reference, which can be from a previous landlord, employer or solicitor. Don't be taken in by a prospective tenant's appearance, as even the most presentable and well spoken people can prove to be a nightmare once you hand over the keys.

Contracts

You must have a rental agreement form that includes all the relevant details for the category of accommodation (see pages 170 and 179). Contracts for lets of more than three months must be in French. You can download various types of rental contract and form letter from the Groupe Express Expansion website (🖥 www.lentreprise.com), but you should always have contracts checked by a *notaire*. To be binding, a rental agreement must be signed by all parties involved.

Restrictions

You must make it clear in the letting agreement if you decide not to allow smokers, pets or children. There are many reasons why you might choose to do this: smell, mess and deterioration apply to all three; pets and children may cause a noise nuisance to neighbours. You will be limiting your market, so consider carefully whether or not to place these restrictions. It might be that your property is simply not suitable, or you may not want to budget for the extra wear and tear involved.

Advertising

In most cases, a small advertisement in the local newspaper should be sufficient to find a tenant for a long-term let. You can also put cards on local supermarket notice boards and a notice in the window of the property itself. If you're letting for shorter periods, or if it's a furnished property, e.g. a town apartment where you might want to attract tenants such as students or businessmen, the above methods would also work, but you might also pay for advertising on the many property websites that are available (see page 89).

Most of the English-language newspapers and magazines listed in **Appendix B** also include advertisements from property owners. There's a demand for medium-length lets among those seeking to buy property in France, most of whom read these magazines.

PROPERTY MANAGEMENT

Using a Management Company

You can use a company to manage your property for you (this may or may not be the letting agent). A management company (*administrateur de bien*) should do the following:

- Read meters (if electricity, gas or water is charged extra).
- Carry out or arrange for routine maintenance of communal areas (if a property is divided into apartments, for example).
- Pay bills (e.g. insurance premiums and taxes).
- Carry out regular inspections of the property.
- Deal with tenants' problems.
- Arrange maintenance, repairs, and replacement of damaged or faulty items and obtain estimates for redecoration or major work.
- Deal with insurance claims.
- Arrange cleaning (between lets) and gardening if appropriate.

You may wish (or need) to make periodic checks on a management company to ensure that your property is being well managed and maintained. Management contracts usually run for a year.

Managing a Property Yourself

You can save money by managing your own property, but be warned that it can be a nightmare and may be impossible if you don't live nearby. However, you will save around 5 to 10 per cent on management fees and will know exactly what's happening with your property – something an agent may not know or tell you. If you're managing a property yourself, you must be well organised and have a team of servicemen, including a cleaner, plumber, electrician, handyman, decorator, gardener (if applicable) 'on call' (although this isn't a concept familiar to most French tradesmen!). You also need to keep records of such things as when your inventory needs updating.

LEASEBACK

A particular way of letting a property 'long term' (i.e. for a number of years, but not necessarily on long-term lets) without any of the hassle of managing it, is a leaseback scheme. Leaseback (*propriété allégée* or *leaseback*) schemes (also known as 'tourism residencies') are a French innovation which has since been adopted in other countries and are designed for those seeking a holiday home for a few weeks each year. There has recently been a considerable increase in leaseback purchases and a corresponding increase in development schemes to meet demand, but prospective buyers should be aware of the disadvantages and possible problems of the scheme, as well as the advantages that are promoted by developers.

Properties sold under a leaseback scheme are always located in popular resort areas, e.g. golf, ski or coastal resorts, where self-catering accommodation is in high demand, and are new or totally rebuilt properties. Leaseback schemes are available in many parts of France, including the Alps and Pyrénées, Brittany, Côte d'Azur and the Atlantic coast, Normandy and Paris. Most estate agents – foreign as well as French – can provide details of properties available on a leaseback basis.

A leaseback scheme allows you to buy a new property at less than its true cost, e.g. 30 per cent less than the list price. In return for the discount, the property must be leased back to the developer, usually for 9 to 11 years, so that he can let it as self-catering holiday accommodation. The buyer (in effect) becomes the landlord and qualifies for a refund of the valued added tax (VAT – 19.6 per cent) that was included in the purchase price, although it can take up to five months for the refund to be made. In addition, the developer usually (but not always) 'guarantees' the buyer a fixed annual return (usually around 2 or 3 per cent of the property's value, adjusted annually for inflation according to the Index of Construction Costs published by INSEE), irrespective of his actual rental income, so that the buyer is effectively given a discount (e.g. 25 or 30 per cent) off the purchase price. The buyer owns the freehold of the property and the full price is shown in the title deed. During the period of the lease, the developer therefore takes all the risks associated with letting and you have a guaranteed income.

The buyer is also given the right to occupy the property for a period each year, usually between two and four weeks, spread over high, medium and low seasons. These weeks can usually be let to provide income or possibly even exchanged with accommodation in another resort (as with a timeshare scheme). The developer furnishes (usually with a standard furnishing 'pack') and manages the property and pays all the maintenance and bills (e.g. for utilities) during the term of the lease (even when the owner is in occupation).

What happens when the lease expires depends on the agreement you make with the developer: in some cases, the property is yours – unless you wish to extend the agreement, which you can usually do for a further three, six or nine years and with a longer usage period (e.g. eight weeks per year); in other cases, the lease must be renewed indefinitely.

Unless you're happy with a 'permanent leaseback', ensure that you will have full and vacant possession at the end of the initial lease period, as with some leaseback agreements you NEVER actually own the property.

Note also that, if you sell a property within 20 years of purchase, you must pay a proportion of the VAT you saved to the government. Owners are also responsible for paying property taxes (see page 216) and income tax on the rent they receive from the developer (see page 212). The amount of tax you pay and the allowances to which you're entitled depend on the letting scheme you adopt: as a leaseback owner, you're normally eligible for the *BIC*, *LMNP* or *LMP* scheme, depending on your circumstances (see **Chapter 5**).

Although the leaseback scheme is generally problem-free, you should beware of developers offering high annual returns (e.g. six or seven per cent), as there's no guarantee that these will be achieved or maintained in the long term.

SURVIVAL TIP
Check the standing of the developer and ask for references before committing to a scheme.

You should also check the penalties for opting out of the scheme should you wish or need to, as these can be high (the developer may have a right to claim 'commercial compensation'), and whether the developer has the right to renew the leaseback period automatically, as he's permitted to by law. The developer may also charge management fees, and you should check what these are and what they cover. Finally, check what happens to the property if the developer goes bankrupt. **It's important to have a leaseback contract checked by a legal expert.**

More information on leaseback schemes is available via the internet, e.g. ⌨ www.europelaw.com, www.leasebackfrance.com and www.themove channel.com.

CASE STUDY 7

My wife, Kate and I moved from Devon in England to Calvados, Normandy, in 1989 after spending our honeymoon in the area. We liked the gentle, peaceful countryside and the fact that at the time we could buy a property here that wouldn't cost us all our savings. We bought a rural cottage, which we restored and lived in happily for many years. Kate's two children integrated into the French school system and are both now grown up and married to French partners. On a trip back to England, Kate suffered a whiplash injury in an accident and the insurance payment enabled her to buy another property on the outskirts of the local village as an investment (we referred to it as 'Whiplash Cottage'!).

We heard about the house through a French friend who had intended to buy it himself, but due to illness decided not to and passed on the opportunity to us. The purchase price was 70,000FF (around €10,000) plus charges. It's a small stone cottage. Downstairs is a living area with a corner kitchen and a separate, smaller sitting room. Upstairs, there are two bedrooms and a bathroom. The property was structurally perfect, but in need of extensive decoration and refurbishment. The plumbing system left a great deal to be desired – the kitchen sink waste went into the gutter and drained off down the road! We rewired the property and installed a larger and more modern septic tank with a grease trap and new kitchen units. The garden was on the opposite side of the road, so with the permission of the *maire* we had around a third of it excavated to create a space for parking. The total cost (purchase and renovation) was around 140,000FF (around €20,000).

We didn't want to run it as a *gîte* for several reasons: it's on the road, its garden is on the other side of the road, and it isn't really attractive enough – *gîtes* need a garden, as people want recreational space when they're on holiday. We decided to explore the possibility of letting it to locals on a longer-term basis, there being a shortage of such accommodation in the area. (There are a lot of empty houses around here that no one can sell or use due to the arcane succession laws.) We took photographs and put up some advertisements on local supermarket notice boards.

Our first tenant was the sister of the owner of the local *épicerie*, a divorcee with three children. We drew up a private contract, which was checked by the *notaire*, who also witnessed the signing. The rent was 2,100FF (around €300) per month, which was paid directly to us, as the woman was in receipt of *RMI* (unemployment benefit). They stayed for two years (they needed a larger house by then) and were perfect tenants, leaving the property in excellent condition.

Then came the catastrophe. We advertised the same way as before and also put a notice in the window of the house. A very beautiful, elegant young woman of around 22 came to view, with her two children and an older, male friend. Before the signing took place, however, she ditched him because he was a Jehovah's Witness and didn't sanction her lifestyle. She told us she was back with her husband, but still wanted the house. We thought this would be a better arrangement, as they were a family unit and he was employed. This time we drew up a more formal agreement through a *notaire*, who warned us against letting to them; the woman's mother worked for another *notaire* in the area and the family had the reputation of being unreliable!

Kate decided to take the chance and give them a new start, but the rent wasn't forthcoming, the neighbours complained about the noise and rows and the property deteriorated. They were there for around 18 months, by which time we had to ask a *huissier* to take action and have them evicted. This took a lot of time and money. They left the house looking as if it had been used by tramps, with piles of rubbish everywhere; they even left their wedding photographs (we'd given them plenty of time to clear their belongings). Everything was damaged. It took several trips to the local tip to clear the mess, and then we had to completely redecorate, which took four weeks. The *huissier* said he had never seen anything like it.

The next time, we asked the *huissier* to arrange the letting. By this time, the village *épicerie* had gone bankrupt and the owner, the sister of the original tenant, wanted to rent the house. The *huissier*, however, refused to handle the letting if we took her as a tenant, as she had a long history of bad debt. This was rather embarrassing, as we'd known them for a long time. The property was eventually let to another single mother with three children who are excellent tenants. The *huissier* charged 10 per cent and handled everything.

John Gibson-Thompson

TOP TEN TIPS FOR LONG-TERM LETTING

- Choose the right type of property in an appropriate location, bearing in mind that you may need to sell if you cannot find tenants.
- Take legal advice, particularly when letting commercial property.
- Familiarise yourself with the legal aspects of the relevant type of letting.
- Make sure you know what's involved if letting unfurnished: be aware of the stringent legislation and be absolutely sure that you're prepared to tie up your property (and investment) on a long-term lease.

- Make sure that short-term tenants of furnished property have a principal residence elsewhere.

- Seriously consider using an agent to manage long-term unfurnished lets – they're professionals in this legal minefield!

- Be prepared to deal with problem tenants and be aware of the steps you can take to deal with them.

- Budget carefully: err on the pessimistic side and allow for vacant periods.

- Make sure you're familiar with the rules for declaring tax on your rental income (see **Chapter 6**).

- Take the advice of your insurance company on security and safety matters.

5.

YOUR HOME AS BUSINESS PREMISES

Business premises (*locaux*) in many parts of France are expensive, particularly those in prime locations. The majority of premises are available on a leasehold (*cession de bail* or simply *cession*) basis only and, as well as paying for the lease, you must pay a monthly rent. Freehold premises are rare – and those at a reasonable price, even rarer! Given the high prices, it isn't surprising that using your home as business premises is an increasingly popular option. **There are, however, strict regulations regarding what sort of business you can set up in your home and (being France) there's plenty of paperwork involved as well.**

This chapter examines the advantages and disadvantages of using your home as your business premises, outlines the rules and regulations that apply, and suggests some ideas for a home-based business.

ADVANTAGES & DISADVANTAGES

Among the many advantages of working from home are a more flexible lifestyle and the saving of time and money commuting and renting business premises. On the other hand, it's sometimes difficult to find motivation to get down to work among all the household distractions, you're limited by law as to what type of business you can run (see below) and clients may take your business less seriously if they must visit you in your home rather than in an office.

RULES & REGULATIONS

Under French law you cannot set up and open just any business in your home: there are extensive regulations concerning what you're permitted to do. Many of these are designed with neighbours in mind and start from the proviso that a residential area is first and foremost somewhere people live rather than work. Activities that interfere with 'normal' life – i.e. anything that causes excessive noise or pollution or is a danger to neighbouring properties – are therefore strictly controlled. Unless your business is limited to you, your telephone and your computer, in which case there are no restrictions, you must be aware of the following regulations.

Whether or not you can run certain businesses from home depends on your neighbours' and, ultimately, the courts' interpretation of what constitutes a nuisance; even a beauty salon or a language academy may be unacceptable in some residential areas. There are, however, many areas where similar home businesses thrive.

When considering whether to set up a business at home, bear your neighbours in mind. If they're the sort that object to the noise made by your children playing in the garden, the chances are that they will be unlikely to tolerate a business in your home. In any case, it's best to avoid business activities that cause noise or those that take place outside normal working hours, which are generally 8am to 8pm Mondays to Fridays. Always check with the town hall whether a home business activity is permitted.

Premises

Unless you already have a designated area in your home for your business, you must probably adapt the property in some way. If this involves any building or conversion work (e.g. an extension or enclosing a terraced area) covering more than 20m² or a change to the use of a building or part of a building (e.g. an attic or barn), you will need a building licence from your local council.

Qualifications & Experience

The most important qualification for working (and living) in France is the ability to speak French fluently. Once you've overcome this hurdle, you should establish whether your trade or professional qualifications and experience are recognised in France. If you're seeking employment, but aren't experienced, French employers expect studies to be in a relevant discipline and to have included work experience (*stage*). Professional or trade qualifications are required to work in most fields in France, where qualifications are also often necessary to be self-employed or start a business. It isn't just a matter of hanging up a sign and waiting for the stampede of customers to your door.

> ## WARNING
> Before starting a business or self-employment, you must make sure that you're legally qualified to carry out your chosen activity in France. The labour market is highly regulated, and restrictions apply to many occupations, not only to 'professional' activities such as being a doctor or lawyer. For example, you must provide proof of qualifications or experience to work as an estate agent, a travel agent, a food producer, a builder or in any of the manual trades or crafts. Depending on your occupation, you may have to obtain authorisation from your *préfecture*, or a *carte professionnelle* (card showing your membership of a profession), a licence to operate, or you may have to register with the appropriate professional body. Many foreign traders are also required to undergo a 'business' course before they can start work in France.

It isn't possible to detail the requirements of every profession here; for information on your particular activity, consult your local *centre de formalités des entreprises* or the appropriate French professional body or trade organisation. You will find their addresses and contact numbers in the directory of the Mouvement des Entreprises de France (MEDEF); for a list of offices where you can consult this directory, go to the MEDEF website (🖳 www.medef.fr/staging/site/page/php?pag_id+2003).

Theoretically, qualifications recognised by professional and trade bodies in one EU country should be recognised in France. However, recognition varies from country to country and in some cases foreign qualifications aren't recognised by French employers or professional and trade associations. All academic qualifications should also be recognised, although they may be given less prominence than equivalent French qualifications, depending on the country and the educational establishment. A ruling by the European Court in 1992 declared that where EU examinations are of a similar standard with just certain areas of difference, individuals should be required to take exams only in those areas.

Certain professions are 'regulated', which means that qualifications obtained in one EU country are valid in another, but you must check that you satisfy the required conditions in terms of qualifications and experience to carry out the activity you've chosen. Regulated professions are broadly those in the fields of architecture, law, medicine and transport. Some are covered by what's called a 'sectoral directive', which means that those with the relevant qualification can exercise their profession freely in any EU state. These include architects, dentists, doctors, midwives, nurses, pharmacists, surgeons and veterinary surgeons. Other regulated professions are covered by a 'general directive' (including most recognised trades), which means that you must check with the relevant French government department or professional body (e.g. the Conseil National de l'Ordre des Architectes, 🖳 www.architectes.org, for architects) that your qualifications are acceptable.

Other occupations are unregulated ('non-regulated' in EU-speak), but you must still register your occupation and be assigned an official status (*statut* or *régime*) , e.g. itinerant tradesmen, estate agent, driving instructor; it's illegal simply to hang up a sign and start business. Acceptance of your status may depend on the assessment of your qualifications and training by individual employers or trade associations. In such cases, you must contact the Chambre de Métiers, the Chambre d'Agriculture or the Chambre de Commerce in the department where you plan to work. You can obtain the address of the relevant body from your local town hall. For information about French Chambers of Commerce contact the Assemblée des Chambres Françaises de Commerce et d'Industrie/APCFCI, 45 avenue d'Iéna, Paris 75016 (☎ 01 53 57 17 00, 💻 www.acfci.cci.fr – available in English). All EU member states issue occupation information sheets containing a common job description with a table of qualifications. These cover a large number of trades and are intended to help someone with the relevant qualifications look for a job in another EU country.

British craftspeople wishing to practise in France can apply to have their experience certified under the UK Certificate of Experience scheme. Contact the Certification Unit, Department of Trade and Industry Trade Policy Europe Branch, Second Floor, 212 Kingsgate House, 66–74 Victoria Street, London SW1E 6SW (☎ 020-7215 4454/4648). Applicants are charged a non-refundable processing fee of around £105 and £45 for a certified translation.

For further information about equivalent qualifications you can contact the Centre d'Études et de Recherche sur les Qualifications (CEREQ), 11 rue Vauquelin, 75005 Paris (☎ 01 44 08 69 10, 💻 www.cereq.fr) or ENIC-NARIC, run by the European Network of Information Centres and the National Academic Recognition Information Centre (💻 www.enic-naric.net). NARIC in the UK doesn't deal directly with individuals, although its website (💻 www.naric.org.uk) will provide you with most of the basic information.

Another source of information about qualifications is the EU website (💻 http://europa.eu.int/eures). Choose 'en' for English and click on 'Living and Working', choose 'France', then 'Living and Working Conditions' and finally, under 'Working Conditions', 'Recognition of Diplomas and Qualifications'.

Further information can be obtained from the Bureau de l'Information sur les Systèmes Educatifs et de la Reconnaissance de Diplômes of the Ministère de la Jeunesse, de l'Education Nationale et de la Recherche, 110 rue de Grenelle, 75357 Paris Cedex 07 (☎ 01 40 65 65 90) and from the Département des Affaires Internationales de l'Enseignement Supérieure, 61–65 rue Dutot, 75015 Paris (☎ 01 40 65 66 19).

A useful booklet, *Europe Open for Professionals*, is available from the UK Department for Education and Skills (☎ 0114-259 4151).

Community Regulations

If your property is part of a community of property owners – and most properties apart from homes on public streets and rural plots are – you must consult the community statutes to find out if you're allowed to operate a business from your home. Even if the statutes don't specifically prohibit businesses within the community, it's wise to obtain permission beforehand. You can take your proposal to the community's Annual General Meeting, where you should explain your plans as fully as possible and be prepared to answer questions. Above all, your neighbours need assurance that your business will cause negligible disruption; if you can give them this (and they have no reason to discriminate against you), they will probably approve your proposal.

SURVIVAL TIP
Obtain approval from your community
before you set up to ensure that you and your business
start off in your neighbours' good books.

BUSINESS IDEAS

In spite of the above restrictions regarding permission and qualifications, there are many businesses that can be legally run from a home with little, if any red tape. The following is a list of ideas:

● **Computer-based Businesses** – Since the advent of email, businesses such as website design and publishing services can be run from almost anywhere in the world. Check that your home has (or can have) a telephone and broadband internet connection (see **Business Communications** on page 246).

● **Financial & Legal Services** – Accounting, financial advisory and legal services can easily be set up in a home, although you're required to register with the relevant professional association.

● **Health Services** – If your qualifications are recognised (see page 199) and you don't intend to install any dangerous machinery (e.g. an X-ray machine), you can usually set up a small health practice (e.g. a general practice, physiotherapy or chiropractic clinic) in your home with few restrictions. Make sure there's adequate parking.

● **Private Classes** – Teaching one-to-one or in small groups (e.g. a maximum of four) is generally permitted in a private home. Music teachers must be aware of potential objections from neighbours, particularly if your home is an apartment or your pupils are learning to play percussion or the trumpet.

For further details of working from home, refer to *Making a Living in France* (Survival Books – see page 317).

LETTING A ROOM

Letting a room in a property is an option worth considering, particularly in cities with universities and business or language schools. For some people, e.g. students and employees on short-term contracts, renting a room is a cheaper and more convenient option than renting a bedsit or studio flat.

Advantages & Disadvantages

Letting a room allows you to make use of otherwise empty space, provides a small income, keeps you in control of your property and gives you the chance to meet interesting people. On the other hand, if you have lodgers in your home, you lose part of your privacy, it can be difficult to go away (unless you have a completely trustworthy lodger) and you may not get on with your lodgers.

Type of Accommodation

The type of accommodation you offer obviously depends on the space you have available in your home. If you let a bedroom only, it's best to let one with an ensuite bathroom, as this provides more privacy for you and for your lodger. Unless your lodger wants to socialise with the other members of the household and you want to socialise with him, it's wise to include a sitting area within the bedroom, e.g. armchair and television.

If your property has a separate studio or guest apartment, e.g. in the basement or an outbuilding, this is ideal for lodgers who want as much independence as possible. Note, however, that if the area has a separate entrance and kitchen and is so large that the tenant doesn't need to use any of the communal areas in your home, this would be classed as separate accommodation, you would be classed as a landlord and you would therefore be bound by long-term letting regulations (see **Chapter 4**).

Type of Board & Services

The type of board you plan to offer should be one of your first considerations. The options are as follows:

- **Lodging Only** – This is the least common option and limits your letting potential.

- **Self-catering** – For this option you must obviously provide a separate kitchen or allow the lodger access to yours, in which case you must also provide cupboard and fridge space and, preferably, establish some house

204 Your Home as Business Premises

rules, such as when the lodger can use the kitchen and how he should clean up afterwards.

- **Half- or Full-board** – If you provide meals, they should be varied and of a reasonable standard. If you aren't prepared to prepare certain types of food (e.g. meat or vegan food), you should state this on your marketing material. Providing meals increases your income and your letting potential, but means that you're tied to the house at certain times of the day and for most of the week.

- **Laundry** – Some owners provide a laundry service for lodgers (if you offer lodging to language school students, the accommodation agreement may include a laundry service). If the lodger is in charge of his own washing, you must agree times for the use of a washing machine and, if applicable, tumble drier.

Finding Tenants

Your two main markets for letting a room are students and employees on temporary or short-term contracts.

Most cities have universities, many have business schools and most large towns and cities have numerous language schools. There are various ways of marketing your services, such as advertising on notice boards in university departments and halls of residence (*résidences universitaires*), leaving your contact details with the accommodation department, and advertising in the local press.

Many large language schools, particularly those attached to universities, offer single-term, as well as annual, courses and are therefore excellent sources of short-term lodgers. Language schools may have minimum requirements for accommodation and may wish to inspect your home beforehand. Language students who choose this option usually want to live in a family environment with the opportunity to practise the language they're learning (usually French).

The best ways to attract employees are to advertise in the local press and contact large companies in your area.

Internet

The internet is a valuable marketing tool and there are several specialist websites, including the following:

- 💻 www.abc-etudiant.com – This site contains accommodation advertisements for university students in university towns across France.
- 💻 www.lindic.fr – A useful site that lists student accommodation in most of France.

- 💻 www.capcampus.com – This site advertises apartments, rooms, houses, studio flats, etc. for student accommodation throughout France.

Vetting Tenants

One of the main disadvantages of letting a room is that you're allowing a stranger to stay in your home and come and go as he pleases. It's therefore vitally important to vet tenants thoroughly beforehand. You should, if possible, ask for references. If the lodger is employed, get a reference from his employer. In the case of students, obtaining a reference is more difficult, but try to obtain one from their previous place of study or, if this is impossible, obtain the address of their normal residence. Banks are also a useful source of references.

If your room is on a language school accommodation list, it may be impossible to vet students beforehand and you probably won't know who the lodger is until he arrives. If this is the case, make sure you agree a procedure with the language school should the tenant turn out to be dishonest, irresponsible or impossible to live with.

Contracts

You're strongly advised to draw up your own 'rules' in the form of a written contract, signed by you and the tenant. This helps to avoid misunderstandings and provide legal proof of the agreement if there are any problems. A written agreement should include at least the following:

- How much the rental is and when it should be paid.
- What services (if any) you're providing for the lodger.
- How much notice should be given when either party wishes to terminate the rental agreement.
- How other bills are to be paid (but note that most lodgers expect their rental payments to cover all utility bills except the telephone).

House Rules

As you're allowing the lodger to use your home and its facilities, it makes life easier for both parties if you agree a basic set of 'house rules'. It's important to strike a balance between too many rules (you aren't the lodger's parent!) and too few, but prevention is always better and easier than cure. House rules might cover the following:

- Security measures the lodger needs to observe, e.g. double locking the front door when leaving the property.

- Which areas of the house the tenant is allowed to use and when.
- Cleaning and tidying up. Decide how tidy you expect the lodger to be and base your rules on this. If you're providing full board, you're usually expected to clean the lodger's room and do his laundry.
- Guests. Do you allow the lodger to invite guests to the house? If so, how many and may they stay the night?
- Noise, e.g. no TV or radio after 11pm.
- Use of the telephone. Telephone companies send out itemised bills so it's easy to work out how much your lodger's calls cost, but you must keep a notebook by the phone for him to record the date and time of calls. Some owners allow lodgers to receive calls only (*service restreint*).

What to Charge

How much you charge for letting a room depends greatly on the services you offer and the extras (e.g. internet access) you provide. Rates for rooms let on a self-catering basis range from €200 to over €500 per month.

Taxation

All rental income from letting a room is subject to income tax at the usual rate for residents (see **Chapter 5**) and should be declared on your annual tax return. You're exempted from tax on the whole of the income if:

- The rooms let are the tenant's principal residence, or the tenants are receiving *RMI* (unemployment benefit) or are students on grants, or the accommodation is let through a recognised organisation.
- The accommodation reaches minimum standards of habitability.
- The annual rent doesn't exceed a certain limit (which varies according to location).

Many owners don't declare income from letting a room, which is often paid in cash, but this is, of course, illegal.

TOP FIVE TIPS FOR A HOME BUSINESS

- Check and double-check local regulations before you do anything.
- Get consent from your community first.
- Keep in your neighbours' good books once you set up.
- Keep noise levels down.

- Discipline yourself to work set hours and to take national holidays.

TOP FIVE TIPS FOR LETTING A ROOM

- Remember that taking a lodger means giving up some of your privacy.
- Find out as much as possible about the lodger before committing yourself.
- Always have a written agreement with your lodger.
- Establish house rules from the start and make sure you both keep to them.
- Self-catering is the option with the least ties for you.

6.

TAX

An important consideration for anyone letting property in France is taxation, which includes property tax, income tax, value added tax (VAT) and capital gains tax – all discussed in this chapter. Note that letting tax (*contribution sur les revenus locatifs*) was abolished in 2005.

Whether you're a French resident or not, you must pay tax in France on all income from property letting, irrespective of any double-taxation or other agreements. Before buying a property for letting, you should obtain expert advice regarding French taxes. This will (hopefully) ensure that you take maximum advantage of your current tax status and that you don't make any mistakes that you will regret later.

Firstly, you must decide whether you're going to let your property furnished or unfurnished, as very different tax rules apply (in addition to different rules and regulations regarding leases – see **Chapter 4**). The principal distinction is that the letting of unfurnished property is classed as a civil activity, whereas letting furnished premises (including bed and breakfast and *gîte* accommodation) is regarded as a business activity; therefore income from it is taxed as business income.

As you would expect in a country with millions of bureaucrats, the French tax system is inordinately complicated and most French people don't understand it. It's difficult to obtain accurate information from the tax authorities and, just when you think you have it cracked, the authorities change the rules or hit you with a new tax. Taxes are levied at national and local levels.

You must complete tax form 2042 (the main tax form) and 2042C for the declaration of letting income. If you have income from outside France, you may be required to complete other forms (e.g. 2047 for the details of your foreign income and 3916 for foreign bank account information). You can now complete your tax returns online (💻 www.impots.gouv.fr) and even earn a concession of €20 if you opt to pay by direct debit (monthly or quarterly).

Late payment of any tax bill usually incurs a surcharge of ten per cent, but there's a five-year statute of limitations on the collection of back taxes: i.e. if no action has been taken during this period to collect unpaid tax, it cannot be collected.

DOMICILE

You're domiciled, and therefore tax resident, in France if **any** of the following applies:

- You live there for 183 days or more each fiscal year.
- Your spouse and family live there for 183 days or more per year.

- You derive the majority of your income from French sources – e.g. if you're retired and your *gîte* business earns more than your UK pension, you're classed as domiciled and tax resident in France, even if you live in the UK!

Residents

As a French resident, you must declare to the French tax authorities all your income, wherever it originates and wherever it's paid. Note that you won't necessarily be sent a tax form – it's your responsibility to obtain, complete and return a tax form, normally before the end of April; ignorance is no excuse!

Non-residents

If you aren't normally resident in France (see above) you must still declare any letting income and pay tax on it in France. **Recently, the tax authorities have been checking on foreign-owned properties in search of undeclared revenue.** If you don't complete a tax return, there are penalties. Overdue tax gathers interest at 0.75 per cent per month, and if you file late there's a penalty of 10 per cent rising to 40 per cent if you fail to respond within 30 days of the first reminder. If a second reminder is sent and ignored, the penalty can rise to 80 per cent.

Non-resident property owners who receive an income from a French source must file a tax return, *Déclaration des Revenus*, no. 2042/2042C, available from local tax offices in France or French consulates abroad. Completed forms must be sent to the Centre des Impôts de Non-Résidents (9 rue d'Uzès, 75094 Paris Cedex 02, ☎ 01 44 76 18 00) before 30th April each year. It's wise to keep a copy of your return and send it by registered post (so that there's no dispute over whether it was received).

Some months after filing you receive a tax assessment detailing the tax due. There are penalties for late filing and non-declaration, which can result in fines, high interest charges and even imprisonment. The French tax authorities can impose tax on 52 weeks' letting income and cancel your entitlement to tax deductions in the future. **The tax authorities have many ways of detecting people letting homes and not paying tax and have been clamping down on tax evaders in recent years.**

Non-residents must declare any income received in France on their tax return in their country of residence, but tax on French letting income is normally paid only in France (see **Double-taxation Treaties** below). However, if you pay less tax in France than you would have paid in your home country, you must usually pay the difference there. On the other hand, if you pay more tax in France than you would have paid on the income in your home country, you aren't entitled to a refund.

If you're a non-resident of France for tax purposes and own residential property there that's available for your use, you're liable for French income tax on the basis of a deemed rental income equal to three times the real rental value of the property. This is usually calculated to be 5 per cent of its capital value. There are, however, exceptions, e.g. if you have French source income that exceeds this level or if you're protected by a double-taxation treaty (see below). Consult a tax accountant to clarify your position.

If you're a British national, information can be obtained from the centre for non-residents in the UK (☎ 0151-210 2222, 🖥 www.inlandrevenue. gov.uk/cnr).

Double-taxation Treaties

Double-taxation treaties mean that citizens of most countries are exempt from paying taxes in their home country when they spend a minimum period abroad, e.g. a year. According to the Convention for the Avoidance of Double Taxation and the Prevention of Fiscal Evasion, France has double-taxation treaties with over 70 countries, including all members of the European Union (EU), Australia, Canada, China, India, Israel, Japan, New Zealand, Pakistan, the Philippines, Singapore, Sri Lanka, Switzerland and the US. Treaties are designed to ensure that income that has already been taxed in one treaty country isn't taxed again in another treaty country. The treaty establishes a tax credit or exemption on certain kinds of income, either in the country of residence or the country where the income is earned. Where applicable, a double-taxation treaty prevails over domestic law. The US is the only country that taxes its non-resident citizens on income earned abroad, although there are exclusions on foreign-earned income (around $76,000 per spouse). If you're in doubt about your tax liability in your home country, contact your nearest embassy or consulate in France.

TAX REGIMES

For individuals with income from letting property there are essentially two tax regimes, depending on the type of property, the level of income and the status of the owner:

- 'Mini'-regime (*micro*) – known as a 'forfeit basis' regime, which means that you forfeit the right to claim actual expenses in exchange for a fixed deduction (which you hope is more than your actual expenses!). This is subdivided into:
  - *Micro-BIC* for furnished property.
  - *Micro-foncier* for unfurnished property.

- 'Real' regime (*régime réel*) – whereby you claim actual expenses. This is subdivided into:
  - Simplified real regime (*regime réel simplifié*), for businesses with a low turnover.
  - Normal real regime (*regime réel simplifié*), for businesses with a higher turnover.

Furnished Letting

You must pay tax on all furnished letting income (subject to the usual allowances and deductions) unless you let or sublet part of your principal residence (i.e. if you let a room or rooms in your home – see page 203).

Régime Micro-BIC

If you receive property income of less than €76,300 per year, you can opt for the *Micro-BIC* tax regime (*BIC* stands for *bénéfices industriels et commerciaux*) and qualify for a 72 per cent tax deduction to cover expenses, paying tax on only 28 per cent of the total income. This regime is obviously beneficial if your actual profit exceeds 28 per cent of income after expenses. It's a simple system: no formal records have to be kept, just a simple account of receipts with dates. You file one tax return a year giving your gross rental income. If you opt for the *régime micro-BIC*, you're tied to it for five years, provided your income doesn't exceed the threshold during that time.

If you're resident in the UK, and your actual profit is more than 28 per cent, take advice when filling in a UK tax return, as the *Micro-BIC* forfeit system isn't recognised by the British tax authorities and you could find yourself taxed twice.

Note also that you cannot show a loss – there will always be a taxable profit – and you cannot use the *régime micro-BIC* if you purchased your property using an *SCI* (see page 216).

 If an *SCI* lets furnished property, it's classed as a commercial activity and you cannot use the *micro-BIC* tax regime.

Régime Réel

The *régime réel* is sub-divided into *simplifié* and *normal*, the difference between the two being the level of gross income. If your gross letting income exceeds €76,300, but is less than €763,000 excluding VAT (*TVA*), you **must** be registered as *régime réel simplifié*. If your gross letting income is below €76,300, you can choose to register under this system rather than *Micro-BIC* (see above), but it would be to your advantage only if the costs incurred on your property exceeded 72 per cent of your rental income. If you have a choice, you must opt in to the *régime simplifié* before 1st February of the tax year and remain opted in for a minimum of two years.

There are some tax advantages of this system over the *micro-BIC* regime: you can offset any annual losses against other income, e.g. a salary; and a tax loss can be carried forward for the next five years and offset against other furnished rental income or business activity.

Régime réel simplifié: Under this system, you deduct from your rental income the actual costs incurred on the property and must provide all invoices relating to these costs. You must prepare accounts quarterly.

Régime réel normal: If your letting income exceeds €763,000 (lucky you!), you **must** use this system, which requires the services of an accountant.

Property owners are eligible for deductions on income of expenses such as repairs, maintenance, security and cleaning costs, mortgage interest payments, management and letting expenses (e.g. advertising), local taxes and insurance fees. There's also an allowance to cover depreciation. Capital expenses (e.g. installation of a swimming pool) aren't deductible.

If you live in the property for part of the year, only a proportion of charges can be deducted. For instance if you let the property for 13 weeks, you can deduct only 25 per cent of the expenses above. You should seek professional advice to ensure that you're claiming everything to which you're entitled; contact your local tax office (don't rely on your accountant).

Unfurnished Letting

Unfurnished letting income comes under a different tax regime and is classified as property rental revenue (*revenu foncier*).

Régime Micro-foncier

If your income is below €15,000, you can opt for the *régime micro-foncier*, by which you benefit from a fixed expense rate of 40 per cent; e.g. you pay tax on 60 per cent of turnover. This is obviously beneficial if your expenses are less than 40 per cent of turnover.

Régime Réel

If your income is below €15,000, but your profit is less than 40 per cent of turnover, you can opt for the *régime réel* and declare your actual expenses. If your income is over €15,000, you **must** be registered as *régime réel*. Deductions allowed are the same as for furnished rental, i.e. repairs and maintenance, improvements, management expenses, mortgage interest payments, local taxes, insurance. You may also claim a deduction of 14 per cent of gross rental to cover depreciation.

INCOME TAX

If you're non-resident in France, you're taxed at the flat rate of 25 per cent on your rental income (less any deductions or allowances). If you're resident (or domiciled – see page 210) in France, your letting income is added to any other taxable income you have and is then taxed at the following rates (2005 income):

Taxable Income (€)	Tax Rate (%)	Tax (€)	Aggregate Tax (€)
Up to 4,262	0	0.00	0.00
4,262 – 8,382	6.83	281.40	281.40
8,382 – 14,753	19.14	1,219.41	1,500.81
14,753 – 23,888	28.26	2,581.55	4,082.36
23,888 – 38,868	37.38	5,599.52	9,681.88
38,868 – 47,932	42.62	3,863.08	13,544.96
Over 47,932	48.09		

The taxable unit is the household. The figures above are for each 'part': a single person is one part; a married couple is two parts; if there are any children, the first two have 0.5 of a part each, any further children one part each. For example, a family with three children will add up to four parts. The total household income is split across those four parts, each of which is separately taxed according to the bands in the table above, the sum of these being added together to result in the amount of tax payable. If our theoretical family's income totals €48,000, it will be taxed on €12,000 four times, the amount of tax due being calculated as follows:

0 percent of the first €4,334	=	€0
6.83 per cent of the next €4,190	=	€286
19.14 per cent of the next €3,476	=	€665
Total €951 x 4	=	**€3,805**

By way of comparison, a couple with no children earning the same amount will be taxed on €24,000 twice, as follows (a big incentive to procreate!):

0 percent of the first €4,334	= €0
6.83 per cent of the next €4,190	= €286
19.14 per cent of the next €6,480	= €1,240
28.26 per cent of the next €8,996	= €2,542
Total €4,068 x 2	**= €8,136**

Further information on French income tax can be found on the Service des Impôts website (🖥 www.impotrevenu.com) and in *Living and Working in France* (Survival Books – see page 317).

Société Civile Immobilière

Many people, especially from the UK, buy their property as a *société civile immobilière* (*SCI*) in order to circumvent French inheritance laws. An *SCI* is a company, usually with family members as shareholders. In France, an *SCI* is a transparent entity for tax purposes, which means that the shareholders are taxed as individuals. If an *SCI* lets furnished property, however, it's classed as a commercial entity and cannot use the *Micro-BIC* tax regime (see page 212). Furthermore the UK and French tax authorities differ on the status of the *SCI*, the Inland Revenue regarding it as a company, which may lead to double taxation.

> **SURVIVAL TIP**
> There's great confusion on this point at present, so it's very important to take proper legal advice (in France and in your home country) before buying property to let through an *SCI*.

PROPERTY TAXES

Taxe d'habitation (residential tax) and *taxe foncière* (property tax) are roughly similar to community tax (rates) in the UK, funding local services and including a contribution towards regional and departmental expenses. They're both based on a notional rental value of the property (*valeur locative cadastrale*), i.e. the assumed value of the property if it were let on the open market, which obviously varies according to the size and type of the property and its location. The rates calculated are set by region, department and commune, and vary enormously from one place to another, generally higher in towns and cities and lower in rural areas and villages, although rates don't necessarily reflect the salubrity of the location: St Germain-des-

Prés, which is one of the most expensive suburbs of Paris, has some of the lowest property tax rates!

Tax rates rise each year. (An overall review of prices was last carried out in 1974 – if the tax authorities were to update their survey again, the resulting figures would probably be a nasty shock for many taxpayers!)

Taxe Foncière

Taxe foncière is payable by the person who's the owner of the property on 1st January. It's divided into two parts, for developed and undeveloped land (*le bâti* and *le non-bâti*). Any development (e.g. conversion, installation of a pool, change of use) must be reported to the tax authorities – so that they can increase your tax!

The amount payable varies by up to 500 per cent with the region, and even between towns or villages within the same region, and may be as little as €300 or as much as €1,500 per year, although there are plans to make the application of the tax 'fairer'. (Strangely, the Paris area has some of the country's lowest rates.)

Taxe d'Habitation

Taxe d'habitation is payable by the occupier of a property (who may or may not be the owner) on 1st January of each year, irrespective of whether he's staying in the property on that date. If the property is furnished, has water and electricity supplies and is available for occupation, the tax is payable.

 Even if you vacate or sell a property on 2nd January, you must pay residential tax for the whole year and have no right to reclaim part of it from a new owner.

Residential tax is levied by the town where the property is located and varies by as much as 400 per cent from town to town. As with *taxe foncière* (see above), the Paris area has some of the country's lowest rates. Generally, you should expect to pay around half the amount paid in *taxe foncière*. Residential tax is usually payable in the autumn of the year to which it applies.

If you have a *gîte* registered with Gîtes de France (or another official organisation), you may be exempt from this tax if the *gîte* is part of the property that's your principal residence (e.g. an outbuilding on the same site as your house).

TAXE PROFESSIONELLE

Taxe professionelle is normally payable by individuals and companies carrying out non-salaried work. It's levied at between around 15 and 20 per cent (the exact percentage varies with the commune) of a 'base', which is currently 8 per cent of your annual income, including VAT. For example, if you earn €30,000 per year, your tax base will be €2,400; if *taxe professionelle* is levied at 20 per cent in your commune, you will pay €480 per year.

Taxe professionelle is assessed as follows: in your first year of French residence, you pay nothing; in your second year, you pay according to your earnings in Year 1 (pro rata if you moved to France part way through the year); in Year 3, your tax is again based on your Year 1 earnings, in Year 4 on your Year 2 earnings, and so on.

A *gîte* owner is exempt if the property is registered with Gîtes de France or another official organisation, e.g. Clévacances or the Comité Départemental de Tourisme. Exemption also applies where the property is your principal residence, provided the rental is 'reasonable'. In effect, most bed & breakfast (B&B), *gîte* and letting businesses aren't liable for *taxe professionelle*, but check with your accountant or local *trésor publique*.

TAXE DE SEJOUR

The local commune may charge you a 'holiday tax' (*taxe de séjour*) for each paying guest. The commune fixes the rate of tax, which varies from €0.20 to €1.50 per person per night according to the standard of accommodation. This might sound like a small sum, but if you have eight people staying for a week at the higher rate it adds up to a not insubstantial €84; multiply this by 30 weeks and your annual bill will amount to €2,520. Children under a certain age (check the age limit locally) aren't counted, and there may be concessions for French families on certain social benefits and those paying with *chèques-vacances* (see page 105). The tariff will be available to consult at your *mairie*. Some communes charge a lump sum per year.

Find out from your *mairie* whether or not this tax is applicable in your commune – ignorance is no excuse for not paying! It's up to your *mairie* to charge you, but you will have to declare how many 'people nights' you've let. The tax is paid to your local *trésor public*, usually found in your *canton* capital.

VALUE ADDED TAX

Unfurnished rentals are generally exempt from VAT (*taxe sur la valeur ajoutée/ TVA*). Furnished rentals are also exempt if you're operating under the *micro-BIC* tax regime (see page 213). If your income exceeds €76,300 and are consequently not eligible for the *micro-BIC* scheme, your income may be subject to VAT. This applies if you offer 'hotel' services, namely three or more of the following:

- Bed linen.
- Reception.
- Daily cleaning.
- Breakfasts.

This means that a B&B business (generating over €76,300) is almost certainly subject to VAT and must therefore charge its clients VAT, whereas most *gîte* businesses are exempt.

If your business is subject to VAT, the accommodation itself is taxed at 5.5 per cent and other services (e.g. meals) at 19.6 per cent.

```
SURVIVAL TIP
You should take advice from an accountant as to
whether you're required to register for VAT.
```

CAPITAL GAINS TAX

Capital gains tax (*impôt sur les plus-values*) is payable on the profit from sales of certain assets in France, including property worth over €15,000 – i.e. anything other than a caravan! (Income tax treaties usually provide that capital gains on property are taxable in the country where the property is located.) Gains net of capital gains tax (CGT) are added to other income and are liable to income tax (see above). If you're a French resident, capital gains are also subject to social security contributions at 8 per cent. Changes to the capital gains regulations were made in the Finance Act, 2004, which also requires a *notaire* handling a property sale to calculate and pay CGT on behalf of the vendor.

Principal Residence

CGT isn't payable on a profit made on the sale of your principal residence in France, provided that you've occupied it since its purchase (or for at least five years if you didn't occupy it immediately after purchase). You're also exempt from CGT if you're forced to sell for family or professional reasons, e.g. the death of a bankrupt relative.

If you move to France permanently and retain a home abroad, this may affect your position regarding capital gains. If you sell your foreign home before moving to France, you're exempt from CGT, as it's your principal residence. However, if you establish your principal residence in France, the foreign property becomes a second home and is thus liable to CGT when it's sold. **EU tax authorities co-operate in tracking down CGT dodgers.**

Second Homes

Capital gains on second homes in France worth over €15,000 are payable by residents and non-residents up to 15 years after purchase (until 2004, the period was 22 years). The basic rates of CGT are 26 per cent for residents, 16 per cent for non-resident EU citizens, and 33.3 per cent for non-resident non-EU citizens. Any inheritance or gift tax paid at the time of purchase is taken into account when determining the purchase price, and there are certain exemptions to the above tax rates, as follows:

● If you've owned a property for more than five years, but less than 15, you're entitled to a 10 per cent reduction in CGT for every year of ownership over five (i.e. 10 per cent for six years' ownership, 20 per cent for seven years', etc.).

● If you've owned a property for at least five years and can produce proof of substantial expenditure on improving it (e.g. receipts for work done by professionals), you can claim a further deduction of 15 per cent of the property's purchase price against CGT (irrespective of the actual cost of the work), but you're no longer entitled to claim for work you've done yourself, nor any materials purchased for DIY improvements.

However, the purchase price of a property is no longer 'indexed' to increases in the cost of living. Note also that, if you make a loss on the sale of a second home, you cannot claim this against other CGT payments, nor against income tax!

Before a sale, the *notaire* prepares a form calculating the tax due and appoints an agent (*agent fiscal accrédité*) or guarantor to act on your behalf concerning tax. If the transaction is straightforward, the local tax office may grant a dispensation (*dispense*) of the need to appoint a guarantor, provided you apply **before** completion of the sale. If you obtain a dispensation, the proceeds of the sale can be released to you in full after CGT has been paid. The *notaire* handling the sale must apply for the dispensation and must declare and pay CGT on your behalf; you're no longer required to make a CGT declaration.

SOCIAL SECURITY CONTRIBUTIONS

France has a comprehensive social security (*sécurité sociale*) system covering healthcare (plus sickness and maternity care), injuries at work, family allowances, unemployment insurance, and old age (pensions), invalidity and death benefits. It's a generous and generally excellent system – social security benefits are among the highest in the EU, the average household receiving around a third of its income from social support payments such as family allowances, state benefits and pensions – but, for this reason, it's **very** expensive. France has one of the highest levels of social security contributions in the EU: over 30 per cent of GDP is spent on 'welfare'.

Total contributions per employee (to around 15 funds) average around 60 per cent of gross pay, some 60 per cent of which is paid by employers (an increasing impediment to hiring staff). The self-employed must pay the full amount. The good news is that, with the exception of sickness benefits, social security benefits aren't taxed.

French social security is an extremely complex subject, and the following is the briefest summary of relevant aspects of it. For further information, refer to *Living and Working in France* (Survival Books – see page 317). There are also a number of books (in French) about social security, including *Tous les Droits de l'Assuré Social* (VO Editions), and consumer magazines regularly publish supplements on various aspects of social security, particularly pensions and health insurance. Some information is available in English on the Service Public website (🖥 www.service-public.fr) and the Assurance Maladie site (🖥 www.ameli.fr – it stands for Assurance Maladie en ligne!).

Registration

If you're working in France, you must register at your local social security office (Caisse Primaire d'Assurance Maladie/CPAM). Your town hall will give you the address of your local CPAM or you can find it under *Sécurité Sociale* in your local yellow pages.

You must provide your personal details, including your full name, address, country of origin, and date and place of birth. You must also produce passports, *cartes de séjour* and certified birth certificates for your dependants, plus a marriage certificate (if applicable). You may need to provide copies with official translations, but check first, as translations may be unnecessary. You also need proof of residence such as a rental contract or an electricity bill. When you've registered, you receive a permanent registration card (*carte d'assurance maladie*, now called a *Carte Vitale*), which looks like a credit card and contains an electronic chip (*puce*) and a certificate (*attestation*) containing a list of those entitled to benefits on your behalf (*bénéficiaires*), i.e. your dependants, and the address of the office where you must apply for reimbursement of your medical expenses.

Contributions

Social security contributions (*cotisations sociales* or *charges sociales*) are calculated as a percentage of your taxable income, although for certain contributions there's a maximum salary level. Note that contributions start as soon as you're employed or start work in France and not when you obtain your residence permit (*carte de séjour*). Social security contributions are paid directly to the Union de Recouvrement des Cotisations de Sécurité Sociale et d'Allocations Familiales (URSSAF), which has 105 offices throughout France. Within a limited period of starting a business, you must register with the Caisse d'Allocations Familiales/CAF (family allowance), the Caisse Nationale de l'Assurance Maladie/CNAM (sickness), and the Caisse Nationale d'Assurance Vieillesse/CNAV (old-age pension).

Self-employed

As a self-employed person you're treated as an employer and must deduct social security contributions from your own earnings and pay them directly to URSSAF. Once registered, you may choose from a selection of recognised organisations providing pensions and health insurance.

Recent legislation has provided some more than welcome respite for the newly self-employed, who, instead of making crippling social security contributions from their start-up, now make contributions (as well as paying income tax) as their business generates income. If you're registered under the *micro-BIC* tax regime (see page 213), you may be entitled to exoneration from part or all of the social security contributions on your letting income.

Payment

Contributions are payable in two lump sums on 1st April and 1st October each year. It's possible to pay contributions monthly (actually, you pay ten monthly instalments from January to October based on an estimated total contribution; any necessary adjustment is made in November or December); you must apply before 1st December of the year preceding the payments.

Employers

If you employ full-time staff, you must make social security contributions for your employees equivalent to over 35 per cent of their salary. If you employ someone to undertake work for you, you should ensure that he has adequate insurance (e.g. accident and third-party liability) or is registered as self-employed and therefore making social security contributions. If you pay someone to do a job on a casual basis (e.g. gardening) and he isn't registered as self-employed, you can make the necessary contributions on his behalf in order to ensure that both he and you are insured in the event of an accident. This can be done by using the *Chèque Emploi Service* system (ask your bank for details).

 If you agree to pay anyone in cash or by ordinary cheque and he has an accident on your premises, you can be sued for a very large sum of money.

7.

OTHER CONSIDERATIONS

This chapter covers various factors that may help you to maximise the income from your property, including accounting, business communications, employing staff, finding help and advice, learning French, obtaining a mortgage and setting up a company.

MORTGAGES

Mortgages or home loans (*hypothèque*) are available from all major French banks (for residents and non-residents) and many foreign banks. It's possible to obtain a foreign currency mortgage, other than in euros, e.g. GB£, Swiss francs or US$. **However, you should be extremely wary before taking out a foreign currency mortgage, as interest rate gains can be wiped out overnight by currency swings and devaluations.** It's generally recognised that you should take out a loan in the currency in which you're paid or in the currency of the country where a property is situated. In this case, if the foreign currency is devalued you will have the consolation of knowing that the value of your French property will have increased by the same percentage when converted back into the foreign currency.

When choosing between a euro loan and a foreign currency loan, be sure to take into account all costs, fees, interest rates and possible currency fluctuations. However you finance the purchase of a home in France, you should obtain professional advice from your bank manager and accountant. Most French banks offer euro mortgages on French property through foreign branches in the European Union (EU) and other countries. Most financial advisers recommend borrowing from a large reputable bank rather than a small one. Crédit Agricole is the largest French lender, with a 25 per cent share of the French mortgage market.

Both French and foreign lenders have tightened their lending criteria in the last few years, as a result of the repayment problems experienced by many recession-hit borrowers in the early '90s. Some foreign lenders apply stricter rules than French lenders regarding income, employment and the type of property on which they will lend, although some are willing to lend more than a French lender. It can take some foreigners a long time to obtain a mortgage in France, particularly if you have neither a regular income nor assets there. If you have difficulty, you should try a bank that's experienced in dealing with foreigners, such as the Banque Transatlantique (🖥 www.transat.tm.fr).

Types of Mortgage

All French mortgages are repaid using the capital and interest method (repayment); endowment and pension-linked mortgages aren't offered.

Interest rates can be fixed or variable, the fixed rate being higher than the variable rate to reflect the increased risk to the lender. The advantage of a fixed rate is that you know exactly how much you must pay over the whole term. Variable rate loans may be fixed for the first two or more years, after which they're adjusted up or down on an annual basis in line with prevailing interest rates, but usually within preset limits, e.g. within 3 per cent of the original rate. You can usually convert a variable rate mortgage to a fixed rate mortgage at any time. There's normally a redemption penalty, e.g. 3 per cent of the outstanding capital, for early repayment of a fixed rate mortgage, although that isn't usual for variable rate mortgages. If you think you may want to repay early, you should try to have the redemption penalty waived or reduced before signing the agreement.

Terms & Conditions

It's customary for a property to be held as security for a loan taken out on it, i.e. the lender takes a charge on the property. Note, however, that some foreign banks won't lend on the security of a French property.

French law doesn't permit French banks to offer mortgages or other loans where repayments are more than 30 per cent of your net income. Joint incomes and liabilities are included when assessing a couple's borrowing limit (usually a French bank will lend to up to three joint borrowers). Note that the 30 per cent limit includes existing mortgage or rental payments, in France and abroad. If your total repayments exceed 30 per cent of your income, French banks aren't permitted to extend further credit. Should they attempt to do so, the law allows a borrower to avoid liability for payment.

To calculate how much you can borrow in France, multiply your total net monthly income by 30 per cent and deduct your monthly mortgage, rent and other regular payments. Note that earned income isn't included if you're aged over 65. As a rough guide, repayments on a €60,000 mortgage are around €600 per month at 6 per cent over 15 years. There are special low mortgage rates for low-income property buyers in some departments. In November 2004, the maximum interest rate a bank could charge on a fixed-rate mortgage was 6.56 per cent and the maximum on a variable-rate mortgage 5.85 per cent.

As a condition of a French mortgage, you must take out a life (usually plus health and disability) insurance policy equal to 120 per cent of the amount borrowed. The premiums are included in mortgage payments. An existing insurance policy may be accepted, although it must be assigned to the lender. A medical examination may be required, although this isn't usual if you're under 50 years of age and borrowing less than €150,000.

Note that a borrower is responsible for obtaining building insurance on a property and must provide the lender with a certificate of insurance.

French mortgages are usually limited to 70 or 80 per cent of a property's value (although some lenders limit loans to just 50 per cent). A mortgage can include renovation work, when written quotations must be provided with a mortgage application. Note that you must add expenses and fees, totalling around 10 to 15 per cent of the purchase price on an 'old' property, i.e. one over five years old. For example, if you're buying a property for €75,000 and obtain an 80 per cent mortgage, you must pay a 20 per cent deposit (€15,000) plus 10 to 15 per cent fees (€7,500 to €11,250), making a total of €22,500 to €26,250.

Mortgages can be obtained for any period from 2 to 20 years, although the usual term is 15 years (some banks won't lend for longer than this). In certain cases, mortgages can be arranged over terms of up to 25 years, although interest rates are higher. Generally, the shorter the period of a loan, the lower the interest rate. All lenders set minimum loans, e.g. €15,000 to €30,000, and some set minimum purchase prices. Usually there's no maximum loan amount, which is subject to status and possibly valuation (usually required by non-French lenders).

In France, a mortgage cannot be transferred from one person to another, as is possible in some countries, but can usually be transferred to another property.

If you fail to maintain your mortgage repayments, your property can be repossessed and sold at auction. However, this rarely happens, as most lenders are willing to arrange lower repayments when borrowers get into financial difficulties.

Application Procedure

To obtain a mortgage from a French bank, you must provide proof of your monthly income and all outgoings such as mortgage payments, rent and other loans or commitments. Proof of income includes three months' pay slips for employees, confirmation of income from your employer and tax returns. If you're self-employed, you require an audited copy of your balance sheets and trading accounts for the past three years, plus your last tax return. French banks aren't particularly impressed with accountants' letters. If you want a French mortgage to buy a property for commercial purposes, you must provide a detailed business plan (in French).

It's possible to obtain agreement in principle to a mortgage, and most lenders will supply a guarantee or certificate valid for two to four months (in some cases subject to valuation of the property), which you can present to the vendor of a property you intend to buy. There may be a commitment fee of around €150. Note that the deposit paid when signing a preliminary property purchase contract (*compromis de vente*) is automatically protected under French law should you fail to obtain a mortgage.

Once a loan has been agreed, a French bank sends you a conditional offer (*offre préalable*), outlining the terms. In accordance with French law, the offer cannot be accepted until after a 'cooling off' period of ten days. The borrower usually has 30 days to accept the loan and return the signed agreement to the lender. The loan is then held available for four months and can be used over a longer period if it's for a building project.

Fees

There are various fees associated with mortgages. All lenders charge an administration fee (*frais de dossier*) for setting up a loan, usually 1 per cent of the loan amount. There's usually a minimum fee, e.g. €350 (plus value added tax/VAT) and there may also be a maximum. Although it's unusual to have a survey, foreign lenders usually insist on a 'valuation survey' (costing around €250) before they grant a loan.

If a loan is obtained using a French property as security, additional fees and registration costs are payable to the notary (*notaire*) for registering the charge against the property.

If you borrow from a co-operative bank, you're obliged to subscribe to the capital of the local bank. The amount (number of shares) is decided by the board of directors and you're sent share certificates (*certificat nominatif de parts sociales*) for that value. The payment (e.g. €75) is usually deducted from your account at the same time as the first mortgage repayment. When the loan has been repaid, the shares are reimbursed (if required).

Note that if you have a foreign currency mortgage or are non-resident with a euro mortgage, you must usually pay commission charges each time you make a mortgage payment or remit money to France. However, some lenders will transfer mortgage payments to France each month free of charge or for a nominal amount.

If you're buying a new property off plan, when payments are made in stages, a bank will provide a 'staggered' loan, where the loan amount is advanced in instalments as required by the *contrat de réservation*. During the period before completion (*période d'anticipation*), interest is payable on a monthly basis on the amount advanced by the bank (plus insurance). When the final payment has been made and the loan is fully drawn, the mortgage enters its amortisation period (*période d'amortissement*).

Remortgaging

If you have spare equity in an existing property, in France or abroad, it may be more cost-effective to remortgage (or take out a second mortgage on) that property than to take out a new mortgage for a second home. Remortgaging involves less paperwork (and you therefore incur lower legal fees), and a plan can be tailored to your requirements. Depending on the equity in your existing property and the cost of a French property, remortgaging may enable you to pay cash for a second home. The disadvantage of remortgaging or a second mortgage is that you reduce the amount of equity available in a property.

French lenders have traditionally been reluctant to remortgage, but they're becoming more willing to do so. On the other hand, it isn't possible to take out a new mortgage with a French lender on a property you already own outright, sometimes known as an 'equity release' mortgage (the concept defies Gallic logic); only offshore lenders offer this facility.

OBTAINING HELP & ADVICE

Finding sources of advice and information is imperative and within France there are numerous places and associations that can provide comprehensive and up-to-date information.

General Information

Your first stop should be the French government's 'Public Service' website (🖳 www.service-public.fr), which contains a wealth of general information in English and French (and German and Spanish) about many aspects of France and specific details about doing business, including statistical, legal and administrative information. The site isn't just aimed at big business, but also at the small entrepreneur who needs simple, basic information. It also contains links to the sites of regional, department and local administrations.

Chambers of Commerce

Among the best sources of help and information is your local chamber of commerce (CCI), of which there are over 160 and at least one in each department (listed on 🖳 www.cci.fr). The website includes a long list of schemes designed to help in the creation or development of a business activity. Most CCIs have good libraries of books, magazines and documents relevant to businesses and setting up small businesses in France, all of which can be consulted free of charge. Most publications are in French, but some CCIs have information in English. Many CCIs organise regular conferences (e.g. once a month) and training programmes on starting a business, business practices, financing small businesses etc., free of charge or for a nominal fee (e.g. €10). However, chambers of commerce aren't professional associations made up of businesses and business owners in France, as chambers of commerce are in the UK and US, but departmental government offices. For further information contact the Assemblée des Chambres Françaises de Commerce et d'Industrie, 45 avenue d'Iéna, 75116 Paris (☎ 01 40 69 37 00, 🖳 www.acfci.cci.fr).

Government Agencies

Information about industry and trade sectors can be found on the websites of the relevant government ministries: enter 🖳 www.[name of ministry].gouv.fr (e.g. 🖳 www.agriculture.gouv.fr). The website of the Agence Pour la Création d'Entreprises (🖳 www.apce.com – see also below) contains a wealth of information (in French) about all the major business areas (e.g. hospitality and leisure); click 'Informations Sectorielles' for lists of relevant organisations, publications and exhibitions and links to related sites.

Specific market studies are undertaken by the Centre de Recherche pour l'Etude et l'Observation des Conditions de Vie (CREDOC), 142 rue du Chevaleret, 75013 Paris (☎ 01 40 77 85 06, 🖳 www.credoc.asso.fr). The website lists the studies available, which can be purchased or consulted at CREDOC's offices, although you must make an appointment, as only a few people are admitted at a time; waiting lists are long. More general economic and demographic studies are available from La Documentation Française, 29 quai Voltaire, 750007 Paris (☎ 01 40 15 70 00, 🖳 www.ladocfrancaise.gouv.fr).

Statistical information is available from the The Institut National de la Statistique et des Etudes Economiques (INSEE, ☎ 08 25 88 94 52, 🖳 www. insee.fr – the site is available in English and lists INSEE's regional offices), the Association Française de Recherches et d'Etudes Statistiques Commerciale (AFRESCO), 46 rue de Clichy, 75009 Paris (☎ 01 48 74 32 80), and the Documentation d'Analyse Financière (Dafsa), 117 quai de Valmy, 75010 Paris (☎ 01 55 45 26 00, 🖳 www.dafsa.fr). The 25 Agences Régionales d'Information Scientifique et Technique (ARIST) are 'regional' agencies providing scientific and technical information; contact details are listed on 🖳 www.arist.tm.fr. There's also a network of Centres Techniques Industriels; contact CTI Réseau, 41 boulevard des Capucines, 75002 Paris (☎ 01 42 97 10 88, 🖳 www.reseau-cti.com).

For information about French and European standards, contact the Association Française de Normalisation (AFNOR), 11 avenue Francis de Pressensé, 93571 Saint-Denis La Plaine Cedex (☎ 01 41 62 80 00, 🖳 www. afnor.fr).

Legal & Professional Advice

Paperwork for almost everything is notoriously complicated and time-consuming in France – so much so that most French people, who can afford to, pay someone to do it for them. This not only guarantees you less stress, but also means that your chances of presenting the right papers to the right people are greatly increased. In any case, if your French is anything less than fluent, you shouldn't contemplate doing the paperwork for your property business yourself.

The best way to find an expert is via personal recommendation – ask others who run a similar business or who have had comparable experiences. In small communities, finding someone with a good reputation is relatively easy, as only the best establish lasting practices. If you're in an area where there's a large foreign population, many of the advisers you come into contact with will speak good English (and often other languages as well). They will also be used to foreign clients and so be familiar with the kind of advice and help you need.

Fees vary; those for some services are regulated by the professional associations while others are set by the individual professional. It pays to shop around and compare fees, bearing in mind that cheaper fees often mean a less professional service and paying more doesn't necessarily mean you receive the best service. It's often cheaper to negotiate an annual fee for services than to pay one-off charges. The following professionals may be especially useful.

Lawyer

Expert, independent legal advice from a qualified lawyer (*avocat*) is highly recommended when you're buying property and essential if you're buying land. The only professionals qualified to give legal advice in France are lawyers and you should take legal advice from no one else. Fees charged are usually between 1 and 1.5 per cent of the property's price, but may depend on the work involved.

ACCOUNTING

French accounting principles derive from the *Code de Commerce* and the *Plan Comptable Général*, which are amended and updated periodically by the Conseil National de la Comptabilité, as well as from the *Code Général des Impôts*. The French make much of the supposed differences between 'French accounting' and what they call *la comptabilité anglo-saxonne*. In practice, however, they aren't all that different, although French accounting – in true Gallic style – involves a host of complex rules that must be observed.

First, it's a legal requirement that accounting records be in French. The principles also specify not only the names, but also the method of numbering for business accounts. Although this can be a nuisance, it simplifies many of the tax reporting requirements, as the instructions refer to the number of a particular account, making it easy to identify. The initial digit of an account number indicates the type of account, as follows:

1... Capital accounts (shareholder equity).

2... Fixed assets (property, plant and equipment).

3... Stock, including raw materials, work in progress and finished goods.

4... 'Third party accounts' (*comptes tiers*), which include all outside parties to which the business owes money or from which it's due money; separate accounts (and account numbers) are required for each social security agency and each taxing authority, a series of VAT accounts and accounts for money owed to shareholders or employees.

5... Bank and other treasury accounts.

6... Expenses.

7... Sales and other income.

There are three legally required journals: the general journal (*le livre-journal*), the inventory journal (*le livre d'inventaire*) and the general ledger (*le grand livre*). (The English terms are approximate – they don't correspond closely to the French journals.)

● **Livre-journal** – The 'general journal' is a chronological list of operations (i.e. journal entries) that track the daily sales and expenditure of the business. The French tend to divide the general journal into sub-journals, dealing with sales, purchases, treasury (i.e. the bank accounts) and 'miscellaneous operations' (*opérations diverses*).

● **Livre d'Inventaire** – The 'inventory journal' isn't strictly speaking confined to inventory or stock taking. It's more of a trial balance, a listing of each account and its balance as of a specific date. Under French accounting law, you're allowed to review the trial balance at the end of the year, and make adjustments, up and down, to those assets and liabilities that have fluctuated in value. This requirement includes the need to verify the status of your stock (of merchandise, raw materials, work in progress and finished goods) and to verify your fixed assets (property, plant and equipment). You must maintain a year-end inventory journal, documenting the final balances in each account, which serves as the basis for your balance sheet.

● **Grand Livre** – The 'general ledger' is the document where the transactions from the general journal (or from the various sub-journals) are summarised and sorted by the accounts affected.

Certain accounting requirements vary according to the type or size of business.

Accountants

French accountants (*experts comptable*) vary greatly in their expertise, helpfulness and cost. Like *notaires*, they tend to view their profession as one designed to enforce the letter of the law, rather than to assist their clients. For example, there are very few (if any) accountants in private practice who do 'write-up' work for clients (i.e. where the client puts all his receipts and invoices in a shoebox and takes them to the accountant every fortnight or so for the accountant to transcribe into the relevant books). In France, you risk being charged by the invoice if you ask your accountant to do this sort of bookkeeping work for you!

You shouldn't expect much in the way of tax saving or tax planning assistance from an *expert comptable*. This is due, in part, to the fact that changes are often made to the current year's tax law as late as October or November in the year, which makes advance tax planning almost impossible. Bear in mind also that, if your accountant makes a mistake, e.g. in calculating your tax, you must pay the correct amount and he's under no obligation to compensate you for his error.

Many small businessmen complain bitterly about how expensive their accountants are, and especially how much they charge for miscellaneous tasks, such as determining which account an invoice should be charged to. (The standard joke is that they charge €60 to tell you which account a €20 invoice should go to – and you must still book the entry yourself!) The chances are an accountant won't save you money on a day-to-day basis, but they can save you hassle with the tax authorities – if only by having the forms correctly filled out. It can also be an advantage to have accountant-prepared financial statements if you must obtain a bank loan or credit of any kind.

French accountants are an excellent source of information on the technicalities of the law, especially tax and accounting law. They may be more knowledgeable than many lawyers when it comes to knowing the various forms of business that are possible, and can advise you about the various social security regimes.

EMPLOYING OTHERS

Hiring employees shouldn't be taken lightly in France and must be taken into account before starting a business. There are around 1.4 million companies in France without employees – and not without reason, as many successful small businesses become less so as soon as they start to recruit!

You must enter into a contract under French labour law and employees enjoy extensive rights. It's also very expensive to hire employees: in addition to salaries, you must pay a 13th month's salary, five weeks' paid annual holiday and 40 to 60 per cent in social security contributions, although there are reductions for hiring certain categories of unemployed people – all of which is detailed below.

There are tax 'holidays' for limited periods for newly formed companies, particularly regarding the first employee. During their first two years' trading, most new businesses are required to pay only around 10 per cent of their first employee's wages in social security contributions. Note, however, that the managing director's spouse doesn't count as a first employee!

Regulations & Employee Rights

General rules and regulations governing the employment of staff are set out in the French Labour Code (*Code du Travail*) as well as collective agreements (*conventions collectives de travail*); specific rules are contained in an individual employee's contract (*contrat de travail*) and the employer's in-house rules and regulations (*règlements intérieurs/règlements de travail*).

Employees have extensive rights under the French Labour Code. The Code details the minimum conditions of employment, including working hours, overtime payments, holidays, trial and notice periods, dismissal conditions, health and safety regulations, and trade union rights. The French Labour Code is described in detail in a number of books, including the *Code du Travail* (VO Editions), and is available online at the Legifrance website (🖳 www.legifrance.gouv.fr).

Employment laws cannot be altered or nullified by private agreements. In general, French law forbids discrimination by employers on the basis of sex, religion, race, age, sexual preference, physical appearance or name, and there are specific rules regarding equal job opportunities for men and women. In 2002, a law was introduced forbidding 'moral harassment'.

It's some consolation for employers that French courts are hesitant to interfere with hiring practices. It's virtually impossible to bring a discrimination action against an employer for not hiring someone. Although discrimination on the job is severely dealt with in the courts, the courts won't normally interfere with the employer's free choice of candidates.

Salaried foreigners are employed under the same working conditions as French citizens, although there are different rules for certain categories of employee, e.g. directors, managers and factory workers. Part-time employees are entitled to the same rights and benefits (on a pro rata basis) as full-time employees.

Recruiting

You're required to notify the government employment service, the Agence Nationale Pour l'Emploi (ANPE, 19 boulevard Gambetta, 92136 Issy-les-

Moulineaux, ☎ 01 46 45 64 85 or 08 10 80 58 05, 🖥 www.anpe.fr), which has some 600 offices throughout France, of all job vacancies, but you're generally free to recruit staff as you wish. You can, of course, make use of the services of ANPE or you can place job advertisements in newspapers, on the internet and even on television and radio. (There's a cable/satellite channel, *Demain*, devoted to career information and job opportunities.) But most recruiting in France is done on a personal 'word-of-mouth' basis, so local networking should be an essential part of your early business plan. Whichever method you use, you must be **absolutely sure** you're engaging the right person, as firing employees is difficult and normally expensive. The hiring process (*embauche*) in France can take several months from initial application to job offer and may involve several repeat visits for interviews, testing, etc. You should take full advantage of this practice and not attempt to short-cut the system, which could be a costly error.

A recruit must be declared to the Union de Recouvrement des Cotisations de Sécurité Sociale et d'Allocations Familiales (URSSAF), using a *document unique d'embauche* (*DUE*), which must be submitted not more than a week before the employee is due to start work. This is known as the *déclaration préalable à l'embauche* (*DPAE*), which must be acknowledged by URSSAF before employment can start. URSSAF pass the *DUE* on to the organisations responsible for registering the employee with social security (health, unemployment and pension benefits, for which you will be told which fund you must contribute to on behalf of your new employee and for health and safety (see **Medical Examinations** on page 227). The only time you might need to contact any of these organisations directly is if there's a change in status of one of your employees, e.g. you promote him from 'rank and file' to management. Details of the *DUE* can be found on URSSAF's dedicated website (🖥 www1.due.urssaf.fr).

Incentives

There are various incentives for employing certain categories of people, including those listed below. Categories and incentives vary from area to area, the latter being most generous in regeneration zones (*zones de redynamisation*). Details of those that apply in your area are available from local offices of ANPE or the Direction Départementale du Travail, de l'Emploi et de la Formation Professionnelle (DDTEFP). Further general information about recruitment incentives can be found on the government website 🖥 www.travail.gouv.fr.

- **Trainees** – People between 16 and 25 who are studying for a vocational qualification. You must give them a contract for between one and three years (subject to a two-month trial period) and pay them between 25 and

78 per cent of the minimum wage (depending on their age and the number of years they've worked for you). You receive an annual payment of between €1,000 and €5,000 (depending on the location of your business) and you don't need to pay the trainee's social security contributions. The trainee must obviously be allowed time off for studying. This is known as a *contrat d'apprentissage*.

- **Long-term Unemployed** – People over 25 who have been unemployed for at least 18 months (12 months if they're over 50). You may give them a fixed term or indefinite contract (see **Contracts** on page 240) and pay them at least the minimum wage. You receive a payment of €330 per month for the first one or two years of employment (€500 per month for up to five years in the case of the over 50s), and the employee may be entitled to continue claiming unemployment benefit. This is known as a *contrat initiative emploi* (*CIE*) and is currently available only to certain types of business, including associations.

- **Young People** – Unemployed people between 16 and 23 who haven't passed their *baccalauréat*. You must give them an indefinite contract, although this can be for part-time work, and pay them at least the minimum wage. You receive a payment of between around €250 and €300 (depending on the employee's salary) per month for the first two years of employment and half of this for the third year. This is known as a *contrat jeunes en entreprise* (*CJE*).

Stagiaires

Many French employers 'hire' students on training courses (*stagiaires*). Nearly all training programmes, including those at university level, involve several periods of 'employment' – usually for a period of three to six weeks, but sometimes as long as six months. In the vast majority of cases, these short-term 'employees' aren't allowed to accept payment (or only a limited amount, e.g. the statutory minimum wage) and their social charges are covered by the school or university (or their parents). This is therefore a cheap (and legal) way of engaging staff for what amounts to a trial period, and many *stagiaires* are highly trained.

At certain times of the year, most small businesses receive telephone calls, letters and even emails from students who must arrange a course (*stage*) related to their study programme. It's up to the *stagiaire* to contact employers and to negotiate the functions they should do to fulfil the requirements of their school or university. Some schools and local governments send out appeals to small businesses to offer internships, summer jobs and other types of employment to various categories of young people.

There are some tax benefits to hiring *stagiaires* or apprentices (*apprentis*). Businesses often re-engage the same *stagiaire* for the whole of their training/school career and then make them an offer of permanent employment when they finish school. By the time they graduate, they know your business reasonably well and can start doing some 'real' work the moment you must start paying them 'real' money!

Titre Emploi Entreprise

A new recruitment system called *Titre Emploi Entreprise* was pioneered in the catering trade and has recently been extended to other sectors. The system offers employers a simplified recruiting procedure for employees on a short-term (less than 100 days in a year) contract, known as *occasionnels*. Pay slips and social security contributions are handled by a centralised office, which provides a standard contract. Further information on this service can be obtained by telephone (☎ 08 10 12 38 33).

Salaries & Minimum Wages

It isn't common practice to specify a salary in a job advertisement and you should negotiate with a prospective candidate according to what you think he's worth! There has been a statutory minimum wage (*salaire minimum interprofessionnel de croissance*, known as *le SMIC*) since 1950. The cost of living index is reviewed annually and, when it rises by 2 per cent or more, the minimum wage is increased. (In practice, the minimum wage rises every year, usually in July and especially when elections are coming up!) The minimum wage is currently €7.61 per hour, equal to gross pay of €1,153.73 per month for 151.67 hours (the new standard under terms of the 35-hour working week), which equates to €859.29 net.

The *SMIC* is lower for juveniles, those on special job-creation schemes and disabled employees. Unskilled workers (particularly women) are usually employed at or near the minimum wage, semi-skilled workers are usually paid 10 to 20 per cent more, and skilled workers 30 to 40 per cent more (often shown in job advertisements as '*SMIC + 10, 20, 30, 40%*'). Details of the legislation relating to minimum wages can be found on the INSEE website (🖥 www.insee.fr/fr/indicateur/smic.htm).

Although many employers pay certain employees, particularly seasonal workers, below the minimum wage, the French government is increasingly clamping down on this practice and penalties can be severe.

Unless you're paying the minimum wage, it may be advantageous to 'pay' part of your employees' salaries in kind, i.e. in the form of benefits and perks such as lunch and holiday vouchers, inexpensive or interest-free home and other loans, rent-free accommodation, travelling expenses, a noncontributory company pension, and a top-up health insurance policy, which may qualify you for tax deductions or allowances and mean that you have to pay less in social charges. **The legalities of doing so are complicated and you should take expert advice on the subject.**

An employee's salary (*salaire*) must be stated in his employment contract, and salary reviews, planned increases, cost of living rises, etc. may also be included. Salaries may be stated in gross (*brut*) or net (*net*) terms and are usually paid monthly (see **Payment** below), although they may be quoted in contracts as hourly, monthly or annually. If a bonus is paid, such as a 13th or 14th month's salary (see below), this must also be stated in the employment contract. General points, such as the payment of a salary into a bank or post office account and the date of salary payments, are usually included in a separate list of employment conditions (*règlement intérieur*), which must be drawn up by any company with 20 or more employees.

Salaries in France must be reviewed once a year (usually at the end of the year), although employers aren't required by law to increase salaries that are above the minimum wage, even when the cost of living has increased. Salary increases usually take effect on 1st January.

13th Month's Salary & Bonuses

Most employers in France pay their employees a bonus month's salary in December, known as the 13th month's salary (*13ème mois*). A 13th month's salary isn't mandatory unless part of a collective agreement or when it's granted regularly in a particular sector, and it should be stated in your employees' contracts. In practice, however, its payment is almost universal and it's often taken for granted. In the first and last years of employment, an employee's 13th month's salary and other bonuses should be paid pro rata if he doesn't work a full calendar year. Some companies also pay a 14th month's salary, usually in July before the summer holiday period, although this isn't recommended until you're earning millions! Where applicable, extra months' salary are guaranteed bonuses and aren't pegged to the company's performance (as with profit-sharing). In some cases, they're paid monthly rather than in a lump sum at the end or in the middle of the year.

Payment

Salaries above €3,000 per month must be paid by cheque or direct transfer (not cash), although it's never wise to pay salaries in cash, as it makes you subject to scrutiny by the tax authorities! You must issue employees with a pay slip (*bulletin de paie*) itemising their salary and deductions.

Computerised payroll programs are widely available, usually as part of a 'management software' package (*logiciel de gestion*), including accounting, payroll, and *gestion commerciale*, which combines purchasing, inventory, and accounts receivable and payable. Among the cheapest are *Ciel* and *ESB*, which can even be bought in hypermarkets; one of the most popular programs is *Sage* (not to be confused with the English software package of the same name, which is incompatible with French accounting practice!).

It's possible to use a payroll service, such as ADP (🖥 www.adp.com), which takes care of all this for you: prepares pay slips and makes the bank transfers, then sends you a report with totals for the various compulsory insurances and withholdings. Ciel also offers online payroll services (🖥 www.ciel.com) for around €15 per pay slip (cheaper if you agree to sign up for a year at a time): you enter the data and Ciel produces a printable pay slip and direct transfers the pay into your employees' accounts.

Taxes

Employees pay their own tax, as France has no pay-as-you-earn (PAYE) system. There has been periodic debate on the introduction of a PAYE system, but the idea has had little support, especially from employers, who are reluctant to 'do the government's work for it', and tax authority employees, who don't want to give the government any excuse for thinning their ranks! It's even unpopular with employees, who consider it a violation of their private lives for their employer to calculate how much tax should be withheld from their pay. As an employer, you must of course declare and pay your own income tax.

Social Security

As an employer, you must pay a significant portion of your employees' social security contributions, which can add up to 40 per cent or more of their salaries (see page 234). Employees are entitled to sickness and maternity, work injury and invalidity, family allowance, unemployment, and old age, widow(er)'s and death benefits, most of which an employer must contribute to. However, employees must earn a minimum salary to qualify for certain benefits. Employers normally continue to pay employees who are off sick for short periods, after which they become entitled to social security sickness benefit.

Contracts

Legally, an offer of employment in France constitutes an employment contract (*contrat de travail/d'emploi*), although it's safer to offer a formal contract. Employers usually issue a formal contract stating such details as job title, position, salary, working hours, benefits, duties and responsibilities, and the duration of employment. Employment contracts usually contain a paragraph stating the date from which they take effect and to whom they apply. **Contracts must be carefully worded and you should take expert advice before drafting them.** For example, whether or not an employee can be required to work at a different location than the one he was hired for or to move if the company moves depends on the wording of his contract.

All employment contracts are subject to French labour law (see page 234), and references may be made to other regulations such as collective agreements. In some sectors, e.g. the catering trade, you must use a standard contract. Anything in contracts contrary to statutory provisions and unfavourable to an employee may be deemed null and void and any exclusion clauses must be 'clear and comprehensible'. All contracts must be written in French.

There are three main types of employment contract in France: a temporary contract, a fixed term contract and an indefinite term contract.

Temporary Contracts

A temporary contract (*contrat de travail temporaire*, also known as an *intérim*), which has no minimum or maximum duration, can be issued in specific circumstances only, as follows:

- For someone who's replacing a staff member who's temporarily absent (except if striking) and whose function is essential to the running of the business.

- For someone who's filling a post on an interim basis until a permanent staff member takes over.

- In the case of a temporary, unforeseen and otherwise unmanageable increase in the workload of existing staff.

- If the business is seasonal and requires additional workers at specific times of year (e.g. in agriculture for harvesting or in catering for peak periods).

- For workers in specific sectors (e.g. the theatre), where the use of temporary contracts is habitual.

Any other type of short-term contract is regarded as a fixed term contract (see below). A worker engaged on a temporary contract is known as a *salarié intérimaire* or simply *intérimaire*. Details of the obligations of employer and employee can be found on the website of the Monster Company (🖥 www. jobpilot.fr/content/service/channel/interim/pratique/contrat.html).

Fixed Term Contracts

A fixed term contract (*contrat à durée déterminée/CDD*) is, as the name suggests, a contract for a limited term. This is normally a maximum of 18 months, although it's limited to nine months if a post is due to be filled permanently and can be extended to two years if the post is due to be suppressed (there's no minimum term). A contract for longer than two years comes under the rules for indefinite term contracts, particularly regarding the dismissal of employees. A term contract must be in writing and for a fixed term or, in the case of temporary employment, for a specific purpose that must be stated in the contract. A term contract ends on the date specified, although it can be renewed twice for a term no longer than the original contract, provided it doesn't exceed two years in total.

A *CDD* can also be for replacement of a specific employee (usually someone on maternity leave) or a general replacement over the summer (to pick up the slack while various employees are off on holiday).

*CDD*s are strictly regulated, mainly because they're considered a contributing factor to the ever-increasing 'precariousness' of employment (*précarité d'emploi*). For example, the salary of an employee hired on a fixed term contract mustn't be less than that paid to a similarly qualified person employed in a permanent job. The employee has the right to an end of contract bonus (*indemnité de fin de contrat*) equal to 10 per cent of his salary, in addition to other agreed bonuses, although this doesn't always apply to seasonal employees.

Contracts for seasonal and temporary workers fall under the same rules as for a *CDD* contract. A *CDD* can be issued when a permanent employee is on leave (including maternity or sick leave), if there's a temporary increase in business, or at any time in the construction industry or for youth employment schemes.

Indefinite Term Contracts

An indefinite term contract (*contrat à durée indéterminée/CDI*) is the standard employment contract for permanent employees. Surprisingly, it isn't necessary for it to be in writing (unlike a term contract), although it's in your interests, as well as the employee's to provide a written contract.

A *CDI* often includes a trial period of one to three months (three months is usual), depending on collective agreements, before it becomes legal and binding on both parties. The trial period doesn't affect the binding nature of the other terms of the contract, just the initial period of time during which either side can terminate the contract without the severance benefits and notice periods taking effect. There can also be a lower rate of pay during the trial period, but the hours and other terms must be in force.

Working Hours

In 2000, France introduced a mandatory 35-hour working week for all large employers, and on 1st January 2002 this became effective for all employers, although the original legislation has since been subject to various amendments, which have 'softened' the obligations of employers and the limitations on employees to exceed a 35-hour week.

Since the introduction of the 35-hour week, time keeping requirements have become much more complex and nearly all employees must be tracked to ensure that weekly, monthly and annual hours and days worked don't exceed the legal limits. For example, employers can establish mandatory break periods (*heures de repos*) to adapt working schedules to the new rules. However, drinks or (if allowed) cigarettes can usually be taken at an employee's workplace at any time.

Overtime

In principle, if an employee works more than 35 hours per week, he must be paid overtime or be given time off in lieu. Employees can be asked to do overtime, but cannot be compelled to do more than 130 hours per year, although this can be altered by collective agreements. The total hours worked per week mustn't exceed an average of 44 over 12 consecutive weeks or an absolute maximum of 48 hours per week.

The minimum legal pay for overtime is the normal rate plus 25 per cent for the first eight hours above the standard 35-hour week (i.e. up to 43) and plus 50 per cent for additional hours (i.e. above 43). Employees can be granted time off in lieu at overtime rates (i.e. 1.25 hours for each hour of overtime worked) instead of being paid. The working week for round-the-clock shift workers is limited to 25 hours, and night work and shift working is usually paid at higher rates, as specified in collective agreements. Employees cannot be obliged to work on Sundays unless collective agreements state otherwise. If an employee agrees to work on a Sunday, normal overtime rates apply.

Holidays & Leave

The French enjoy generous holiday and leave entitlements compared with employees in most other countries (and especially the US).

Annual Holidays

Under French labour law, an employee is entitled to 2.5 days' paid annual holiday (*congé/vacances*) for each full month he works. Annual holiday entitlement is calculated assuming that Saturdays are work days, a legacy of the time when the usual working week consisted of six days. After working for a full year, an employee is entitled to 30 days off (12 months x 2.5 days per month), which equals five weeks (including Saturdays).

Legally, holiday entitlement is earned over the course of a year that runs from 1st May to 30th April. So, if an employee starts work in January, by 1st May he will have earned ten days of holiday, which he can take during the subsequent year (i.e. starting 1st May). By the next 1st May, he should have accrued a full five weeks of holiday, which is available to him over the next 12 months. Employers cannot include official French public holidays (see below) as annual holidays.

French employees are legally entitled to take up to four weeks' paid holiday in a single block between 1st May and 31st October (known as the *période légale*), unless business needs dictate otherwise (although other agreements are possible). However, if you oblige employees to take more than two days off outside the *période légale*, they're entitled to additional holiday: an extra day for three to six days outside the *période légale*; an extra two days for six or more days outside. Before taking on staff, check what holidays they've booked or planned. If these fall within their trial period, you aren't obliged to allow them.

Public Holidays

Since 2004, there have been ten public holidays in France, which are listed below. Surprisingly, the only public holiday an employer in France is legally obliged to grant with pay is 1st May (irrespective of which day of the week it falls on). Nevertheless, most collective agreements allow paid holidays on several public holidays and it's usual for employers to grant all of them.

Officially, after the heatwave of 2003, which supposedly killed tens of thousands of people, Pentecost Monday was 'sacrificed' to save money to pay for better care for old people (it wasn't clear how). In typical French style, however, employers were offered a compromise: if you don't want to do away with the Pentecost holiday (e.g. because your business is too busy at that time), you can cancel any of the other holidays (except 1st May) instead.

Date	Holiday
1st January	New Year's Day (*Nouvel An/Jour de l'An*)
March or April	Easter Monday (*Lundi de Pâques*)
1st May	Labour Day (*Fête du Travail*)
8th May	VE Day (*Fête de la Libération/Victoire 1945/ Anniversaire 1945*)

May	Ascension Day (*Ascension*) – the sixth Thursday after Easter
14th July	Bastille Day (*Fête Nationale*)
15th August	Assumption (*Fête de l'Assomption*)
1st November	All Saints' Day (*Toussaint*)
11th November	Armistice Day (*Fête de l'Armistice*)
25th December	Christmas Day (*Noël*)

When a public holiday falls on a Saturday or Sunday, you aren't obliged to offer another day (e.g. the previous Friday or following Monday) as a holiday instead. However, when a public holiday falls on a Tuesday or Thursday, you must decide whether to allow the day before or the day after (i.e. Monday or Friday respectively) as a holiday. This practice is called 'making a bridge' (*faire le pont*) and you may make yourself unpopular with your employees if you don't allow them to do so. (Some even expect to be allowed to bridge from a Wednesday to the previous or following weekend!) Depending on how the public holidays fall, you can gain or lose a significant number of days' work.

Sick Leave

Employees in France don't receive a quota of sick days, as in some countries (e.g. the US), and there's no limit to the amount of time an employee may take off work due to sickness or accidents, although they're entitled to social security benefits for long-term illnesses or disabilities. For this reason, many French employers take out salary insurance). An employee is normally required to notify you immediately of sickness or an accident that prevents him from working. He must also obtain a doctor's certificate (*arrêt de travail*) on the first day of his sickness; otherwise it counts as a day's holiday.

Trial & Notice Periods

For most jobs in France, there's a trial period (*période d'essai*) of one to three months, depending on the type of work and the employer (three months is usual). The trial period isn't required by law, although there's no law forbidding it. The length of a trial period is usually stated in collective agreements. During the trial period, either party may terminate the employment contract without notice or any financial penalty, unless otherwise stated in a collective agreement.

Notice periods are governed by law and collective agreements and usually vary with length of service. The minimum notice period is usually a month for clerical and manual workers, two months for foremen and supervisors, and three months for managerial and senior technical staff. The minimum notice period for employees with over two years' service is two months.

A term contract can be terminated before the end of its period only in specific circumstances, i.e. when the employer or employee has committed a serious offence (*faute grave*), in the case of an event beyond the control of both parties (*force majeure*), or with the agreement of both parties. Under recently passed regulations designed to modernise labour law, an employee may terminate a temporary contract without penalty if he accepts a job with an indefinite contract.

BUSINESS COMMUNICATION

Although you wouldn't think so from the postal service, communications have improved in France during the last decade. If you're running a bed & breakfast (B&B) or letting a property, you will need access to fixed and mobile telephones, and the internet. Note that broadband (*haut-débit*, usually known as *ADSL*) connection isn't available in all areas of France (see page 248). The following is a brief guide to telephone and internet services and the postal service.

Telephone Services

The telephone network is operated by France Télécom (FT), which is 55 per cent state-owned (and one of the most indebted companies in the world!), but since 2002 call services have been open to competition, which has resulted in an intense price war. Despite this 'market liberalisation', however, FT is still the only company that offers a complete service, including the installation of telephone lines, others providing only call services. Nevertheless, some other companies may offer call charge packages that suit your business needs and it's worth investigating the alternatives. There's a variety of tariffs, so make sure you thoroughly investigate the alternatives, particularly if your business relies heavily on telephone communications.

Alternative Providers

There are currently around 20 alternative telephone service providers (i.e. other than France Télécom) in France, some of which advertise in the English-language press (see **Appendix B**). If you wish to use another provider (or several providers, for different types of call), you must open a separate account with each one. You must still have an account with FT for line rental.

It's possible to have subscriptions with several different telephone providers, and each one will indicate what numbers you must dial to route your calls correctly. Alternatively, you can notify FT of your default provider and they will set up your telephone line to automatically route calls to whichever of the alternative telephone providers you prefer, without having to use the extra numbers. This facility costs around €11 and takes a week or two to set up (during which time you can use a prefix).

If you have all your calls automatically routed via another provider, it's possible to revert to the FT system by dialling 8 before the number. This service, which is useful if there's a problem with your alternative provider, must be ordered in advance from FT and it's free.

To help you find your way through the maze of alternative telephone providers, you may want to consult a service such as BudgeTelecom (💻 www.budgetelecom.com), where you can compare the available tariffs based on your own calling pattern and review customer evaluations of the services available from each provider.

Installation & Registration

If you're planning to move into a property without an existing telephone line, you will need to have one installed. In this case, you must visit your local France Télécom agent, which you will find in the yellow pages under *Télécommunications: service*. You must prove that you're the owner or tenant of the property in question, e.g. with an electricity bill, confirmation of purchase (*attestation d'acquisition*) or a lease. You also require your passport or residence permit (*carte de séjour*).

If you buy a property in a remote area without a telephone line, it may be expensive to have a telephone installed, as you must pay for the line to your property. Contact FT for an estimate. You should have trenches dug for the telephone cable if you want a below-ground connection (you may be able to have an above-ground connection via a wire from the nearest pylon). This work can be carried out by FT, but their charges are high and it's possible to do it yourself, although you must observe certain standards. Details of the required depth of trenches and the type of conduit (*gaine*) to use, etc. can be obtained from FT.

When you go to the FT agency, you must know what kind of telephone sockets are already installed in the property, how many telephones you want, where you want them installed and what kind of telephone you want (if you're buying from FT). If you want a number of telephone points installed, you should arrange this in advance. You may also want to upgrade a line (e.g. to ADSL – see **Broadband** below).

You will also be asked whether you want a listed or unlisted number and must inform FT where you want your bill sent and how you wish to pay it (see page 239). If you wish to pay your bill by direct debit, you must provide your account details (*relevé d'identité bancaire*). You can also request an itemised bill at the same time.

You may be given a telephone number on the spot, although you should wait until you receive written confirmation before giving it to anyone. It isn't possible simply to take over the telephone number of the previous occupant. You will receive a letter stating that you have a mixed line (*ligne mixte*), which is simply a line allowing incoming and outgoing calls.

To have a line installed takes from a few days in a city, to weeks or possibly over a month in remote rural areas, although 90 per cent of new customers have a line installed within two weeks. In certain areas, there's a waiting list and you can have a line installed quickly only if you need a telephone for your safety or security, e.g. if you're an invalid, in which case a medical certificate is required. Business lines may be installed quicker than domestic lines.

Broadband

There are two types of broadband (*haut-débit*) connection: Asymmetric Digital Subscriber Lines (ADSL) and Integrated Services Digital Network (ISDN). France Télécom is committed to extending the availability of ADSL, but it isn't available in all areas and may even be available in one part of a village, but not another! To find out if ADSL is available in your area, go to 🖥 www.francetelecom.fr, click on '*internet et multimédia*' (on the left) and '*abonnement express*' and enter your current telephone number (or a neighbour's) or the number of the department in which you live or intend to live. France Télécom expects broadband to be available throughout France by 2007.

If available, it's possible to upgrade an existing line to ADSL at no extra charge; if it isn't available and you aren't in a 'cabled' area, ISDN (*RNIS*, but referred to by FT as *Numéris*) is the only option. An ISDN 'line' actually provides you with three telephone numbers, but only two lines (at least, you can use only two at once!) and you must use both lines simultaneously to achieve 128kbps download speed; check whether your internet service provider (ISP) allows this.

France Télécom also offers various combined telephone and internet access packages (see **Internet** on page 251). Installation of ADSL costs the same as a standard line (normally €104), but an ISDN line costs an additional €90 (for private use) or €123 (for business use).

Bills

France Télécom bills its customers every two months and allows you two weeks to pay your bill (*facture*). Bills include VAT (*TVA*) at 19.6 per cent, although an ex-VAT figure (*HT*) is shown as well as the total, including VAT (*TTC*). You can request an itemised bill (*facturation détaillée*), which lists all calls with the date and time, the number called, the duration and the charge. This service is free, but must be requested a month in advance.

Bills can be paid by post by sending a cheque to France Télécom, at a post office or at your local FT office. Simply detach the tear-off part of your bill and send or present it with payment. You can pay your telephone bill by direct debit (*prélèvement automatique*) or have the payments spread throughout the year. If you pay your bills by direct debit, your invoice specifies the date of the debit from your account, usually around 20 days after receipt of the invoice. Contact your local FT agent for information. France Télécom is trying to encourage customers to pay by direct debit, payment by telephone, or by *Titre Interbancaire de Paiement* (*TIP*), whereby your bank account details are pre-printed on the tear-off part of the bill, which you simply date and sign and return. Most alternative providers insist on payment by direct debit, and you may be billed monthly.

Charges

Deregulation of the telecommunications market has resulted in an intense price war, and considerable savings can be made on national, as well as international, calls by shopping around for the lowest rates (see **Alternative Providers** on page 246). However, as there are around 20 alternative providers, it's impossible to list all their tariffs here, and only FT's are given in detail. Comparisons between the rates offered by different service providers can be found via the internet (e.g. ▣ www.comparatel.fr and www.budgetelecom.com) or you can contact the Association Française des Utilisateurs de Télécommunications (AFUTT, BP1, 92340 Marne-la-Coquette, ☎ 01 47 41 09 11, ▣ www.afutt.org) on Mondays to Thursdays between 10.30 and 12.30. Line rental and call charges are explained below; for information about installation and registration charges, see page 247.

Line Rental: A monthly line rental or service charge (*abonnement*) of €14 is payable to France Télécom irrespective of the service provider you choose. If you use an alternative provider (see page 246), there may be a separate monthly fee in addition to your call charges, although most providers have dropped these.

Domestic Calls: France Télécom's tariffs depend on the destination and time of calls. Calls at peak times (*heures pleines*), which are Mondays to Fridays from 08.00 to 19.00 and Saturdays from 08.00 to 12.00, are charged at the 'normal' rate (*tarif normal*); calls at all other times (*heures creuses*), including all day on public holidays, are charged at a reduced rate (*tarif réduit*).

Call charges are based on an initial 'connection' charge (*mise en relation* or *crédit-temps*), which pays for a minute or 39 seconds depending on whether the call is local (i.e. calls to numbers starting with the same four digits as your own) or not, plus a per-minute rate after that time. The term 'unit' (*unité*) is sometimes used for the initial charge, although you may receive different definitions of the term, even from FT staff! France Télécom's current standard charges for calls from and to fixed lines are shown below.

	Initial Charge	Peak Minute	Off-peak Minute
Local Calls	€0.09 (60 seconds)	€0.033	€0.018
Other Calls	€0.11 (39 seconds)	€0.090	€0.063

France Télécom no longer publicises these rates, however, but offers instead an array of 'all-inclusive' packages (*forfait*), of which there are currently around 20. Packages require a fixed monthly payment (e.g. between €1.50 and €10) in return for reduced price or, in some cases, 'free' calls, which makes it all but impossible to calculate what you're paying for each call or to compare rates with those of other providers. A recent comparison between rates charged by the five major providers showed a price variation between €0.13 and €0.16 for a three-minute, off-peak local call, and between €0.27 and €0.40 for a ten-minute, peak rate local call, with FT's charges – not surprisingly – generally the highest, although if you're a telephone-addict you may find their 'unlimited use' (*illimité*) packages good value.

Alternative telephone service providers also offer a variety of call packages, consisting of a combination of varying initial charges and lengths followed by different per-minute charges and, in some cases, a single rate for all times of day and all destinations. Cégétel, for example, charges a connection fee of €0.118 followed by a standard per-minute charge of €0.013 to all fixed lines in France, irrespective of the distance or time of the call.

International Calls: France Télécom has eight tariff levels for international calls, listed on its website. All international calls are subject to a 'connection charge' (*mise en relation*) of €0.12 (unless you're using the *Option Plus* or *Les Heures* package, in which case it's €0.11 – big deal!). Calls to other Western Europe and North America are charged at the cheapest tariff and cost €0.22 per minute during peak periods (see above) and €0.12 per minute off-peak. Calls to Australia and New Zealand are the most expensive, costing €1.14/0.94 per minute.

Other telephone providers have different tariff structures for international calls. Most alternative providers also offer a variety of discount plans, such as half price on all calls to a designated 'favourite country' or to specific overseas numbers frequently called.

Mobile Telephones

After a relatively slow start in introducing mobile phones (*téléphone portable* or simply *portable*, but increasingly *mobile*), France has one of Europe's fastest growing cellular populations and it's estimated that over 60 per cent of people in France use mobiles. Mobile phones are now so widespread that some businesses (e.g. restaurants, cinemas, theatres, concert halls) ban them and some even use mobile phone jammers that can detect and jam every handset within 100m.

There are currently three mobile phone service providers: Bouygues ☎ 08 10 63 01 00, 🖳 www.bouyguestelecom.fr), France Télécom, operating under the Orange trademark (☎ 08 00 83 08 00, 🖳 www.orange.fr), and SFR (☎ 08 00 10 60 00, 🖳 www.sfr.fr). Buying a mobile phone is a minefield, as there aren't only different networks to choose from, but also a wide range of tariffs covering connection fees, monthly subscriptions, insurance and call charges. To further complicate matters, all three providers have business ties to one or more of the fixed telephone services (SFR with Cégétel, for example) and offer various deals for those who combine mobile and fixed telephone services.

Internet

The internet in France got off to rather a slow start due to competition from Minitel (France's pioneering telephone information service) and the market is still expanding rapidly, which has led to a proliferation of internet service providers (*fournisseur d'accès/FAI* or *serveur*), over 200 currently offering a variety of products and prices. France Télécom offers Wanadoo, a package that includes email (see below), Minitel (of course) and online shopping. AOL Compuserve France is the other major internet contender. Between them, Wanadoo and AOL have some two-thirds of the market. Contact details of some of the major French ISPs are as follows:

- Alice France (formerly Tiscali) (☎ 1033, 🖳 www.aliceadsl.fr).
- AOL (☎ 08 92 02 03 04, 🖳 www.aol.fr).
- Club Internet (☎ 3204, 🖳 www.club-internet.fr).
- Free (☎ 3244, 🖳 www.free.fr).
- FreeSurf (☎ 08 26 00 76 50, 🖳 www.freesurf.fr).
- Wanadoo (☎ 08 90 71 99 99, 🖳 www.wanadoo.fr).

For details of all the French ISPs, go to 🖳 www.lesproviders.com; for a comparison of ISP services and charges, consult one of the dedicated internet magazines, such as *Internet Pratique* and *Net@scope*, or visit the

Budgetelecom website (⌨ www.budgetelecom.com), which carries a list of internet access providers in France, with information on current offers, customer evaluations and direct links to provider websites.

Charges: France has a number of 'free' internet access services, where you pay only for your telephone connection time, not for access to the internet provider. Alternatively, most service providers (including the free ones) offer various monthly plans which include all telephone charges for your online connections, usually at a rate that's lower than the telephone charges alone. For as little as €6 to €10 per month, you can usually have five or ten hours online. For an ordinary connection, Wanadoo offers 100 hours per month for €25 (with a reduction to €5 for the first three months). If you exceed your allotted time, you're billed a flat rate (usually around €0.05 per minute) for the excess time. AOL is currently offering 60 hours for €17 (€5 for the first three months) and Alice France offers a *forfait illimité*, whereby you can spend as much time online as you wish for €30 per month, and FT offers a combined telephone/internet access package, including unlimited 'free' dial-up. Charges for broadband connection are around twice as high, although in Paris and other urban centres with cable television, it's often possible to have a combined television and broadband internet access package.

Postal Services

The French Post Office (La Poste) is a state-owned company, and post offices (*la poste* also means 'post office') in France are always staffed by post office employees, who are French civil servants (*fonctionnaires*); there are no post offices run by private businesses, as in the UK, for example. Privatisation of the postal service began in 2003 and La Poste's monopoly on the handling of letters between 50 and 100g ends in 2006. There are around 17,000 post offices, 60 per cent of them in communes of fewer than 2,000 inhabitants and, as in other countries, those in the least populated areas are gradually being closed. (La Poste made a loss of millions of euros in 2001 after many years in the black.)

In addition to the usual post office services, a range of other services are provided, although post offices generally have fewer facilities than those in the UK, for example. These include telephone calls, telegram and fax transmissions, domestic and international cash transfers, payment of telephone and utility bills, and the distribution of mail-order catalogues. Recently, La Poste has also started offering email services on the internet, including free and permanent email addresses, as well as e-commerce services for small businesses. The post office also provides financial and banking services, including cheque and savings accounts, mortgage and retirement plans, and share prices. Post offices usually have photocopy machines and telephone booths.

The Post Office produces numerous leaflets and brochures, including the *Tarifs Courrier – Colis*, or you can obtain information on ☎ 08 20 80 80 00 for general information or 08 10 82 18 21 for information regarding international post. La Poste has a website where you can find information on all its services, although only limited information is available in English (🖳 www. laposte.fr). The site offers a search tool to help you find the address and telephone number of your nearest post office, according to the town name or postcode. The listings don't include the opening hours or the times for the last collection each day.

Note that French companies are usually slow to reply to letters and it's often necessary to follow up a letter with a telephone call.

Parcels

The post office provides a (confusing and ever-changing) range of parcel (*colis*) services, domestic and international, now collectively called *ColiPoste*. Parcel services are also provided by French railways and airlines and international courier companies such as DHL, Fedex and UPS. First-class parcels are limited to a maximum weight of 3kg, and parcels containing printed matter (e.g. books and magazines) are limited to 5kg. Parcels heavier than 5kg must be taken to a main post office. International parcels are usually limited to 30kg, although there are lower limits, e.g. 20kg, for some countries. Parcels to addresses outside the European Union (EU) must have an international green customs label (*déclaration de douane*) affixed to them. Recent security regulations require you to present identification when sending parcels over 250g.

Registered & Recorded Post

Registered post is commonly used in France when sending official documents and communications, when proof of despatch and/or receipt is required. You can send a registered letter (*lettre recommandée*) with (*avec*) or without (*sans*) proof of delivery (*avis de réception*). There are three levels of compensation (*indemnité forfaitaire*) for domestic registered letters and parcels. The sender's address must be written on the back of registered letters. You receive a receipt for a registered letter or parcel.

LEARNING FRENCH

If you don't already speak good French, don't expect to learn it quickly, even if you already have a basic knowledge and take intensive lessons. It's common for foreigners not to be fluent after a year or more of intensive lessons in France. If your expectations are unrealistic, you will become frustrated, which can affect your confidence. **It takes a long time to reach the level of fluency needed to be able to work in French.** If you don't speak French fluently, you should consider taking a menial or even an unpaid voluntary job on arrival in France, as this is one of the quickest ways of improving your French.

Although it isn't easy, even the most non-linguistic person can acquire a working knowledge of French. All that's required is a little hard work, some help and perseverance, particularly if you have only English-speaking colleagues and friends. **Your business and social enjoyment and success in France will be directly related to the degree to which you master French.**

Most people can teach themselves a great deal through the use of books, tapes, videos and even computer and internet-based courses.

A good place to start, and a resource you can continue to use wherever you are, is the impressive languages section of the BBC website (💻 www. bbc.co.uk/languages/french), which is comprehensive and informative. You can test your ability to find out which level is best for you and learn French online at your own pace. The site also contains news and features about France, to help you get a feel for the country and its people, and there's a fascinating section entitled 'French for Work'. Here, you can find out what it's like working in a French business environment and get help with specialist language practice for a variety of business situations. Particularly valuable are the experiences of those who have already taken the plunge and the expert tips from those who have been in the world of work in France for some time.

Other websites offering free tutorials include 💻 www.france-pub/com /french, www.frenchassistant.com, www.frenchlesson.org and www.french tutorial.com. There are also self-study French courses you can buy – if you've paid money for a course, you're more likely to see it through! – including those offered by Eurotalk (💻 www.eurotalk.co.uk) and Linguaphone (💻 www.linguaphone.co.uk). A quarterly publication, *Bien-dire* (sic), is aimed at adult learners (💻 www.learningfrench.com).

There are several things you can do to speed up your language learning before and after your arrival in France, including watching television (particularly quiz shows where the words appear on the screen as they're spoken) and DVDs (where you can select French or English subtitles), reading (especially children's books and product catalogues, where the words are accompanied by pictures), joining a club or association, and (most enjoyable) making French friends!

Lessons

However, even the best students require some professional help. Teaching French is big business in France, with classes offered by language schools,

French and foreign colleges and universities, private and international schools, foreign and international organisations (such as the British Institute in Paris), local associations and clubs, and private teachers. There are many language schools (*école de langues*) in cities and large towns, most universities provide language courses, and many organisations offer holiday courses year-round, particularly for children and young adults (it's best to stay with a local French family). Tuition ranges from courses for complete beginners, through specialised business or cultural courses to university-level courses leading to recognised diplomas. If you already speak French, but need conversational practice, you may prefer to enrol in an art or craft course at a local institute or club. You can also learn French via a telephone language course, which is particularly practical for busy executives and those who don't live near a language school.

In some areas, the *Centre Culturel* provides free French lessons to foreigners. If you're officially registered as unemployed and have a residence permit (*carte de séjour*), you can obtain free lessons (*perfectionnement de la langue française*), although complete beginners don't qualify (contact your local ANPE office for information).

One of the most famous French language teaching organisations is the Alliance Française (AF), 101 boulevard Raspail, 75270 Paris Cedex 06 (☎ 01 42 84 90 00, 🖳 www.alliancefr.org), a state-approved, not-for-profit organisation with over 1,000 centres in 138 countries, including 32 centres in France, mainly in large towns and cities. The AF runs general, special and intensive courses, and can also arrange a homestay in France with a host family.

Another non-profit organisation is Centre d'Echanges Internationaux, 1 rue Gozlin, 75006 Paris (☎ 01 43 29 60 20), offering intensive French language courses for juniors (13 to 18 years) and adults throughout France. Courses include accommodation in their own international centres, with a French family, or in a hotel, bed and breakfast, or self-catering studio. Junior courses can be combined with tuition in a variety of sports and other activities, including horse riding, tennis, windsurfing, canoeing, diving and dancing.

Another well known school is Berlitz (☎ 01 40 74 00 17, 🖳 www.berlitz. com) with around 16 schools in France, including five in Paris. The British organisation CESA Languages Abroad (☎ 01209-2211800, 🖳 www.cesa languages.com) offers advice and arranges language courses.

Most language schools run various classes depending on your language ability, how many hours you wish to study a week, how much money you want to spend and how quickly you wish to learn. Language classes generally fall into the following categories: Extensive (four to ten hours per week); Intensive (15 to 20 hours); Total Immersion (20 to 40 or more).

Don't expect to become fluent in a short time unless you have a particular flair for languages or already have a good command of French. Unless you must desperately learn French quickly, it's better to arrange your lessons over a long period. However, don't commit yourself to a long course of study, particularly an expensive one, before ensuring that it's the right course. The cost for a one-week total immersion course is usually between €2,500 and €3,000! Most schools offer free tests to help you find your appropriate level and a free introductory lesson.

You may prefer to have private lessons, which are a quicker, although more expensive, way of learning a language. The main advantage of private lessons is that you learn at your own speed and aren't held back by slow learners or left floundering in the wake of the class genius. You can advertise for a teacher in your local newspapers, on shopping centre/supermarket bulletin boards and university notice boards, and through your or your spouse's employer. Otherwise, look for advertisements in the English-language press (see **Appendix B**). Don't forget to ask your friends, neighbours and colleagues if they can recommend a private teacher. Private lessons by the hour cost from around €50 at a school or €15 to €35 with a private tutor, although you may find someone willing to trade French lessons for English lessons. In some areas (particularly in Paris), there are discussion groups which meet regularly to talk in French and other languages; these are usually advertised in the English-language press (see **Appendix B**).

Our sister-publication, *The Best Places to Buy a Home in France* (Survival Books – see page 317) includes lists of language schools in the most popular regions of France. A comprehensive list of schools, institutions and organisations providing French language courses throughout France is contained in a booklet, *Cours de Français Langue Étrangère et Stages Pédagogie de Français Langue Étrangère en France*. It includes information about the type of course, organisation, dates, costs and other practical information, and is available from French consulates or from the Association pour la Diffusion de la Pensée Française (ADPF), 6 rue Ferrus, 75683 Paris Cedex 14 (☎ 01 43 13 11 00, 🖳 www.adpf.asso.fr).

Regional Languages & Dialects

As well as French, there are a number of regional languages in France, including Alsatian (spoken in Alsace), Basque (Pyrénées), Breton (Brittany), Catalan (Roussillon), Corsican (Corsica) and Occitan (Languedoc). Although you're unlikely to have to deal with anyone who speaks **only** a regional language, you should bear in mind that your linguistic life will be even more complicated if you decide to live and work in any of these areas. If you have school-age children, you should note that in some areas, schools teach in the regional language, as well as in French.

As well as regional languages, France has a plethora of local dialects (*patois*), which are often incomprehensible even to native French speakers! Add to all this the various accents of 'standard' French, particularly the typical twang of southerners (who pronounce the word *accent* 'aksang') and you will appreciate the importance of mastering the language before you even **think** about working in France!

APPENDICES

APPENDIX A: USEFUL ADDRESSES

Holiday Letting Agencies

Allez France (UK ☎ 0845-330 2056, 🖳 www.allezfrance.com). A well established company with over 300 properties and a printed brochure.

Bowhills (UK ☎ 01489-872727, 🖳 www.bowhills.co.uk). 350 properties. 30,000 copies of a colour brochure printed annually. Strongest in the Dordogne, Provence, Languedoc and Brittany. UK-based bilingual representatives and a dedicated owners' telephone helpline. Looking for properties with pools or within 20 minutes of a beach or perhaps a river frontage.

Brittany Ferries Holiday Homes (UK ☎ 0870-536 0360, 🖳 www. brittanyferries.com). The official UK representative of Gîtes de France, with 850 *gîtes* and 450 cottages in its brochure, some villas with pools in southern France. Ferry fares 15 per cent lower than public fares.

Crystal France (UK ☎ 0800-980 3381, 🖳 www.crystalfrance.co.uk). Nearly 300 mid to up-market properties, covering most French regions.

French Affair (UK ☎ 020-7381 8519, 🖳 www.frenchaffair.com). Operating to France since 1986. Villas on the Atlantic Coast and in Corsica, Dordogne, Languedoc-Roussillon, Lot, Pays Basque and Provence.

Gites Direct (🖳 www.gitesdirect.com). Booking service on commission basis, owners otherwise liaising directly with clients.

Holiday Cottages Group: One of the largest companies in this field, which also owns **Chez Nous** (see **Advertising Sites** below). Its brands include:

- **Easycottages** (UK ☎ 0870-197 2799, 🖳 www.easycottages.com).
- **French Country Cottages** (UK ☎ 0870-078 1500, 🖳 www. french-country-cottage.co.uk, 🖳 www.countrycottagesin-france.co.uk, 🖳 www.cottages4you.co.uk). 900 French lets. 200,000 preview brochures sent to mailing list plus 200,000 main brochures to past and potential customers in November. Dedicated owner helpline and bilingual representatives in the UK. Annual inspections by regional

representatives in France. Full back-up for owners. French Country Cottages pay up front any monies received, deposits and full payments, which are non-refundable in the case of late cancellation by the client. 50 per cent of properties have pools.

- **French Life** (UK ☎ 0870-197 6675, 🖳 www.frenchlife.co.uk). 1,000 cottages and villas, priced between French Country Cottages and Welcome Cottages.

- **Welcome Cottages** (UK ☎ 0870-197 6420, 🖳 www.welcome cottages.com). Less expensive cottages, villas and apartments across France.

Individual France (UK ☎ 0870-077 1771, 🖳 www.individualtrav-ellers.com). Formerly Vacances en Campagne. 400 properties, around half of which have pools. Prices include short Channel crossing or car hire. Properties to be submitted by May for inclusion in the following year's brochure, but can immediately go on the website.

Just France (UK ☎ 020-8780 4480, 🖳 www.justfrance.co.uk). Website booking and printed brochure.

VFB Holidays (UK ☎ 01242-240340, 🖳 www.vfbholidays.co.uk). Properties are mostly French-owned. Each property is inspected every year. Printed brochure. Cleaning included in holiday price.

Advertising Sites – Gîtes and Bed & Breakfast

Anglo-French Bed & Breakfast (🖳 www.anglofrenchbedand-breakfast.com). Bed & breakfast (B&B) for English speakers. €39 for one year's subscription including an advertisement with up to three photographs.

Bedbreak.com (🖳 www.bedbreak.com). B&B in France. Site in six languages and printed guidebook in association with Thomas Cook.

Bonnes Vacances (UK ☎ 0870-760 7073, 🖳 www.bvdirect.co.uk). Advertises in national newspapers, publishes a brochure and offers travel discounts and an insurance service. Listing cost: from £200 per year.

Brittany Ferries Owners in France (UK ☎ 0870-901 3400, 🖳 www. ownersinfrance.co.uk). The well known ferry company's agency division with an easy-to-navigate site and a well distributed brochure. Offers ferry fare and other travel discounts. Listing cost: from £215 + value added tax (VAT) per year.

Chez Nous (UK ☎ 0870-197 1000, 🖳 www.cheznous.com). An easy-to-navigate site and a well distributed brochure listing over 4,000 properties plus extensive advertising in the UK national press. Listings can be on the website only or also in the brochure. Listing cost: from £225 + VAT.

Easy-Gite (🖳 www.easy-gite.co.uk). Simple, easy-to-navigate site with free listings and paid upgrades.

France Direct (🖳 www.francedirect.net). A UK company, also registered in France (95 per cent of owners are English-speaking). Has an easily navigated site, but no brochure. A sister company of Gites Direct (see above), its commission-based agency. There are several subscription levels. Listing cost: from €150 per year.

France One Call (UK ☎ 0871-717 9092, 🖳 www.franceonecall.com). Web based advertising with a referral system: when members receive enquiries for weeks that are already booked they give the enquirer the France One Call number or forward the email. Listing cost: £180 per year for one property, £30 for each additional property.

France Renting Abroad (🖳 http://france.renting-abroad.com). Three-month free trial, then £50 per year. Has excellent search engine visibility.

French Accommodation (🖳 www.frenchaccommodation.co.uk). Privately owned *gîtes*, chalets, villas and B&B accommodation. Listing cost: from €110 per year.

French Connections (🖳 www.frenchconnections.co.uk). Has a fast, easy-to-search site including plenty of details. Listing cost: from £150 per year.

Gite.com (🖳 www.gite.com). US-based company. Good photography tips on the site. Listing cost: from $180 for six months.

Gites-in-France (UK ☎ 0870-720 2966, 🖳 www.gites-in-france. co.uk). Advertise from £15, with photograph from £75.

Homelidays (France ☎ 01 70 75 34 03, 🖳 www.homelidays.com). The site is available in French, Spanish, German, Italian and

Portuguese. Listing cost: €90 per year (you can choose to advertise for 1, 4, 8 or 12 months).

JML Villas (🖥 www.jmlvillas.com). Holiday villas, apartments and cottages. Listing cost: £11.75 per year.

Paris-Apts.com (France ☎ 01 40 28 01 28, 🖥 www.paris-apts.com). Short-term Paris apartment rentals.

Rentals France (🖥 www.rentalsfrance.com). Good site with plenty of additional information and useful links. Flexible payment plans – pay per enquiry or from £24. (Also 🖥 www.rentalsfrance.com/paris/index.html – Paris apartments.)

Vacation Rentals by Owner/VRBO (🖥 www.vrbo.com). The fast site provides comprehensive details of accommodation worldwide; France can be searched by region. Listing cost: US$148 per year (includes three photographs).

Visit France (UK ☎ 0870-350 2808, 🖥 www.visitfrance.co.uk). Has an easily navigated site (no brochure) listing over 500 properties, including *gîtes* and B&B. Listing cost: from £100.

Appendix B: FURTHER READING

English-language Newspapers & Magazines

The publications listed below are a selection of the dozens related to France and, in particular, French property. Most of these include advertisements by estate agents and companies offering other services for house hunters and buyers as well as an ordering service for books about France and the French.

The Connexion, BP25, 06480 La-Colle-sur-Loup, France (☎ 04 93 32 16 59, 🖳 www.connexionfrance.com). Monthly newspaper.

Everything France Magazine, Brooklands Magazines Ltd, Medway House, Lower Road, Forest Row, East Sussex RH18 5HE, UK (☎ 01342-828700, 🖳 www.everythingfrancemag.co.uk). Bimonthly lifestyle magazine.

Focus on France, Outbound Publishing, 1 Commercial Road, Eastbourne, East Sussex BN21 3XQ, UK (☎ 01323-726040, 🖳 www. outboundpublishing.com). Quarterly property magazine.

France Magazine, Archant Life, Archant House, Oriel Road, Cheltenham, Gloucestershire GL50 1BB, UK (☎ 01242-216050, 🖳 www.francemag.co.uk). Monthly lifestyle magazine.

France Magazine (US) (🖳 www.francemagazine.org). Quarterly magazine published by the French-American Cultural Foundation in Washington, DC.

France-USA Contacts, FUSAC, 26 rue Bénard, 75014 Paris, France (☎ 01 56 53 54 54, 🖳 www.fusac.fr). Free biweekly magazine.

French Magazine, Merricks Media Ltd, Cambridge House South, Henry Street, Bath BA1 1JT, UK (☎ 01225-786840, 🖳 www.french magazine.co.uk). Monthly lifestyle and property magazine.

French News, SARL Brussac, 225 route d'Angoulème, BP4042, 24004 Périgueux Cedex, France (☎ 05 53 06 84 40, 🖳 www.french-news.com). Monthly newspaper.

French Property News, Archant Life, 6 Burgess Mews, London SW19 1UF, UK (☎ 020-8543 3113, 🖳 www.french-property-news. com). Monthly property magazine.

The Irish Eyes Magazine, The Eyes, 2 rue des Laitières, 94300 Vincennes, France (☎ 01 41 74 93 03, 🖳 www.irisheyes.fr). Monthly Paris cultural magazine.

Living France, Archant Life, Archant House, Oriel Road, Cheltenham, Gloucestershire GL50 1BB, UK (☎ 01242-216050, 🖳 www.livingfrance.com). Monthly lifestyle/property magazine.

Normandie & South of England Magazine, 330 rue Valvire, BP414, 50004 Saint-Lô, France (☎ 02 33 77 32 70, 🖳 www. normandie-magazine.fr). News and current affairs about Normandy and parts of southern England, published eight times a year mainly in French, but with some English articles and translations.

Paris Voice/Paris Free Voice, 7 rue Papillon, 75009 Paris, France (☎ 01 47 70 45 05, 🖳 www.parisvoice.com). Free weekly newspaper.

The Riviera Reporter, 56 chemin de Provence, 06250 Mougins, France (☎ 04 93 45 77 19, 🖳 www.riviera-reporter.com). Bimonthly free magazine covering the Côte d'Azur.

The Riviera Times, 8 avenue Jean Moulin, 06340 Drap, France (☎ 04 93 27 60 00, 🖳 www.rivieratimes.com). Monthly free newspaper covering the Côte d'Azur and Italian Riviera.

French Property Magazines

Franchise Magazine (🖳 www.franchise-magazine.com). Information regarding all types of franchise.

ICF l'Argus des Commerces (🖳 www.argus-commerce.com). Magazine of interest to all businesses.

Immobilier en France (🖳 www.immobilierenfrance.com). Magazine with advertisements for property to buy and rent.

Info Presse (🖳 www.info-presse.fr). Subscription service for over 5,000 magazines, e.g. *Artisans Magazine, l'Officiel de la Franchise* and *l'Officiel des Commerciaux*.

L'Hôtellerie (🖳 www.lhotellerie.fr). Magazine for those in the hotel and restaurant industry.

Living France (🖳 www.livingfrance.com). English-language guide to France and French property.

Logic-immo (🖳 www.logic-immo.com). Monthly magazine with advertisements for property for sale and rent.

Books

The following books about France and the French are published by Survival Books and can be ordered using the form on page 317.

The Alien's Guide to France, Jim Watson. A light-hearted look at life in France.

Brittany Lifeline, Val Gascoyne. A directory of services, amenities and facilities in Brittany for visitors and residents.

Dordogne/Lot Lifeline, Val Gascoyne. A directory of services, amenities and facilities in Dordogne, Lot and Lot-et-Garonne for visitors and residents.

Foreigners in France: Triumphs & Disasters, Joe & Kerry Laredo (eds). Real-life stories of people from all over the world who have moved to France.

Living & Working in France, David Hampshire. Everything you need to know about life and employment in France.

Making a Living in France, Joe Laredo. The ins and outs of self-employment and starting a business in France.

Normandy Lifeline, Val Gascoyne. A directory of services, amenities and facilities in Upper and Lower Normandy for visitors and residents.

Poitou-Charentes Lifeline, Val Gascoyne. A directory of services, amenities and facilities in Poitou-Charentes for visitors and residents.

Provence-Côte d'Azur Lifeline, Val Gascoyne. A directory of services, amenities and facilities in Provence-Alpes-Côte-d'Azur for visitors and residents.

Renovating & Maintaining Your French Home, Joe Laredo. How to realise the renovation dream and avoid nightmares.

Surprised by France, Donald Carroll. An expatriate's view of the idiosyncrasies of French life.

APPENDIX C: USEFUL WEBSITES

Property Websites in English

1st For French Property (🖥 www.1st-for-french-property.co.uk). French property for sale in all regions, from chateaux, *gîtes* and farmhouses to mobile homes; a portal for over 50 agents.

A Vendre A Louer (🖥 www.avendrealouer.fr/en). Network for advertising all types of property for sale and rent.

Blue Homes (🖥 www.bluehomes.de/blue-en). Network of estate agents, working in five languages.

Coast-Country (🖥 www.coast-country.com). Thousands of properties; nine multilingual agents throughout France.

Domus Abroad (🖥 www.domusabroad.com). UK-based agency.

Find Your Property (🖥 www.findyourproperty.com). Global property finder.

Francophiles (🖥 www.francophiles.co.uk). UK-based property company specialising in all areas of France.

French Connections (🖥 www.frenchconnections.co.uk). Advertising portal for property owners and agents selling or renting in France.

French Property News (🖥 www.french-property-news.com). Site containing advertisements from estate agents, solicitors, financial advisers, builders, removal companies, surveyors, etc.

Gites in France (🖥 www.gites-in-france.co.uk). Gîte businesses for sale.

Green Acre (🖥 www.green-acre.com). Private sales, no agents, contact vendors directly. Well-arranged site, easy to search. The French version is (🖥 www.immofrance.com).

Internet French Property (🖥 www.french-property.com). Property website with advertisements of properties for sale, rental and ancillary services.

Links French Property Services (🖥 www.linksproperty.co.uk). Properties for sale, with guidance through the purchase process.

Outbound Publishing (🖥 www.outboundpublishing.com). Information on emigration, jobs and property.

Properties in France (🖥 www.propertiesinfrance.com). Properties include *gîte* complexes, vineyards and stud farms.

Renovation-EU (🖥 www.renovation.eu.com). Excellent site with properties for sale and extensive information on renovation and links to UK press articles on all aspects of living in France.

La Résidence (🖥 www.laresidence.co.uk). Gîte complexes and B&Bs for sale in the north, west and south-west.

Salut-France (🖥 http://salut-france.com). Property search agency providing an English-language service in Brittany and Loire-Atlantique.

United Residence (🖥 www.united-residence.com/france). Network of estate agents.

Property Websites in French

Agency Sites

123 Immo (🖥 www.123immo.fr). Displays over 4,000 estate agencies' advertisements.

3d Immo (🖥 www.3d-immo.com). Portal displaying advertisements from individuals and estate agents.

Abimmo (🖥 www.abimmo.com). Many properties for sale – new and old, houses and apartments.

Abonim (🖥 www.abonim.com). Displays advertisements from individuals and estate agents.

L'Argus du Logement (🖥 http://universimmo.services alacarte.wanadoo.fr/argus). Estimates of property values.

Century 21 (🖥 www.century21.fr). Estate agent with offices throughout France.

FNAIM (🖥 www.fnaim.fr). French national estate agents' organisation with advice on buying property and property advertisements.

Guy Hoquet (🖥 www.guy-hoquet.com). Property company for buying or renting private or business premises.

Logic-immo (🖥 www.logic-immo.com). Monthly magazine listing houses for sale and rent.

Nota (🖳 www.nota.fr). *Notaires'* website covering Calvados and Manche.

Orpi (🖳 www.orpi.com). Displays over 1,000 estate agencies' advertisements.

Panorimmo (🖳 www.panorimmo.com). Links to property websites.

Le Partenaire Européen (🖳 www.partenaire-europeen.fr). Property search agency helping buyers and sellers of property throughout France.

Propriétés de France (🖳 www.proprietesdefrance.com). Website providing advice and listing estate agencies for top-of-the-range properties.

Le Site Immobilier (🖳 www.lesiteimmobilier.com). Website containing many estate agents' advertisements.

SNPI (🖳 www.snpi.fr). Website of the estate agents' organisation, containing advertisements and advice.

Le Tuc (🖳 www.letuc.com). Estate agent with offices throughout France.

UNPI (🖳 www.unpi.org). Website of the estate agents' organisation.

Private Advertisement Sites

L'Annonce (🖳 www.lannonce.com/immobilier/index.html). Property for sale and to rent.

Appel Immo (🖳 www.appelimmo.fr).

La Centrale (🖳 www.lacentrale.fr/home_immo.php). Property for sale and to rent.

E-immo (🖳 www.e-immo.biz). Private and estate agency advertisements.

Entreparticuliers (🖳 www.entreparticuliers.com). Property for sale and to rent.

Explorimmo (🖳 www.explorimmo.com). Property for sale and links to other useful sites.

Immobilier-particulier (🖳 www.immobilier-particulier.net). Property to buy and rent throughout France.

Immosurcartes (⌨ www.immosurcartes.com). Property for sale and to rent.

Immo-web (⌨ www.immo-web.net). Private and estate agents' advertisements for property to buy and rent.

Le Journal des Particuliers (⌨ www.journaldesparticuliers.fr). Property for sale and holiday homes to rent throughout France.

Kitrouve (⌨ www.kitrouve.com). Property for sale and to rent.

Mister Annonces (⌨ www.misterannonces.com/fr/houses). Property for sale and to rent.

De Particulier à Particulier (⌨ www.pap.fr).

ParuVendu (⌨ www.bonjour.fr). Property for sale and to rent.

Petites Annonces (⌨ www.petites-annonces.fr). Property for sale and to rent.

Holiday Rental Sites

Café-Couette (⌨ www.cafe-couette.com). B&B advertising free; 'VIP' subscription at €32.

Clévacances (⌨ www.clevacances.com). Official French organisation for B&B and *gîtes*.

Fleurs de Soleil (⌨ www.fleursdesoleil.fr). Up-market B&B.

Gîtes de France (⌨ www.gites-de-france.fr). Official French organisation for B&B and *gîtes*.

Guide Vacances (⌨ www.guidevacances.com). Holiday listing site. Basic listing free, with several optional paid extras (e.g. €15 for a photograph).

Le Petit Futé (⌨ www.lepetitfute.com). Well known French guide. Website entries cost €120 (including a photo).

Vacances (⌨ www.vacances.com). Advertisements translated into seven languages; from €83 per year.

General Property Sites

All sites are in French unless otherwise stated.

Agence Nationale pour l'Information sur le Logement (🖳 www.anil.org). Information on letting, with rules and regulations and guidance for both owners and tenants.

Agence Pour la Création d'Entreprises (🖳 www.apce.com). Official government site with information on starting a business. Some information in English.

Assemblée des Chambres Françaises de Commerce et d'Industrie/ACFCI (🖳 www.acfci.cci.fr). Association of French Chambers of Commerce.

Conseil Géneral (🖳 www.cg00.fr). To find the *Conseil Géneral* site for your department, substitute your department number for the '00' (e.g. for department 42 enter 🖳 www.cg42.fr).

Direct Gestion (🖳 www.directgestion.fr). Useful site providing templates for letters, contracts and leases.

L'Entreprise (🖳 www.lentreprise.com). Useful site providing templates for letters and contracts.

European Union (🖳 www.europa.eu.int). General information about working in France (and other EU countries) and details of the economic situation and employment situation in each region (English).

FEEF (🖳 www.feef.org). Site of the Fédération des Entreprises et Entrepreneurs de France, providing general information about starting a business.

Fiducial (🖳 www.fiducial.fr). Information for small businesses.

France Initiative Réseau (🖳 www.fir.asso.fr). Information about loans and other assistance for entrepreneurs.

Government Portal (🖳 www.premier-ministre.gouv.fr – in English). French official government site.

Info Travail (🖳 www.infotravail.com). Government site with information on the legal aspects of employment.

Inforeg (🖳 www.inforeg.ccip.fr). Paris-based site containing legal information with a good section on holiday letting.

Institut National de la Statistique et des Études Économiques (🖳 www.insee.fr). Official French site for national statistics, censuses and surveys.

Internet French Property Co. (🖳 www.french-property.com – in English). This property site also has a good community section with news, finance, legal, and travel information and a discussion forum.

Kifaikoi (🖳 www.kifaikoi.com – in English). Information for holiday accommodation businesses, with a very good forum (in French).

Lay My Hat (🖳 www.laymyhat.com – in English). Advice for rental owners, from rental owners, with a good discussion forum.

Logement.org (🖳 www.logement.org). General information on renting or letting out a property, including legalities.

Ministry of Employment (🖳 www.travail.gouv.fr). Site of the Ministère de l'Emploi, du Travail et de la Cohésion Sociale.

Ministère de l'Équipement, Transport et Logement (🖳 www. logement.equipement.gouv.fr and 🖳 www.equipement.gouv.fr). Government site with rules and regulations for letting and housing.

Ministère des Petites et Moyennes Enterprises (🖳 www.pme. gouv.fr). Official French site for information on small and medium businesses.

Notaires (🖳 www.notaires.fr – available in English). A site which explains the role of *notaires* and their services and lists properties for sale (click on *'Rechercher un bien'*).

Monter une Entreprise (🖳 www.montermonentreprise.com). Online magazine with information about starting a business.

Panoranet (🖳 www.panoranet.com). Mortgage and insurance information.

Paris Entreprises (🖳 www.paris-entreprises.com). Official site for information about setting up a business in the Paris area, but offers clear information relevant to all areas of France.

Perval (🖳 www.immoprix.com). General land and property prices.

Petites Affiches (🖳 www.petites-affiches.presse.fr). Legal information.

Total France (🖳 www.totalfrance.com – in English). Properties to buy or rent, plus fact sheets, news, events, advertising, and a useful forum.

URSSAF (🖳 www.urssaf.fr). Official site of the main social security agency, with details of social security contributions.

Financial Information Sites

French Entrée (🖥 www.frenchentree.com). A general site about living in France which has a good financial section.

French Mortgage Connection (🖥 www.french-mortgage-connection.com). A UK-based broker which arranges mortgages with banks in France; the site has a good information section.

Impôt Revenue (🖥 www.impotrevenu.com). Official French tax site.

Ministère des Finances (🖥 www.finances.gouv.fr). This government site has financial news plus practical information and services.

PropertyFinance4Less (🖥 www.propertyfinance4less.com). Contains information on French mortgages and a buyers' guide.

UK Inland Revenue (🖥 www.inlandrevenue.gov.uk) UK inland revenue (tax) site; add /cnr for the centre for non-residents.

Miscellaneous Sites

Anglo Info (🖥 www.angloinfo.com). General information site with a useful forum.

Discover France (🖥 www.discover-france.info). Comprehensive travel and tourism information site.

Gîte Courses (🖥 www.gitecomplexes.co.uk). Chloe and Tim Williams.

Lay My Hat (🖥 www.laymyhat.com). Advice for rental owners, from rental owners, with a good discussion forum.

Living France (🖥 www.livingfrance.com). General information site with a lively forum.

Maison de la France (🖥 www.franceguide.com). Official French tourism website, available in many languages. Lots of information, holidays, guide, festivals, heritage & culture.

This French Life (🖥 www.thisfrenchlife.com). Includes articles about setting up a variety of necessary services, from bank accounts to internet connections.

APPENDIX D: MAPS

The map opposite shows the 22 regions and 96 departments of France (excluding overseas territories), which are listed below. Departments 91 to 95 come under the Ile-de-France region, which also includes Ville de Paris (75), Seine-et-Marne (77) and Yvelines (78), shown in detail opposite. The island of Corsica consists of two departments, 2A and 2B. The maps on the following pages show major airports and ports with cross-Channel ferry services, high-speed train (*TGV*) routes, and motorways and other major roads.

01 Ain	32 Gers	64 Pyrénées-Atlantiques
02 Aisne	33 Gironde	65 Hautes-Pyrénées
2A Corse-du-Sud	34 Hérault	66 Pyrénées-Orientales
2B Haute Corse	35 Ille-et-Vilaine	67 Bas-Rhin
03 Allier	36 Indre	68 Haut-Rhin
04 Alpes-de-Hte-Provence	37 Indre-et-Loire	69 Rhône
05 Hautes-Alpes	38 Isère	70 Haute-Saône
06 Alpes-Maritimes	39 Jura	71 Saône-et-Loire
07 Ardèche	40 Landes	72 Sarthe
08 Ardennes	41 Loir-et-Cher	73 Savoie
09 Ariège	42 Loire	74 Haute-Savoie
10 Aube	43 Haute-Loire	75 Paris
11 Aude	44 Loire-Atlantique	76 Seine-Maritime
12 Aveyron	45 Loiret	77 Seine-et-Marne
13 Bouches-du-Rhône	46 Lot	78 Yvelines
14 Calvados	47 Lot-et-Garonne	79 Deux-Sèvres
15 Cantal	48 Lozère	80 Somme
16 Charente	49 Maine-et-Loire	81 Tarn
17 Charente-Maritime	50 Manche	82 Tarn-et-Garonne
18 Cher	51 Marne	83 Var
19 Corrèze	52 Haute-Marne	84 Vaucluse
21 Côte-d'Or	53 Mayenne	85 Vendée
22 Côte-d'Armor	54 Meurthe-et-Moselle	86 Vienne
23 Creuse	55 Meuse	87 Haute-Vienne
24 Dordogne	56 Morbihan	88 Vosges
25 Doubs	57 Moselle	89 Yonne
26 Drôme	58 Nièvre	90 Territoire de Belfort
27 Eure	59 Nord	91 Essonne
28 Eure-et-Loir	60 Oise	92 Hauts-de-Seine
29 Finistère	61 Orne	93 Seine-Saint-Denis
30 Gard	62 Pas-de-Calais	94 Val-de-Marne
31 Haute-Garonne	63 Puy-de-Dôme	95 Val-d'Oise

REGIONS & DEPARTMENTS

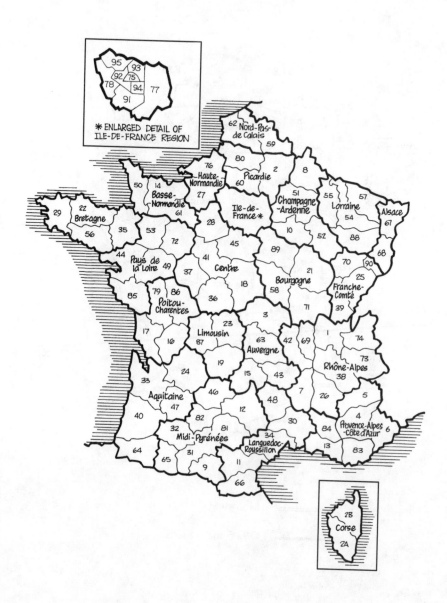

Motorways & Major Roads

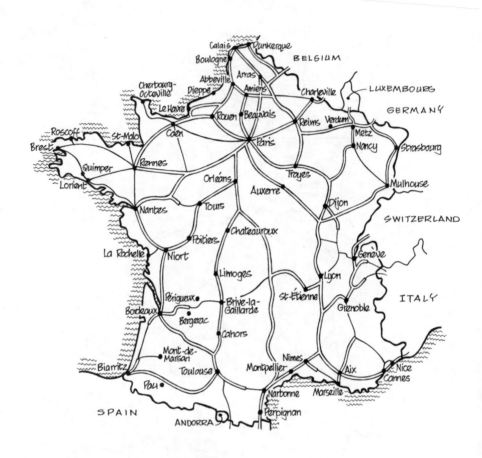

	Motorways
	Other main roads

TGV NETWORK

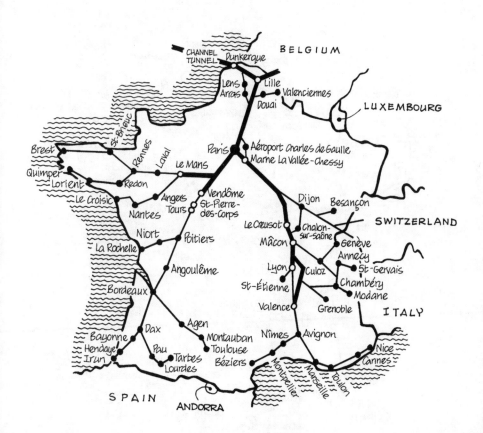

━━━━━━ Special track, on which trains can run at up to 300kph (187mph).

───── Ordinary track, on which trains are restricted to around 200kph (122mph).

AIRPORTS & PORTS

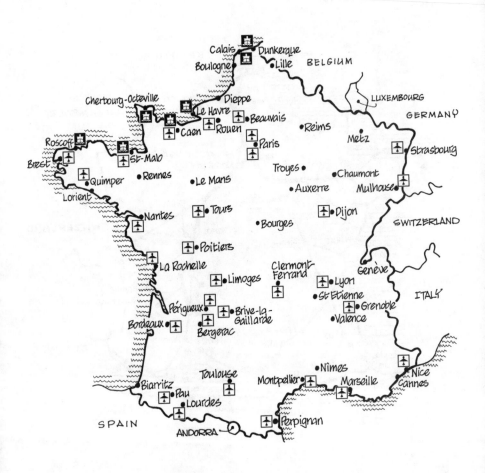

Airports

Ferry ports

APPENDIX E: AIRLINE SERVICES

The tables on the following pages indicate scheduled flights operating from UK and Irish airports to France. Details were current in April 2003. Airlines are coded as shown below (note that these aren't all official airline codes). Airport telephone numbers and website addresses are also shown below. Telephone numbers in italics are Irish numbers; all other numbers are UK numbers.

Code	Airline	Telephone	Website
AF	Air France	0870-142 4343	www.airfrance.com
AL	Aer Lingus	*0813-365 000*	www.aerlingus.com
AS	Air Scotland	0141-222 2363	www.air-scotland.com
BA	British Airways	0870-850 9850	www.ba.com
BB	BMIbaby	0870-264 2229	www.bmibaby.com
BM	BMI	0870-607 0555	www.flybmi.com
EJ	EasyJet	0871-750 0100	www.easyjet.com
FB	Flybe	0871-700 0123	www1.flybe.com
FG	Flyglobespan	0870-556 1522	www.flyglobespan.com
GB	GB Airways (British Airways)	0870-850 9850	www.gbairways.com
J2	Jet 2	0870-737 8282	www.jet2.com
RA	Ryanair	0871-246 0000	www.ryanair.com

Airport	Telephone	Website
Aberdeen	0870-040 0006	www.aberdeenairport.com
Belfast International	028-9448 4848	www.belfastairport.com
Birmingham	0870-733 5511	www.bhamintlairport.com
Bristol	0870-121 2747	www.bristolairport.co.uk
Cardiff	01446-71111	www.cwlfly.com
Cork	*021-431 3131*	www.cork-airport.com
Dublin	*01-814 1111*	www.dublin-airport.com
Durham/Tees Valley	01325-332811	www.teessideairport.com
Edinburgh	0870-040 0007	www.edinburghairport.com

Exeter	01392-367433	www.exeter-airport.co.uk
Glasgow Prestwick	0870-040 0008	www.glasgowairport.com
Leeds/Bradford	0113-250 9696	www.leedsairport.co.uk
Liverpool	0870-750 8484	www.liverpooljohnlennon airport.com
London City	020-7646 0088	www.londoncityairport.com
London Gatwick	0870-000 2468	www.gatwickairport.com
London Heathrow	0870-000 0123	www.heathrowairport.com
London Luton	01582-405100	www.london-luton.co.uk
London Stansted	0870-000 0303	www.stanstedairport.com
Manchester	0161-489 3000	www.manchesterairport.co.uk
Newcastle	0870-122 1488	www.newcastle international.co.uk
Norwich	01603-411923	www.norwichairport.co.uk
Nottingham/East Midlands	0871-919 9000	www.nottinghamema.com
Shannon	*061-712000*	www.shannonairport.com
Southampton	0870-040 0009	www.southamptonairport.com

	Aberdeen	Belfast International	Birmingham	Bristol	Cardiff	Cork	Dublin	Durham/Tees Valley	Edinburgh	Exeter	Glasgow Prestwick	Leeds/Bradford
Beauvais							RA					
Bergerac			FB[1]	FB[1]								
Bordeaux			BB	FB[1]			AF AL					
Brest			FB[1]							FB[1]		
Carcassonne							RA					
Chambéry			FB[1]							FB[1]		J2
Grenoble				EJ								
La Rochelle			FB[1]									
Lyon			BA				AL					
Marseille							AL					
Nice		EJ	BA BB	EJ			AL		FG		FG	J2
Paris CDG	AF	EJ	AF BA	BA	BB	AL	AF AL	BB BA	AF	FB[1]	AS BM	BB J2
Perpignan			FB[1]									
Toulouse			FB[1]	FB[1]			AL					

NOTES:

1. Flybe's schedules are planned only around six months in advance. All flights shown here were operating in winter 2005/06; summer '06 schedules were to be fixed in December 2005.
2. From May 2006.
3. Winter only

Flights from Bournemouth and Brighton to St-Brieuc in Brittany via the Channel Islands are offered by Rockhopper (UK ☎ 01481-824567, 🖥 www.rockhopper.aero).

Lydd Air (UK ☎ 01797 322207, 🖥 www.lyddair.co.uk) operates regular flights on a 16-seat plane between Lydd airport (near Ashford in Kent) and Le Touquet in Pas-de-Calais.

Some tour operators, e.g. First Choice, Monarch, Thomas Cook and Thomson, sell seats on their 'charter' flights to Toulouse and other airports; Thomsonfly offers flights from Bournemouth, Coventry and Doncaster/Sheffield to Lyon (winter only) and Paris CDG (summer) or Orly (winter).

	Liverpool	London City	London Gatwick	London Heathrow	London Luton	London Stansted	Manchester	Newcastle	Norwich	Nottingham/East Midlands	Shannon	Southampton
Ajaccio			GB2									
Bastia			GB2									
Beauvais												
Bergerac						RA						FB1
Biarritz						RA						
Bordeaux			BA				BB					
Brest												FB1
Carcassonne						RA						
Chambéry									FB1			
Dinard					RA	RA						
Grenoble			EJ		EJ	RA						
La Rochelle						RA						
Limoges						RA						FB1
Lyon				AF BB BM		EJ	BA					
Marseille			BA EJ									
Montpellier			GB2			RA						
Nantes			AF GB3			RA						
Nice	EJ		BA EJ	AF BB BM	EJ	EJ	J2	EJ				
Nîmes					RA	RA						
Paris CDG	EJ	AF		AF BA BB BM	EJ		AF BA	AF EJ				AF
Paris Orly		AF										
Pau						RA						
Perpignan						RA						
Poitiers						RA						FB1
Rennes												
Rodez						RA						FB1
St Etienne						RA						
Strasbourg			AF									
Toulon						RA						
Toulouse			BA EJ				BB BM					

APPENDIX F: USEFUL INFORMATION

OFFICIAL ORGANISATIONS

There are several official organisations with which a *chambers d'hôtes* or *gîte* business may register. Although they're all national organisations, they operate at departmental level. Whereas some of their criteria might apply to all properties, and most are broadly similar, there are many variations between departments. The requirements listed below should therefore be taken as typical, but you should contact the relevant office in your own department (also listed below) for a definitive list.

Accueil Paysan

Accueil Paysan Féderation Nationale (9 rue de la Poste, 38000 Grenoble, ☎ 04 76 43 44 83, 💻 www.accueil-paysan.com) works in conjunction with farmers, marketing holidays whereby the guests experience the countryside, animals, plants and 'the rhythm of the seasons'. The organisation includes *chambres d'hôtes*, *gîtes* and campsites. There are currently 502 farms in the scheme.

Bienvenue à la Ferme

5,000 farmers are members of the Bienvenue à la Ferme network, at various levels from simply opening their farms for visits and sale of regional products to running *gîtes* and *chambres d'hôtes* businesses. For details, contact the **Assemblée Permanente des Chambres d'Agriculture (APCA)**, 9 avenue Georges V, 75008 Paris (☎ 01 53 57 11 44, ✉ bienvenue-a-la-ferme@apca.chambagri.fr, 💻 www. bienvenue-a-la-ferme.com).

Clévacances

Clévacances classifies self-catering properties with one to five *clés* (keys), as detailed below. Reasons for non-acceptance, apart from non-compliance with the requirements listed below, include the following:

● Dampness.
● Little or no natural light.

- Insufficient ventilation in any room.
- Unsatisfactory arrangement of rooms – e.g. access to the bathroom or lavatory from the kitchen (except studio flats).
- Outside lavatory.
- Difficult vehicle access.
- Environmental problems (e.g. noise, smells, right of way across land).
- Rooms too small (see **Dimensions** on page 290).

The usual criteria for each classification are listed below; for further details contact the head office, Fédération Nationale des Locations de France Clévacances, 54 boulevard de l'Embouchure/BP2166, 31022 Toulouse Cedex 2 (☎ 05 61 13 55 66, 🖳 www.clevacances.com). You should, however, check local variations by contacting the Clévacances representative at the Comité Départemental de Tourisme.

1 Clé

Individual apartment or house for the exclusive use of the clients; no access allowed by the owner or others.

Bathroom(s): Must be independent, inside the building, with a door or partition, and equipped with a ventilation system (window, *ventilation méchanique contrôlée/VMC*, or ventilation grilles). For more than six people there must be two bathrooms, one of which must be separate. Each bathroom must contain a shower, bath or bath with a shower head, basin with mixer tap, soap holder fixed to the shower, wall-mounted towel rail, mirror, shelf, bathroom waste bin, coat peg or hook, razor socket and light over the basin.

Bedding: Bedding (mattress and divan base) must be clean, in perfect condition and fitted with a mattress protector. Mattresses must be good quality and in perfect condition. Metal bases and horsehair aren't allowed. One bedspread and two blankets or one duvet minimum per bed (in the south, except in the mountains, one blanket may be allowed in summer), one bolster and/or one pillow per person, one bedside table per occupant or one between twin beds, clothes rail with hangers. Any other bedding must be of good quality and in good condition. In overseas departments, a mosquito net for each bed is advised.

Bedrooms: Single beds must be 90cm wide and 190cm long (80cm bunk beds might be allowed). Double beds must be 140cm wide and 190cm long. Excepting studio flats, bedrooms must be separated from day rooms by a door or partition (for alcoves by a curtain, for cabins by a door). All bedrooms must have natural ventilation (window or roof opening). Shutters, blinds or curtains must obscure all light.

Cupboards: For two people: 2.5m². For each extra person: 1m².

Curtains & Blinds: Exterior shutters must be fitted to windows in rooms occupied at night unless the curtains ensure obscurity. When rooms are overlooked, net curtains must be used.

Electricity: The electrical system must conform to electrical standards. Electricity must be available in all rooms. There must be at least one socket per room and one or two lights totalling at least 15W per m² or equivalent. There must be free access to the fuse box.

Entrance Hall: Must have a doormat!

Exterior: Roofs must be covered with traditional regional materials, and tiles or slates must be in good condition. The facade must conform to the architecture of the site, and approaches to the house must be in good condition and unobstructed. If the accommodation allows, there must be a set of garden furniture with a parasol (unless there's natural shade), and a light for eating outside in the evening. Parking for visitors must be near the accommodation.

Floors: Must be in good condition and easily cleaned, soundproof and waterproof (e.g. parquet, tiles, paving, plastic flooring, carpets). No bitumen or cement floors.

Furniture: Must be in good condition, clean and suitable for its purpose: hanging cupboards, chests of drawers, wardrobes, chairs, sideboards, armchairs, sofas, divans, cupboards, table lamps, side tables and bedside tables according to the capacity of the accommodation.

Heating: The heating in each room must ensure a minimum temperature of 19°C during the letting period. For overseas territories, air-conditioning or ventilators are obligatory.

Kitchen or Kitchen Area: Ventilation or air-conditioning must be installed (an extractor hood in studio apartments), and there must be enough room for the maximum number of people accommodated. There must be a double or triple burner and mini-oven, sink with mixer tap, wooden or plastic draining rack (unless there's a dishwasher), pressure cooker, electric coffee maker, salad spinner, refrigerator (e.g. 140 litres for five people). The cooking utensils and dishes (two for each person) must be in perfect condition, not chipped or unmatched. Matching cutlery must be of sufficient quantity and quality (no aluminium or plastic).

Lavatory: Must be indoors, separate or in the bathroom, with ventilation and everything necessary for its use (e.g. brush, cover and paper holder).

Living/Dining Room: There must be an eating area adjacent to or independent of the kitchen with a table and chairs in perfect condition and sufficient for the capacity of the accommodation. If there's a fireplace, it must be well restored and in good working order, possibly with an insert (not a wood stove).

Walls & Ceilings: Walls and ceilings must be covered with materials such as painted plaster, paint, wallpaper, tiles or fabrics. They must be waterproof and in good condition, with good acoustic qualities. Wood is allowed where it guarantees comfort and insulation. Ceilings must be a minimum height of 2.2m (1.80m in attic spaces).

Water: Hot and cold water must be available at all times in all facilities. There must be a minimum of 40 litres of hot water per person per day.

Windows, etc: Sufficient ventilation and lighting for all rooms. One opening window for each living room.

Other Facilities & Equipment: There must be an iron and ironing cloth, vacuum cleaner (if there's carpet), indoor clothes line, waste bin (not a bucket), broom, bucket, shovel and floor cloth. Cleaning products advisable. Bathroom and kitchen towel hire must be available, as well as a folder with emergency numbers and practical information, and tourist leaflets. If an apartment is higher than the third floor, there must be a lift. No shared landings.

2 Clés

As for 1 *clé* with the following limitations or additions:

Bathroom(s): Shower with curtain or bath with a shower system. Ventilation must be by *VMC*.

Bedrooms: Apart from studio flats, the main bedroom must be independent with a double bed (140 x 190cm) or two single beds (90 x 190cm). Studio flats and apartments may have 80cm single beds. Hanging space and shelves with a door – for two people: $3m^2$; for each extra person: $1m^2$. The main light must have switches at the entrance and next to the bed. Sheet hire must be available. Overseas departments must have a mosquito net for each bed.

Entrance Hall: Must have a coat rack.

Exterior: Apartments must have a balcony or terrace with exterior lighting. A portable barbecue (unless forbidden by bylaws).

Kitchen or Kitchen Area: Must have an extractor hood, a *maxi-four* oven (for more than two people), a washing machine (which may be shared with the owner and other tenants).

Living Room: Must have a television socket, armchairs or sofas sufficient for the number of people, and a coffee table.

Windows, etc.: Rooms must be well ventilated and have sufficient natural light.

Other: Ironing board.

3 Clés

As for 2 *clés* with the following limitations or additions:

Bathroom(s): Must have a shower with plastic or glass doors, ceiling light and fan heater.

Bedrooms: There must be a chair or armchair and net curtains or double curtains in each bedroom.

Exterior: Houses must have a private yard or outside area (minimum $50m^2$) with grass and flowers, and one reserved parking space for clients.

Kitchen: Must have *VMC*, a four-burner hob (gas or electric), oven, microwave oven, double sink, food processor, refrigerator with freezer compartment, washing machine, toaster, electric knife and *raclette* set. For more than four people, there must be a dishwasher large enough for eight place settings. There must be three times the number of dishes as people.

Lavatory: For more than six people, there must be two lavatories, one of which must be separate.

Other: Cleaning products, colour television (TV), telephone with *téléséjour* service or *service restreint*. A cleaning service must be available at a moderate cost. The accommodation must be furnished 'in good taste', with matching furniture co-ordinating with the decor.

4 Clés

As for 3 *clés* with the following limitations or additions:

Bathroom: For more than six people, there must be two bathrooms, one of which must be independent. Both must have a bath with a shower screen in excellent condition, a mixer tap with a single swivel control (*mitigeur*), good quality lighting (low wattage or halogen).

Bedrooms: There must be a TV socket in the main bedroom and not more than one double bed or two single beds per room. Double beds must be 160 x 190cm. Each bedroom must have a wardrobe with hangers.

Exterior: Apartments must have a loggia or terrace (minimum 9m²). Houses must have a well kept garden with shade. There must be a paved area or terrace, good quality garden furniture (e.g. teak or cast iron) including sunloungers, a swimming pool (which may be shared with the owner or other tenants), and a good view. There must be private parking, indoor or covered.

Kitchen: Must have a window, tumble dryer, freezer or fridge/freezer. For more than six people, there must be a dishwasher for 12 places.

Lavatory: Must have a window.

Living Room: There must be a sitting room separate from the main room.

Other: Vacuum cleaner, folder with tourist information, hi-fi system and board games. All rooms must have direct fresh-air ventilation. Main rooms must have good natural light. Decoration must be to a high standard.

5 Clés

As for 4 *clés* with the following limitations or additions:

Bathroom(s): Heated towel rail.

Bedrooms: Colour TV in the main bedroom. Linen must be included in the rental price. At least one bedroom must have an ensuite bathroom.

Exterior: The house must be surrounded by enclosed grounds and have a private swimming pool.

Kitchen: Must be separate from the living room.

Other: Video/DVD player. Sheets and towels must be provided. Cleaning at the end of stay must be included in the rental price.

Dimensions

Generally, the living space must be in proportion to the capacity of the accommodation. The following criteria may vary according to the accommodation as well as the department:

- Minimum total area including kitchen or kitchen area, but excluding bathroom and lavatory for accommodation for two people (over five years old):
  - 1 *clé*: 12m^2.
  - 2 *clés*: 14m^2.
  - 3 *clés*: 16m^2.
  - 4 *clés*: 18m^2.
  - 5 *clés*: 24m^2.

Add 3m^2 for each additional person.

- The minimum area of extra bedrooms must usually be as shown below:
  - 1 *clé*: 7m^2.
  - 2 *clés*: 8m^2.
  - 3 *clés*: 9m^2.
  - 4 *clés*: 10m^2.
  - 5 *clés*: 12m^2.

Fleurs de Soleil

The 'Fleurs de Soleil' label is awarded by the organisation Les Maisons d'Amis en France to chambres d'hôtes businesses. Members must conform to the conditions in its 'quality charter', the main requirements of which are listed below. Further details and addresses of departmental offices can be obtained from the head office: Fleurs de Soleil, Domaine du Frère, Les Milles, 1382 Aix-en-Provence, Cedex 3 (☎ 08 26 62 03 22, 🖥 www.fleursdesoleil.fr). The label also applies to upmarket self-catering accommodation, but only around 400 properties are labelled, so details aren't included here; for information, contact Fleurs de Soleil.

General

Detached properties with character, whether old or modern, are preferred, and they should be set in pleasant, well maintained gardens with climbing plants, trees, shrubs and flowers. There must be no hotel or restaurant business on the site. If in a town, a property must be away from noise such as busy roads or a railway, or any noisy commercial activities. When activities such as swimming or tennis are mentioned in the description of the accommodation, these may not be subject to any supplementary charge.

Accommodation

There must be one to five bedrooms, with bathrooms, catering for up to 12 guests; breakfast must be included in the rental price. The guest rooms must be situated in the hosts' house or in an annexed building. Guests must have rooms, shared by the hosts or by other guests, where they can eat breakfast, socialise, read, and maybe listen to music or watch television.

Bathroom: Each bedroom must normally have its own bathroom and WC. When a bathroom is shared by two rooms, these must be described as a suite and the bathroom cannot be be shared without the assent of their occupants. In all cases, a basin and a shower or bath must be available, with a bathroom waste bin, all clean and in perfect working order, fresh soap and paper tissues. Towels and flannels must be renewed at least every three days. Cleaning and emptying of waste bins must be done every day.

Bedrooms: Bedrooms must have an area of at least 12m² (excluding areas under eaves, for example) and a height of 1.8m. Ventilation and heating must be provided, with at least one window or roof opening offering a view of the surrounding countryside. Double beds must be at least 140cm wide (160cm is recommended); single beds must be at least 80cm wide (90cm recommended). Twin beds must be identical. Beds must be not less than 40cm high and have a divan base and mattress in perfect condition. There must be a bedside rug, table and light for each person, a writing table, shelving or wardrobe, hanging space and clothes hangers. Blankets or duvets must be of good quality, as must bedspreads and pillows. Sheets and pillowcases are to be changed at least every five days. A cold drink (bottle or carafe with glasses) must be provided in each room. Facilities for preparing hot drinks (kettle, cups and sachets) are appreciated. Eating in bedrooms isn't allowed.

Stairs: If the layout of the accommodation means that guests have to use a staircase, this must be solid and not too steep. Stairs with treads higher than 18cm or narrower than 25cm must be mentioned in the description of the accommodation.

Meals

Breakfast: Breakfast must be included in the rental price. It must be plentiful and prepared with care from fresh ingredients: fresh tea, coffee or chocolate, a variety of breads, butter and jams (often home-made), regional and seasonal products. The host must be able to respond to special requests (if not excessive), e.g. cereals, yoghurts, eggs. Breakfast should be taken at a reasonable time for all involved according to their schedules.

Evening Meal: Evening meals are extra, as described in the details of accommodation, with an all-inclusive set price, and booked according to how long the host needs to prepare the meal. The service need be available only to those without special dietary requirements. Two things are imperative: cleanliness and freshness.

Welcome

Emphasis is put on the welcome given to guests, and the hosts' sharing of their lifestyle and culture. The family opens its house to visitors, helping them to discover the region's cultural and natural attractions. After booking, the visitor must be sent a map and directions, making the house easy to find. Arrival time is between 5pm and 7pm, unless otherwise agreed. The guests must be welcomed with a drink while their plans are discussed, then shown to their room(s), which must have been carefully prepared, with personal touches such as flowers, snacks and fruit. Hosts must be attentive and available to assist their guests with the language and local customs, supply maps and tourist information and materials for everyday needs such as sewing, writing and shoe polishing.

Gîtes de France

Gîtes de France (GdF) properties are classified by *épis* (wheatears), 1 being the lowest and 5 the highest. The requirements for the different types of *gîte* (see page 56) are given below. Departmental addresses are listed below; for general information, contact the head office, La Maison des Gîtes de France et du Tourisme Vert, 59 rue Saint-Lazare, Paris 75439 CEDEX 09 (☎ 01 49 70 75 75, 💻 www. gites-de-france.fr).

Departmental Offices

Ain: 21 place Bernard/BP198, 01005 Bourg-en-Bresse Cedex (☎ 04 74 23 82 66, ✉ gites-de-france-ain@wanadoo.fr, 💻 www.gites-de-france-ain.com).

Aisne: Comité Départemental du Tourisme, 24–28 avenue Charles de Gaulle, 02007 Laon Cedex (☎ 03 23 27 76 76, ✉ s.chamaux@cdt-aisne.com, 💻 www.gites-de-france-aisne.com).

Allier: Pavillon des Marronniers, Parc de Bellevue, 6 rue Jean Vidal/BP65, 03402 Yzeure Cedex (☎ 04 70 46 81 56, ✉ gites defrance@pays-allier.com, 💻 www.gites-de-france-allier.com).

Alpes-de-Haute-Provence: Maison du Tourisme, Rond Point du 11 Novembre/BP201, 04001 Digne-les-Bains Cedex (☎ 04 92 31 30 40, 💻 www.gites-de-france-04.fr).

Alpes-Maritimes: CRT 55-57 promenade des Anglais/BP1602, 06011 Nice Cedex 01 (☎ 04 92 15 21 30, 💻 www.gites-de-france-alpes-maritimes.com).

Ardèche: 4 cours du Palais/BP402, 07004 Privas Cedex (☎ 04 75 64 70 70, 💻 www.gites-de-france-ardeche.com).

Ardennes: 29 rue du Petit Bois/BP370, 08106 Charleville-Mezières Cedex (☎ 03 24 56 89 65, ✉ contact@gitardennes.com, 💻 http://212.234.53.212/GDF/08).

Ariège: 31bis avenue du Général de Gaulle/BP143, 09004 Foix Cedex (☎ 05 61 02 30 80, ✉ gites-de-france.ariege@wanadoo.fr, 💻 www.gites-de-france-ariege.com).

Aube: Chambre d'Agriculture, 2bis rue Jeanne d'Arc/BP4080, 10014 Troyes Cedex (☎ 03 25 73 00 11, ✉ gites.aube@wanadoo.fr, 💻 www.gites-de-france-aube.com).

Aude: Maison du Tourisme Vert, 78ter rue Barbacane, 11000 Carcassonne (☎ 04 68 11 40 70, ✉ gitesdefrance.aude@wanadoo.fr, 🖳 www.gites-de-france-aude.com).

Aveyron: APATAR Maison Départementale du Tourisme, 17 rue Aristide Briand/BP 831, 12008 Rodez Cedex 9 (☎ 05 65 75 55 55, ✉ apatar@wanadoo.fr, 🖳 www.gites-de-france-aveyron.com).

Bas-Rhin: 7 place des Meuniers, 67000 Strasbourg (☎ 03 88 75 56 50, ✉ alsace@gites67.com, 🖳 www.alsace-gites-de-france.com).

Bouches-du-Rhône: Domaine du Vergon, 13370 Mallemort (☎ 04 90 59 49 40, ✉ gitesdefrance@visitprovence.com, 🖳 www.gdf 13.com).

Calvados: 6 promenade de Madame de Sévigné, 14050 Caen Cedex 4 (☎ 02 31 82 71 65, 🖳 www.gites-de-france-calvados.fr).

Cantal: 34 avenue des Pupilles de la Nation/BP631, 15006 Aurillac Cedex (☎ 04 71 48 64 20, ✉ gites-de-france-cantal@wanadoo.fr, 🖳 www.gites-de-france-cantal.fr).

Charente: 23 avenue des Maréchaux, 16000 Angoulème (☎ 05 45 69 48 62, 🖳 www.gitescharente.com).

Charente-Maritime: Association GDF et du Tourisme Vert, 1 perspective de l'Océan, Résidence le Platin/BP32, 17002 La Rochelle Cedex 01 (☎ 05 46 50 63 63, 🖳 www.itea.fr/GDF/17).

Cher: 5 rue de Séraucourt, 18000 Bourges (☎ 02 48 48 00 18, ✉ tourisme.berry@cdt18.tv, 🖳 www.gites-du-cher.com).

Corrèze: Gîtes de France, Immeuble Consulaire/BP30, 19001 Tulle Cedex (☎ 05 55 21 55 61, ✉ gites-de-france@correze.chambagri.fr, 🖳 www.gites-de-france-limousin.com).

Corse: 77 cours Napoléon/BP10, 20181 Ajaccio Cedex 01 (☎ 04 95 10 06 14, 🖳 www.gites-corsica.com).

Côte-d'Or: 15 rue de l'Arquebuse/BP 90452, 21004 Dijon Cedex (☎ 03 80 45 97 15, ✉ gites.de.france21@wanadoo.fr, 🖳 www.gites-de-france-cotedor.com).

Côtes-d'Armor: 7 rue St Benoit/BP 4536, 22045 Saint-Brieuc Cedex 2 (☎ 02 96 62 21 73, ✉ contact@gitesdarmor.com, 🖳 www.gites darmor.com/voyageencotesdarmor.asp).

Creuse: Loisirs Accueil, 8 rue Martinet/BP7, 23001 Gueret Cedex (☎ 05 55 52 87 50, ✉ SLA.resa.creuse@wanadoo.fr, 💻 www.gites-de-france-limousin.com).

Deux-Sèvres: 15 rue Thiers/BP8524, 79025 Niort Cedex 9 (☎ 05 49 77 15 90, ✉ gites-de-France-deux-sevres@wanadoo.fr, 💻 www.itea.fr/GDF/79/F).

Dordogne: 25 rue Wilson/BP2063, 24002 Périgueux Cedex (☎ 05 53 35 50 24, ✉ dordogne.perigord.tourisme@wanadoo.fr, 💻 www.dordogne-perigord-tourisme.fr).

Doubs: 4ter Faubourg Rivotte, 25000 Besançon (☎ 03 81 82 80 48, ✉ loisirs.accueil.doubs@wanadoo.fr, 💻 www.gites-de-france-doubs.fr).

Drôme: Plateau de Lautagne, 42 avenue des Langories Bât. C/BP169, 26906 Valence Cedex 09 (☎ 04 75 83 16 42, 💻 www.gites-de-france-drome.com).

Essonne: Maison du Tourisme, 19 rue des Mazières, 91000 Evry (☎ 01 64 97 23 81, 💻 www.gites-de-france-essonne.com).

Eure: 9 rue de la Petite Cité, 27008 Evreux Cedex (☎ 02 32 39 53 38, 💻 www.gites-de-france-eure.com).

Eure-et-Loir: Loisir Accueil, 10 rue du Docteur Maunour, 28002 Chartres (☎ 02 37 84 01 02, ✉ loisirs.accueil28@tourisme28.com, 💻 www.france-bonjour.com/gites-chartres).

Finistère: Accueil Rural Finistère, 5 allée Sully, 29322 Quimper Cedex (☎ 02 98 64 20 20, ✉ reservation@gites-de-france-finistere.fr, 💻 www.gites-finistere.com).

Gard: Gîtes de France Gard, Maison du Tourisme, 3 place des Arènes, 30007 Nîmes Cedex 4 (☎ 04 66 27 94 94, 💻 www.gites-de-france-gard.fr).

Gers: Maison de l'Agriculture, Route de Tarbes/BP161, 32003 Auch Cedex (☎ 05 62 61 79 00, ✉ loisirs.accueil.gers@wanadoo.fr, 💻 www.gers-gites-france.com).

Gironde: Maison du Tourisme, 21 cours de l'Intendance, 33000 Bordeaux (☎ 05 56 81 54 23, ✉ gites-de-france-gironde@wanadoo.fr, 💻 www.gites-de-france-gironde.com).

Haut-Rhin: Maison du Tourisme, 1 rue Schlumberger/BP371, 68007 Colmar Cedex (☎ 03 89 20 10 62, ✉ reservation@tourisme68.asso.fr, 🖥 www.itea.fr/GDF/68).

Haute-Garonne: 14 rue Bayard/BP845, 31015 Toulouse Cedex 06 (☎ 05 61 99 70 60, 🖥 www.gites-de-france-31.com).

Haute-Loire: Hôtel du Département/BP332, 43012 Le Puy-en-Velay Cedex (☎ 04 71 07 41 56, ✉ sla43@auvergnevacances.com, 🖥 www.gites-de-france-haute-loire.com).

Haute-Marne: Cours Marcel Baron/BP2048, 52902 Chaumont Cedex 2 (☎ 03 25 30 39 03, ✉ gites@tourisme-hautemarne.com, 🖥 www.gites-de-france-hautemarne.com).

Haute-Saône: Relais des Gîtes de France, Vesoul Technologia, rue Max Devaux/BP50077, 70002 Vesoul Cedex (☎ 03 84 97 10 75, ✉ info@gites-de-france70.com, 🖥 www.itea.fr/GDF/70).

Haute-Savoie: Maison du Tourisme Vert, 16 rue Guillaume Fichet, 74000 Annecy (☎ 04 50 10 10 11, 🖥 www.gites-de-france-haute-savoie.com).

Haute-Vienne: Maison de l'Agriculture, 32 avenue du Général Leclerc, 87065 Limoges Cedex (☎ 05 55 79 04 04, ✉ sla87@wanadoo.fr, 🖥 www.gites-de-france-limousin.com).

Hautes-Alpes: 1 place du Champsaur/BP55, 05002 Gap Cedex (☎ 04 92 52 52 92, ✉ gdf05@free.fr, 🖥 www.gites-de-france-hautes-alpes.com/francais).

Hautes-Pyrénées: Maison de l'Agriculture, 2 place du Foirail, 65000 Tarbes (☎ 05 62 34 31 50, ✉ contact@gites-france-65.com, 🖥 www.gites-de-france-65.com).

Hérault: Maison du Tourisme, Avenue des Moulins, 34184 Montpellier Cedex 4 (☎ 04 67 67 71 62, 🖥 www.gites-de-france-herault.asso.fr).

Ille-et-Vilaine: 107 avenue Henri Fréville, BP70336, 35203 Rennes Cedex 2 (☎ 02 99 22 68 68, ✉ gitesdefrance35@wanadoo.fr, 🖥 www.gitesdefrance35.com).

Indre: 7bis rue Bourdillon, 36000 Châteauroux (☎ 02 54 22 91 20, ✉ gites36@wanadoo.fr, 🖥 www.itea.fr/GDF/36).

Indre-et-Loire: 38 rue Augustin Fresnel/BP139, 37171 Chambray-les-Tours (☎ 02 47 27 56 10, 🖥 www.gites-touraine.com).

Isère: Maison des Agriculteurs/BP2646, 38036 Grenoble Cedex 2 (☎ 04 76 40 79 40, ✉ relais.gites38@wanadoo.fr, 🖥 www.gites-de-france-isere.com).

Jura: 8 rue Louis Rousseau, 39000 Lons-le-Saunier (☎ 03 84 87 08 88, 🖥 www.jura-tourism.com).

Landes: Chambre d'Agriculture, Cité Galliane/BP279, 40005 Mont-de-Marsan Cedex (☎ 05 58 85 44 44, ✉ gites-de-france@landes.chambagri.fr, 🖥 www.gites-de-france-landes.com).

Loir-et-Cher: 5 rue de la Voûte du Château/BP249, 41001 Blois Cedex (☎ 02 54 58 81 64, ✉ GITES41@wanadoo.fr, 🖥 www.gites-de-france-blois.com).

Loire: 43 avenue Albert Raimond/BP20048, 42272 St-Priest-en-Jarez Cedex (☎ 04 77 79 18 49, ✉ contact@gites42.com, 🖥 www.gites-de-france-loire.com).

Loire-Atlantique: 3-5 rue Félibien/ BP93218, 44032 Nantes Cedex 1 (☎ 02 51 72 95 65, 🖥 www.gites-de-france-44.fr).

Loiret: 8 rue d'Escures, 45000 Orleans (☎ 02 38 62 04 88, ✉ gitesdefrance@loiret.chambagri.fr, 🖥 www.gites-de-france-loiret.com).

Lot: Maison du Tourisme, Place François Mitterand, 4600 Cahors (☎ 05 65 53 20 90, ✉ loisirs.accueil.lot@wanadoo.fr, 🖥 www.gites-de-france-lot.com).

Lot-et-Garonne: 11 rue des Droits de l'Homme, 47000 Agen (☎ 05 53 47 80 87, ✉ gites-de-france.47@wanadoo.fr, 🖥 www.gites-de-france-47.com).

Lozère: 14 boulevard Henri Bourillon, 48001 Mende Cedex (☎ 04 66 65 60 00, 🖥 www.lozere-tourisme.com).

Maine-et-Loire: Gîtes de France Anjou/BP52425, 49024 Angers Cedex 02 (☎ 02 41 23 51 42, ✉ gites-de-france-anjou@wanadoo.fr, 🖥 www.gites-de-france-anjou.com).

Manche: 98 route de Candol, Maison du Département, 50008 Saint-Lô Cedex (☎ 02 33 56 28 80, ✉ manchetourisme@cg50.fr, 🖥 www.manche-locationvacances.com/gites-de-france.htm).

Marne: Complexe Agricole du Mont Bernard, Route de Suippes/BP525, 51000 Chalons-en-Champagne (☎ 03 26 64 95 05, 🖥 www.gites-de-france-marne.com).

Mayenne: 84 avenue Robert Buron/BP0325, 53009 Laval Cedex (☎ 02 43 53 58 78, ✉ gites-de-france-53@wanadoo.fr, 🖥 www.gites-de-france-mayenne.com).

Meurthe-et-Moselle: Square Herzog, ZAC Ban la Dame, 54390 Frouard (☎ 03 83 23 49 50, ✉ gites-de-france54@wanadoo.fr, 🖥 www.gites54.com).

Meuse: Relais des Gîtes Ruraux de la Meuse, Hôtel du Département, 55012 Bar-le-Duc Cedex (☎ 03 29 45 79 76, 🖥 www.gites-de-meuse.fr).

Morbihan: 42 avenue Wilson/BP30318, 56403 Auray Cedex (☎ 02 97 56 48 12, ✉ gites-de-france.morbihan@wanadoo.fr, 🖥 www.gites-de-france-morbihan.com).

Moselle: Gîtes de Moselle, 6 rue de l'Abattoir, 57630 Vic-sur-Seille (☎ 03 87 01 18 50, ✉ gitesdefrance.moselle@wanadoo.fr, 🖥 www.gites57.com).

Nièvre: 3 rue du Sort, 58000 Nevers (☎ 03 86 59 14 22 ✉ gites-de-france-nievre@libertysurf.fr, 🖥 www.gites-de-france-nievre.com).

Nord: 89 boulevard de la Liberté/BP1210, 59800 Lille (☎ 03 20 14 93 93, ✉ gites.de.france.nord@wanadoo.fr, 🖥 www.itea.fr/GDF/59).

Oise: 8 rue Auguste Delaherche/BP80822, 60008 Beauvais Cedex (☎ 03 44 06 25 85, ✉ gites@oisetourisme.com, 🖥 www.itea.fr/GDF/60/F).

Orne: CDT/BP50, 61002 Alençon Cedex (☎ 02 33 28 07 00, ✉ info@ornetourisme.com, 🖥 www.itea.fr/GDF/61).

Pas-de-Calais: La trésorerie, Wimille/BP79, 62930 Wimereux (☎ 03 21 10 34 40, ✉ gitesdefrance@pas-de-calais.com, 🖥 www.gitesdefrance-pas-de-calais.com).

Puy-de-Dôme: Relais des Gîtes du Puy-de-Dôme, Place de la Bourse, 63038 Clermont-Ferrand Cedex 1 (☎ 04 73 42 22 61, ✉ gitesdefrance63@planetepuydedome.com, 🖥 www.gites-de-france-puydedome.com).

Pyrénées-Atlantiques: 20 rue Gassion/BP537, 64010 Pau Cedex (☎ 05 59 11 20 64, 🖥 www.gites64.com).

Pyrénees-Orientales: 3 boulevard de Clairfont, Bât. D, Naturopôle, 66350 Toulouges (☎ 04 68 68 42 88, 🖥 www.gites-de-france-66.com).

Rhône: 1 rue Général Plessier, 69002 Lyon (☎ 04 72 77 17 50, ✉ gites69.adtr@wanadoo.fr, 🖳 www.gites-de-france-rhone.com).

Saône-et-Loire: Esplanade du Breuil/BP522, 71010 Mâcon Cedex (☎ 03 85 29 55 60, ✉ gites71@sl.chambagri.fr, 🖳 www.itea.fr/GDF/71).

Sarthe: 78 avenue du Général Leclerc, 72000 Le Mans (☎ 02 43 40 22 60, ✉ gites-de-France-72@wanadoo.fr, 🖳 www.gites-de-france-sarthe.com).

Savoie: Maison du Tourisme, 24 boulevard de la Colonne, 73024 Chambéry Cedex (☎ 04 79 85 01 09, ✉ gites.france.savoie@wanadoo.fr, 🖳 www.gites-de-france-savoie.com).

Seine-et-Marne: 9-11 rue Royale, 77300 Fontainebleau (☎ 01 60 39 60 39, ✉ mdt@tourisme77.net, 🖳 www.itea.fr/GDF/77/F).

Seine-Maritime: Seine-Maritime Tourisme Réservation (SMTR), Chambre d'Agriculture, Chemin de la Bretèque/BP59, 76232 Bois-Guillaume Cedex (☎ 02 35 60 73 34, ✉ info@gitesdefrance76.com, 🖳 www.gitesdefrance76.fr).

Somme: 21 rue Ernest Cauvin, 80000 Amiens (☎ 03 22 71 22 70, ✉ accueil@somme-tourisme.com, 🖳 www.itea.fr/GDF/80/F).

Tarn: Maison des Agriculteurs, 96 rue des Agriculteurs/BP80332, 81027 Albi Cedex (☎ 05 63 48 83 01, ✉ gitesdutarn@free.fr, 🖳 www.gites-tarn.com).

Tarn-et-Garonne: CDT, 7 boulevard Midi-Pyrénées/BP534, 82000 Montauban Cedex (☎ 05 63 21 79 61, ✉ info@tourisme82.com, 🖳 www.gitesdefrance82.com).

Territoire-de-Belfort: 2bis rue Clémenceau, 90000 Belfort (☎ 03 84 21 27 95, ✉ gitesdefrance@ot-belfort.fr, 🖳 www.itea.fr/GDF/90).

Val d'Oise: Château de la Motte, rue François de Ganay, 95270 Luzarches (☎ 01 30 29 51 00, ✉ gites@val-doise-tourisme.com, 🖳 www.gites-val-doise.com).

Var: Conseil Général du Var, Rond Point du 4/12/74/BP215, 83006 Draguignan Cedex (☎ 04 94 50 93 93, 🖳 www.gites-de-france-var.fr).

Vaucluse: BP164, 84008 Avignon Cedex 1 (☎ 04 90 85 45 00, 🖳 www.itea.fr/GDF/84).

Vendée: Relais des Gîtes de France et du Tourisme Vert, 124 boulevard Aristide Briand/BP735, 85018 La Roche-sur-Yon (☎ 02 51 37 87 87, ✉ gites-de-France-vendee@wanadoo.fr, 🖥 www.gites-de-france-vendee.com).

Vienne: 1bis rue Victor Hugo/BP287, 86007 Poitiers (☎ 05 49 49 59 11, 🖥 www.gitesdefrance-vienne.com).

Vosges: 31 rue François de Neufchâteau, 88000 Epinal (☎ 03 29 35 50 34, ✉ gites-88@wanadoo.fr, 🖥 www.vosges-gites.com).

Yonne: Chambre d'Agriculture, 14bis rue Guynemer, 89015 Auxerre Cedex (☎ 03 86 72 92 15, ✉ gitesdefrance@yonne.chambagri.fr, 🖥 www.itea.fr/GDF/89).

Yvelines: Hôtel du Département, 2 place André Mignot, 78012 Versailles Cedex (☎ 01 30 21 36 73 ✉ gitesdefrance@cg78.fr, 🖥 www.gites-de-france-yvelines.com).

Gîte Rural

1 *épi*: Outside area, garden furniture, one shower room with WC for up to six people, second shower room for more than six people, rotisserie or mini-oven, hob unit, pressure cooker, fridge, cooking utensils and basic household cleaning products, iron. High chair to be provided on request.

2 *épis*: In addition to the above: barbecue (where bylaws permit), washing machine (for six or more guests), mixer, electric coffee maker, television socket. Sheets, table and bath linen on request.

3 *épis*: In addition to the above: separate entrance and private garden, two WCs (for seven or more guests), washing machine, dishwasher (for five or more guests), oven, colour television, telephone. Cleaning service on request.

4 *épis*: In addition to the above: house with character, high-quality setting and interior decoration, log fireplace or stove (where bylaws permit), microwave, refrigerator with freezer compartment, clothes dryer (for six or more guests).

5 *épis*: In addition to the above: private landscaped garden or grounds, use of leisure facilities (e.g. tennis court, swimming pool, sauna and Jacuzzi), stereo, video recorder, garage or shelter, dishwasher and clothes dryer (for three or more guests).

Gîte d'Étape

Living room, dining area, kitchen or equipped kitchen area for guests' use, telephone, clothes drying area, storeroom. Relaxation area or activity room, dishwasher, clothes dryer, sheets and towels on request. Up to 50 per cent of sleeping facilities may be 'board beds'.

Gîte de Séjour

Living room, dining area, relaxation area or activity room, telephone, clothes drying area, storeroom, adjacent laid-out or equipped grounds, library, board games or musical instruments, dishwasher, washing machine and dryer, sheets and towels on request. No 'board beds'.

TOURIST BOARD

Each department has a tourist board (*comité départemental du tourisme*); look in the local yellow pages under *Offices de tourisme, syndicats d'initiative*.

Standards

Tourist board standards are rated by *étoiles* (stars) at five levels, as follows:

1 Etoile

Accommodation must have the following:

- Floors, walls, ceilings in good condition and watertight.
- Fixed partitions between rooms.
- Light and air sufficient for all rented rooms (interior rooms with no outside doors aren't counted in the number of rooms rented).
- Exterior blinds, interior curtains/blinds.
- Floor coverings (carpet, tiles, parquet, etc.).
- Soundproofing according to housing regulations.

- Electric socket in each room and one or more lamps (minimum 15W per m²).
- Central or electric heating sufficient for a minimum temperature of 19°C in each room.
- Enough furniture for the number of occupants, in good condition.
- Mattresses clean, in good condition with protectors, and bases in good condition.
- One bolster or pillow per bed.
- Bedside lamp for each person.
- Two covers (one wool) or one duvet per bed.
- Mixer tap (*mélangeur*) in bathroom.
- In a property for up to six people, indoor bathroom with ventilation, basin and shower or a bath with shower attachment.
- In a property for more than six people, two bathrooms, one with independent access.
- Indoor WC.
- Hob (with two rings for up to five people, four rings for more than five people).
- Oven or rotisserie.
- Refrigerator large enough for the number of people.
- Utensils and matching dishes for the number of people.
- Pressure cooker.
- Cleaning equipment appropriate for the accommodation.
- Washing line or dryer.
- Iron.
- Ironing cloth.
- High-chair (on request).
- Telephone nearby (within 500m).
- Lift to reach the fourth floor.
- Parking nearby.
- Brochures and leaflets (practical and tourist information).

2 Etoiles

As above, with the following limitations and additions:

- TV socket in living room.
- Sheets available on request (may be at extra charge).
- Towels on request (at extra charge).
- Mixer tap in kitchen.
- Matching dishes.
- Three sets of cutlery, dishes and glasses per person.
- Table linen on request (at extra charge).

3 Etoiles

As above, with the following limitations and additions:

- TV socket in living room and TV set.
- Bolster and pillow per bed.
- Extra WC (separate or in one of the bathrooms).
- Hob with four rings.
- Oven.
- Cooker hood or controllable ventilation.
- Electric mixer and coffee maker.
- Dishwasher for more than four people.
- Ironing board.
- Telephone in the building, billed for the period of the let.
- Colour TV.
- Lift to reach the third floor.
- Private parking.
- Well kept balcony, terrace, loggia or garden of at least 4m².
- Cleaning service on request (at extra charge).

4 Etoiles

As above, with the following limitations and additions:

- Matching furniture.
- High-quality furniture and decoration.
- Electric hairdryer.
- In a property for up to six people, an indoor bathroom with ventilation, basin and bath with shower above.
- In a property for more than six people, two bathrooms with a bath with a shower above.
- Microwave oven.
- Refrigerator with freezer compartment.
- Washing machine for more than five people.
- Tumble dryer for more than five people.

5 Etoiles

As above, with the following limitations and additions:

- Portable TV set and sockets in each main room.
- Mixer tap with a single swivel control (*mitigeur*) in bathroom.
- Dishwasher for more than two people.
- Washing machine for more than two people.
- Tumble dryer for more than two people.
- Cordless telephone.
- Hi-fi system.
- Video/DVD player.
- Well kept balcony, terrace, loggia or garden of at least 9m^2.
- Leisure equipment (e.g. tennis court, pool, sauna, Jacuzzi).

Dimensions

Area: The minimum total area of the accommodation (excluding bathroom and WC, but including kitchen) is as follows:

- One-room accommodation for two people:
  - 1 *étoile*: 12m^2.
  - 2 *étoiles*: 14m^2.

- 3 *étoiles*: 16m².
- 4 *étoiles*: 18m².
- 5 *étoiles*: 24m².
- Add 3m² for each extra person.
- Add the following for each extra bedroom:
  - 1 *étoile*: 7m².
  - 2 *étoiles*: 8m².
  - 3 *étoiles*: 9m².
  - 4 *étoiles*: 10m².
  - 5 *étoiles*: 12m².

Beds: The following restrictions apply:

- Single beds must be at least 80cm wide (1 to 3 *étoiles*) or 90cm wide (4 to 5 *étoiles*).
- Double beds must be at least 140cm wide (1 to 4 *étoiles*) or 160cm wide (5 *étoiles*).
- Single and double beds must be at least 190cm long (1 to 4 *étoiles*) or 200cm long (5 *étoiles*).

Cupboards: There must be at least the following cupboard or shelf space in two-person accommodation:

- 1 *étoile*: 2.5m².
- 2 to 4 *étoiles*: 3m².
- 5 *étoiles*: 4m².
- Add 1m² for each extra person.

Inventory

The following is a typical kitchen inventory for a property accommodating four to six people:

- 12 each of the following: glasses, dinner plates, soup plates, dessert plates, forks, knives, dessert spoons, soup spoons.
- 1 cutlery tray.
- 6 coffee bowls.

- 6 cups.
- 1 serving plate.
- 1 serving bowl.
- 2 salad bowls.
- 2 ovenproof dishes.
- 1 cake or flan tin.
- 4 saucepans.
- 2 saucepan lids.
- 1 or 2 casserole dishes.
- 2 frying pans (1 non-stick).
- 1 each of the following: sieve, egg timer, measuring jug, vegetable mincer, lemon squeezer, salad spinner, grater, chopping board, bread knife, carving knife, scissors, vegetable peeler, spatula, wooden spoon, set of salad servers, ladle, corkscrew, tin opener, sardine tin key.

INDEX

G

H

I

L

LIVING AND WORKING SERIES

Living and Working books are essential reading for anyone planning to spend time abroad, including holiday-home owners, retirees, visitors, business people, migrants, students and even extra-terrestrials! They're packed with important and useful information designed to help you **avoid costly mistakes and save both time and money.** Topics covered include how to:

- Find a job with a good salary & conditions
- Obtain a residence permit
- Avoid and overcome problems
- Find your dream home
- Get the best education for your family
- Make the best use of public transport
- Endure local motoring habits
- Obtain the best health treatment
- Stretch your money further
- Make the most of your leisure time
- Enjoy the local sporting life
- Find the best shopping bargains
- Insure yourself against most eventualities
- Use post office and telephone services
- Do numerous other things not listed above

Living and Working books are the most comprehensive and up-to-date source of practical information available about everyday life abroad. They aren't, however, boring text books, but interesting and entertaining guides written in a highly readable style.

Discover what it's really like to live and work abroad!

Order your copies today by phone, fax, post or email from: Survival Books, PO Box 3780, YEOVIL, BA21 5WX, United Kingdom (☎/🖷 +44 (0)1935-700060, ✉ sales@survivalbooks.net, 🖥 www.survivalbooks.net).

BUYING A HOME SERIES

Buying a Home books, including **Buying, Selling & Letting Property**, are essential reading for anyone planning to purchase property abroad. They're packed with vital information to guide you through the property purchase jungle and help you **avoid the sort of disasters that can turn your dream home into a nightmare!** Topics covered include:

- Avoiding problems
- Choosing the region
- Finding the right home and location
- Estate agents
- Finance, mortgages and taxes
- Home security
- Utilities, heating and air-conditioning
- Moving house and settling in
- Renting and letting
- Permits and visas
- Travelling and communications
- Health and insurance
- Renting a car and driving
- Retirement and starting a business
- And much, much more!

Buying a Home books are the most comprehensive and up-to-date source of information available about buying property abroad. Whether you want a detached house, townhouse or apartment, a holiday or a permanent home, these books will help make your dreams come true.

Save yourself time, trouble and money!

Order your copies today by phone, fax, post or email from: Survival Books, PO Box 3780, YEOVIL, BA21 5WX, United Kingdom (☎/▤ +44 (0)1935-700060, ✉ sales@survivalbooks.net, 🖥 www.survivalbooks.net).

OTHER SURVIVAL BOOKS

The Alien's Guides: *The Alien's Guides to Britain and France* will help you to appreciate the peculiarities (in both senses) of the British and French.

The Best Places to Buy a Home in France/Spain: The most comprehensive homebuying guides to France and Spain, containing detailed profiles of the most popular regions for home-buying.

Buying, Selling and Letting Property: The most comprehensive and up-to-date source of information on buying, selling and letting property in the UK.

Earning Money From Your Home: Essential guides to earning income from property in France and Spain, including short- and long-term letting.

Foreigners in France/Spain: Triumphs & Disasters: Real-life experiences of people who have emigrated to France and Spain, recounted in their own words.

Lifelines: Essential guides to life in specific regions of France and Spain. See order form for a list of current titles in the series.

Making a Living: Essential guides to self-employment and starting a business in France and Spain.

Renovating & Maintaining Your French Home: The ultimate guide to renovating and maintaining your dream home in France.

Retiring Abroad: The most comprehensive and up-to-date source of practical information available about retiring to a foreign country.

Shooting Caterpillars in Spain: The hilarious experiences of an expatriate who sent to Spain in search of . . . she wasn't quite sure what.

Surprised by France: Even after living there for ten years, Donald Carroll finds plenty of surprises in the Hexagon.

Broaden your horizons with Survival Books!

Order your copies today by phone, fax, post or email from: Survival Books, PO Box 3780, YEOVIL, BA21 5WX, United Kingdom (☎/📠 +44 (0)1935-700060, ✉ sales@survivalbooks.net, 🖥 www.survivalbooks.net).

Qty.	Title	Price (incl. p&p)			Total
		UK	Europe	World	
	The Alien's Guide to Britain	£6.95	£8.95	£12.45	
	The Alien's Guide to France	£6.95	£8.95	£12.45	
	The Best Places to Buy a Home in France	£13.95	£15.95	£19.45	
	The Best Places to Buy a Home in Spain	£13.95	£15.95	£19.45	
	Buying a Home Abroad	£13.95	£15.95	£19.45	
	Buying a Home in Australia & NZ	£13.95	£15.95	£19.45	
	Buying a Home in Cyprus	£13.95	£15.95	£19.45	
	Buying a Home in Florida	£13.95	£15.95	£19.45	
	Buying a Home in France	£13.95	£15.95	£19.45	
	Buying a Home in Greece	£13.95	£15.95	£19.45	
	Buying a Home in Ireland	£11.95	£13.95	£17.45	
	Buying a Home in Italy	£13.95	£15.95	£19.45	
	Buying a Home in Portugal	£13.95	£15.95	£19.45	
	Buying a Home in South Africa	£13.95	£15.95	£19.45	
	Buying a Home in Spain	£13.95	£15.95	£19.45	
	Buying, Letting & Selling Property	£11.95	£13.95	£17.45	
	Earning Money From Your French Home	£11.95	£13.95	£17.45	
	Earning Money From Your Spanish Home	£11.95	£13.95	£17.45	
	Foreigners in France: Triumphs & Disasters	£11.95	£13.95	£17.45	
	Foreigners in Spain: Triumphs & Disasters	£11.95	£13.95	£17.45	
	Costa Blanca Lifeline	£11.95	£13.95	£17.45	
	Costa del Sol Lifeline	£11.95	£13.95	£17.45	
	Dordogne/Lot Lifeline	£11.95	£13.95	£17.45	
	Normandy Lifeline	£11.95	£13.95	£17.45	
	Poitou-Charentes Lifeline	£11.95	£13.95	£17.45	
	Provence-Côte d'Azur Lifeline	£11.95	£13.95	£17.45	
	Living & Working Abroad	£14.95	£16.95	£20.45	
	Living & Working in America	£14.95	£16.95	£20.45	
	Living & Working in Australia	£16.95	£18.95	£22.45	
	Living & Working in Britain	£14.95	£16.95	£20.45	
	Living & Working in Canada	£16.95	£18.95	£22.45	
	Living & Working in the European Union	£16.95	£18.95	£22.45	
	Living & Working in the Far East	£16.95	£18.95	£22.45	
	Total carried forward (see over)				

ORDER FORM

Qty.	Title	UK	Europe	World	Total
			Total brought forward		
		Price (incl. p&p)			
		UK	Europe	World	
	Living & Working in France	£14.95	£16.95	£20.45	
	Living & Working in Germany	£16.95	£18.95	£22.45	
	L&W in the Gulf States & Saudi Arabia	£16.95	£18.95	£22.45	
	L&W in Holland, Belgium & Luxembourg	£14.95	£16.95	£20.45	
	Living & Working in Ireland	£14.95	£16.95	£20.45	
	Living & Working in Italy	£16.95	£18.95	£22.45	
	Living & Working in London	£13.95	£15.95	£19.45	
	Living & Working in New Zealand	£16.95	£18.95	£22.45	
	Living & Working in Spain	£14.95	£16.95	£20.45	
	Living & Working in Switzerland	£16.95	£18.95	£22.45	
	Making a Living in France	£13.95	£15.95	£19.45	
	Making a Living in Spain	£13.95	£15.95	£19.45	
	Renovating & Maintaining Your French Home	£16.95	£18.95	£22.45	
	Retiring Abroad	£14.95	£16.95	£20.45	
	Shooting Caterpillars in Spain	£9.95	£11.95	£15.45	
	Surprised by France	£11.95	£13.95	£17.45	
				Grand Total	

Order your copies today by phone, fax, post or email from: Survival Books, PO Box 3780, YEOVIL, BA21 5WX, United Kingdom (☎/📠 +44 (0)1935-700060, ✉ sales@ survivalbooks.net, 🖥 www.survivalbooks.net). If you aren't entirely satisfied, simply return them to us within 14 days for a full and unconditional refund.

I enclose a cheque for the grand total/Please charge my Amex/Delta/Maestro (Switch)/MasterCard/Visa card as follows. (delete as applicable)

Card No. _ _ _ _   _ _ _ _   _ _ _ _   _ _ _ _   Security Code* _ _ _

Expiry date _____   Issue number (Maestro/Switch only) _____

Signature _____   Tel. No. _____

NAME _____

ADDRESS _____

_____

* The security code is the last three digits on the signature strip.

NOTES

NOTES